MEDIA REPORTING

MEDIA REPORTING

N. Afaque Shamsi

ANMOL PUBLICATIONS PVT. LTD.
NEW DELHI - 110 002 (INDIA)

ANMOL PUBLICATIONS PVT. LTD.
H.O.: 4374/4B, Ansari Road, Darya Ganj,
New Delhi-110 002 (India)
Ph.: 23261597, 23278000
B.O.: No. 1015, Ist Main Road, BSK IIIrd Stage
IIIrd Phase, IIIrd Block,
Bangalore - 560 085 (India)
Visit us at: www.anmolpublications.com

Media Reporting

First Published, 2006

ISBN 81-261-2665-5

PRINTED IN INDIA

Published by J.L. Kumar for Anmol Publications Pvt. Ltd., New Delhi - 110 002 and Printed at Mehra Offset Press, Delhi.

Contents

Preface

Media is the plural of 'Medium' and 'mass' means a large number. Thus, by mass-media, what is meant is 'the main means of communication at a large number' i.e., all those means, which are used to communicate with people on a vast level or at a great number, as, newspapers, magazines, radio and television, etc.

Though communication has always been an important need of life, it assumed the status of the most essential and one of the basics of life in the later half of the 20th century. As a result, a number of different and diverse forms of media emerged and institutions imparting their thorough knowledge mushroomed throughout the width and length of the country and world.

In this battle of survival and cut-throat comptetion, the one which won the greatest appreciation and applaud of the masses is the Electronic Media by virtue of its being capable of communicating to people, live and pulsating coverage of news and events occurring in every nook and corner of the world and in all the strata of the society ranging from the laymen to the top brass of Government, Semi-Government and non-Government administrations.

Given the above-discussed situation, there was an urgent demand for such an Encyclopaedia, which may cater to the maximum requirements of the seekers of knowledge in this regard. This series has been prepared with a view to encapsulating most of the stuff required by a media-lover.

Should we succeed in our attempt and get a favouring feedback excluding unnecessary brickbats, we would put a more enlightening, informative and comprehensive ocean of knowledge in the hold of your hands.

Editor

1

Reporting Skill

The heroes of journalism are reporters. What they do is find things out. They go in first, amid the chaos of now, battering at closed doors, sometimes taking risks, and capture the beginnings of the truth. And if they do not do that, who will? Editors' Commentators? There is only one alternative to reporters: accepting the authorised version, the one the businesses, bureaucrats and politicians choose to give us. After all, without reporters, what would commentators know.

Key Players : Reporters are, like almost all heroes, flawed. As a group, they have a more soiled reputation than most; for enough of them routinely exaggerate, simplify and contort the truth to have made parts of the trade a by-word for calculated dishonesty. Not for nothing do screen writers and dramatists, in search of a booable villain, regularly opt for a tabloid reporter. It saves time. They don't have to spend pages establishing a lack of morals, the mere announcement of the character's line of work is enough for audiences to grasp that this person is going to wheedle and deceive. Then there are the lazy — those who opt for spoon-feeding and the facile, rather than the hard, painstaking, often exposed job of getting it as right as they can.

There is, to be sure, a lot of calculated malice and shoddy workmanship in the history of journalism.

But there is a lot that is heroic, and far, far more of it than most media critiques and journalism schools would have the beginner believe. There is John Tyas's exposure for *The Times* of British atrocities against demonstrators in Manchester in 1819; William Howard Russell's accounts of the bungling of the British army in the Crimea; William Leng's exposure in the *Sheffield Telegraph* of corruption and violence in that city (he was threatened so often that he kept a loaded revolver on his desk and had a police escort home every night); Emily Crawford, who incessantly risked her life to report the 1871 Paris Commune for the *Daily News* and then scooped the world at the subsequent Versailles Conference; Nellie Bly, who feigned mental illness to get inside an asylum and wrote a series for the *New York World* that described the terrors and cruelties she found and which led to improved conditions; W.T. Stead's exposure in the *Pall Mall Gazette* of child prostitution; and Ida Tarbell's articles in *McClure's* that documented the corruption and intimidation of the Standard Oil Company 1902–1904 and prepared the way for the dissolution of the firm.

Then there is Emilie Marshall, who broke several all-male preserves in becoming the first woman reporter in the House of Commons' press gallery and the first woman staff reporter on both the *Daily Mail* and *Daily Express;* John Reed's reporting of the Russian Revolution; the unmasking of the violently racist Ku Klux Klan by Roland Thomas of the *New York World;* Ilya Ehrenburg's reporting for *Red Star* that first revealed the Nazi extermination camps; John Hersey and Wilfred Burchett's reporting from Hiroshima that disproved the official lie that there was no such thing as radiation sickness; the courageous opposition of the *Observer* and *Manchester Guardian* to the Suez invasion of 1956; the relentless pursuit of high-level security breaches by the whole British press in the early 1960s, the uncovering by Seymour Hersch, then a young freelance, of the full horrors of the My Lai massacre in 1968; the *Sunday Times'* campaign for the limbless victims of the drug thalidomide; Carl Bernstein and Bob Woodward's Watergate investigation in the *Washington Post* that proved a US President to be a corrupt liar; and Robert Fisk's refusal to swallow the NATO line (or, for that matter, anyone's line) in reporting the Kosovo conflict in the *Independent* in 1999.

Able Reporters

There are also those whose names are read fleetingly, but rarely remembered; the ones whose efforts to inform their communities are met, not with an obstructive official or evasive answer, but with intimidation or worse. Every year, thousands of reporters are arrested or threatened, hundreds imprisoned, and scores killed. In its most extreme form, this is what Peruvian journalist Sonia Goldenburg has called 'censorship by death'. In 1982 nine journalists were killed around the world. In 1994 no fewer than 103 journalists died for getting too close to the truth. By the turn of the twentieth century, each month saw 40 journalists threatened, 20 arrested, 90 in jail and three killed. Each one of them is a definitive answer to those, both inside and outside the business, who think that journalism is a branch of marketing that organises and exaggerates trivia. After all, no authority would bother obstructing, jailing or murdering people for that.

Finally, there are the tens of thousands of other, often local, journalists whose lot is nothing more glamorous or heroic than discovering the most complete version of what happened in their areas and reporting it. They don't expect gold or glory, and there is no particular reason why they should get it. But they are, nevertheless, an antidote, socially and professionally, to those who have traded in their credibility for a high salary or easy life.

Motives and Purposes : And all these good reporters share something. They may keep it well hidden under the journalists' obligatory, hard-bitten mask, but the immortals, the persecuted and the unsung all share a belief in what the job is about. This is, above all things, to question; and, by so doing, then to:

- Discover and publish information that replaces rumour and speculation.
- Resist or evade government controls.
- Inform, and so empower, voters.
- Subvert those whose authority relies on a lack of public information.
- Scrutinise the action and inaction of governments, elected representatives and public services.
- Scrutinise businesses, their treatment of workers and customers, and the quality of their products.
- Comfort the afflicted and afflict the comfortable, providing a voice for those who cannot normally be heard in public.
- Hold up a mirror to society, reflecting its virtues and vices and also debunking its cherished myths.
- Ensure that justice is done, is seen to be done and investigations carried out where this is not so.
- Promote the free exchange of ideas, especially by providing a platform for those with philosophies alternative to the prevailing ones.

If you can read that list without the hairs on the back of your neck beginning to stand up, then maybe journalism is not for you.

To meet the aims listed above on a regular basis is a tough assignment. The idea, common among those outside journalism, that what a reporter needs more than anything is the ability to write well is not even the half of it. Literary ability is only part of the job, and often not the largest part. Neither is good reporting a matter of acquiring a little bag of tricks and tools, out of which the appropriate one is selected according to circumstance. What is needed to succeed as a reporter are the right attitudes and character.

The most important equipment reporters have is that which is carried around between their ears. Some of these attitudes are instinctive, others are learnt quickly, but most are built up through years of experience – by researching and writing, re-researching and re-writing hundreds and hundreds of stories.

You need a keen news sense and for three reasons. First, in the positive sense of knowing what makes a good story and the ability to find the essential news point in a mass of dross. Second, in the negative sense of not wasting time by pursuing stories that will never amount to much. Often you have to ask yourself: 'What is the best this story can be? What is the strongest news point it will have if one gets all the information I need?' And sometimes the answer is that it will not be much of a tale. So drop it. The third reason is that if you don't have a news sense, or have it but don't use it, you will miss things and make a fool of yourself. Take the case of Duncombe Jewell, a reporter for the Daily Mail in its early days. He was sent to cover the launch of HMS Albion at the Thames Ironworks in London and in due course returned to the office with a piece of purple prose that was, in his own words, 'the nearest thing to a Turner sunset that you could get in manuscript'. As he handed it in, news reached the paper that 30 people had drowned at the launching. His news editor was beside himself with anger. 'Well,' said Jewell, 'I did see some people bobbing about in the water as I came away but...'

As a news editor, passion and precision is the one attribute which is valued more than any other in reporters. Could one rely on their work and trust their accuracy? As a reporter you also speedily appreciate that your reputation for accuracy and not exaggerating, either in print or beforehand, is a valuable commodity. Lose it, and it will be very difficult to regain.

Precision means three things. First, the obvious one of recording and writing accurately what people tell you. Second, taking care that however accurate each little part of your story, the whole thing is true to the spirit and atmosphere of the situation or events — which means adding background and context. Third, not falling into the dangerous and widespread habit of saying, 'Well if that happened and the other happened, then this other thing must be true.' You should not wish but report your stories into print. If there are any gaps in a sequence of events that you are reporting, find out precisely what is missing: don't think that if A happened, then something else and then C, then the missing part must be B. It may not be.

Making assumptions applies to all assumptions — either of logic, identity, fact or motives. The great problem with assumptions is that most of them turn out to be correct; that is what makes them so dangerous and tempting. Play safe, report only what you know, not what you think you know. That way you will avoid being inaccurate, dishonest and misleading — or sacked.

There was a famous occasion when a freelance photographer gave a British mass-market newspaper a picture of Prince Charles putting his arms around a lady who was not his wife at a time when he was known to be unhappily married. The paper published the picture under a headline that suggested a romantic relationship, because the editors assumed that was what was taking place. They were wrong. Unknown to them, the picture was taken at the funeral of the woman's child, who had died of leukaemia at the age of four. The Prince was doing what any of us might have done in a similar situation — he was comforting the distressed mother. However rudimentary you may imagine your ignorance to be, if you don't know, ask; if you don't understand, request an explanation. Don't worry if anyone laughs at you. The really stupid reporters are the ones who pretend to know, who sit there nodding throughout an interview they only partly understand and who then try to write the story — and find that they can't. The place to show your ignorance is when questioning people, not on paper in your subsequent story.

An essential general attitude for reporters, indeed all journalists, is to be suspicious of all sources. Why is this person telling me this? What is their motive? And are they really in a position to know what they claim to know?

You cannot be expected to shed all your cherished beliefs, but you should never allow them consciously to affect your work. Reporters should accurately relate what happened, not strain everything through the sieve of their own prejudices, cultured and intelligent though they imagine these to be.

This invocation applies to newly minted prejudices as well as old ones. Don't let the opinions you form early on in the research prematurely colour your judgement of the story. A great sin of some reporters, particularly those often asked to write colour and atmosphere pieces, is that they will write the intro in their heads on the way to an interview. Their intro may be smart, it may be a beautiful piece of writing, but the chances are that it will say more about them than their subject.

Reporters are subject to what editors want. By all means argue with them, shout at them and try to sweet-talk them, but, in the end, you have to accept their decision — or go and work elsewhere. That is professionalism. So, too, is the acceptance of the discipline of the schedule of your paper. A lot of reporters think it is somehow a mark of a literary talent in full flower to be late and over length. It is not. It is the sign of an unreliable amateur. So too is the reporter who, when out on a story, fails to call into the office regularly. You can often, however, use the paper's needs to your advantage, getting prominence for your stories by calculating when in your paper's production cycle they are most in need of early stories or ones illustrated by pictures, graphics, sidebars, etc. — and delivering them.

Unless people read your story, you might as well be muttering it to yourself in a darkened room. They will read it if you consider them — when you write, but especially when you research. What will readers want to know? What do they need explained? And what will bring this story home to them? Find anecdotes, show how the events will impact on readers' lives, or impact on other lives; use examples that will be relevant to their own experience; above all, where possible, tell the story in terms of real people.

Sooner or later the new reporter experiences the dawning realisation that the rest of the world is not run for the convenience of newspapers. Stories happen at bad times and in awkward places, telephones are not always available or working; and, if you are out of the city or country, you can be running out of money, time, food, drink and energy. You need a strong desire to beat whatever circumstances are strewn in your path, get to the story and then file as fast as possible. To be like Ed Cody of the *Washington Post*.

Mort Rosenblum's excellent book *Who Stole the News*, tells the story of how Cody was in Paris one night in December 1988 when word reached him that a Pan Am jumbo jet had crashed on Lockerbie, a little town in Scotland. It was 8.20 p.m. and the last flight to Britain that evening had already left. Cody found a charter operator, persuaded his foreign editor in the United States to authorise the cost and, a few hours later, the reporter was in Glasgow. Lockerbie was 60 miles south and by that time had been sealed off by police roadblocks. Miraculously, Cody found a cab driver who was from the town and, with his local knowledge and contacts, Cody made it to the scene. The driver even had a friend who owned a pub, which he opened up so that the reporter could call Washington to file his story.

The crash, in which all 259 passengers and 11 people on the ground died, was one of the biggest stories of the 1980s. Cody's excellent job on it was possible because he had the will to win. He may also have had a paper prepared to pay $6,000 for a charter aircraft, but, on most occasions, a reporter's desire to get to the story will not cost as much and it will always bring rewards.

Newspapers want their reporters to file the earliest and fullest account of a story that they can get. A little healthy, or even unhealthy, competition to be first is part of the reality—and fun— of the job. And it serves readers well, just so long as not too many corners are cut.

Beating the rival agency, for instance, was uppermost in the minds of the Associated Press (AP) and United Press International (UPI) photographers who were assigned to take pictures of the Dalai Lama as he fled Tibet in 1959. Both chartered planes and organised relays of motorcyclists so that they could get their pictures from the Chinese borders to the nearest transmitter in India. When the Dalai Lama emerged from his aircraft, the photographers leapt forward, took their pictures and ran to their already-revving planes. After a break-neck race in the air and on the ground, UPI won.

The AP man was devastated. He went back to his hotel room and sat there, full of recrimination about what might have been and the shame of being beaten. Then he received a cable from his office: 'Opposition's Dalai Lama has long shaggy hair. Yours bald. How please %'The AP man cabled back: 'Because my Dalai right Dalai.' In his desperation to be first, the UPI man had photographed the interpreter.

Acceptable rivalry has its limits, however, and they were surely reached — and considerably exceeded — by the former *New York Post* journalist Steve Dunleavy who as a young man worked as a reporter when his father was with the opposition paper. Both were assigned the same story and he was so keen to be first to the scene that he immobilised his father's car. by slashing its tyres.

Collecting News

All around the world governments are getting ever more sophisticated in their management of news, tightly controlling what information they distribute and who gets it. In some places access to these channels even involves reporters joining a kind of informal 'club', with rules about what constitutes 'responsible' behaviour and the threat of exclusion from the official information for those who stray. This is unhealthy, as is the habit of reporters sometimes to cooperate with each other, sharing quotes and phone numbers. But good reporters should always be prepared to strike out on their own when necessary, to go where no one else is going, and — when it does not work out — take the flak. They are ready to spurn predigested meals from the official spoon because they know there is something far tastier to be found if only they go foraging for themselves.

Almost any intelligent human being can, with sufficient application, learn how to be a competent reporter. But to rise above that, to be good or great, you must have real talent and flair for either research, or writing, or both. And you should have the right kind of character; for if there is one thing that separates outstanding reporters from the ordinary, it is this.

If one was to select one piece of reporting that in its quality and impact represents the best of journalism, one could do a lot worse than go back a century and a quarter to a Central Europe riven by nationalist claims and systematic violence. In what follows, any resemblance to contemporary events in that part of the world is almost certainly not a coincidence.

The story started with allegations of atrocities, the simultaneous lying of several governments, censorship and a dying empire. It drew in Turkey. Russia, Britain and a nascent Bulgaria, continued with heroism and a war, and concluded with nothing less than the creation of several new nations in the re-drawing of the map of Europe. And what drew all these disparate strands together was a former St. Petersburg correspondent, an Irish-American called Januarius Aloysius MacGahan.

Even by the adventurous standards of his day, MacGahan was a thrill-seeker of the first order. In an age when men in an international hurry used the horse and the steamship, MacGahan in five hasty years reported from the Paris Commune (where he was imprisoned), the court of St. Petersburg, Central Asia, Cuba, the Arctic, the Caucasus and the Pyrenees. Famously distinguished for his impartiality and sharp eye, MacGahan was also never one to shirk a challenge. In 1875 he sailed through the Arctic's ice-choked waters in a wooden boat and two years earlier he defied a Russian embargo on reporters to make a remarkable ride over the Central Asian steppes. His goal was to catch up with a Russian military expedition on its way to Turkestan. Cossacks bent on his destruction pursued him for nearly 1,000 miles but after 29 days, accompanied by two attendants, sometimes forced to wade knee-deep in sand and several times lost, he reached the camp. His towering reputation for reliability and bravery reached new peaks.

By the summer of 1876, this 32-year-old reporter was in London with his Russian-born wife, Barbara, and a young son. He was planning a third book and some rest. But his relaxation was short-lived. The *Daily News*, a prominent liberal London paper, contacted him. They had an urgent assignment.

The *News* was in some trouble. A day or so before, on 23 June, they had published a story from their man in Constantinople, Sir Edwin Pears, based on rumours of terrible atrocities in southern Bulgaria by Turkish forces against the Christian population. The British Foreign Office was furious. So too was the pro-Turkish Prime Minister, Benjamin Disraeli. Describing the reports as 'coffee-house babble', he flatly denied them and openly charged the paper with misreporting and with, that old standard whine of the politicians, 'irresponsibility'. The Turks, who had imposed a total censorship on events, denied the whole thing.

It was now up to the *News* to prove their charges, or humiliatingly to climb down. So they sent for MacGahan and commissioned him to go to Bulgaria and try to discover the truth. By early July he was on his way; by the middle of the month he was there, investigating and interviewing hundreds of survivors. What he found was beyond even his hardened imagining: the frenzied and wholesale butchery of some 12,000 Bulgarian men, women and children.

In the first of his dispatches, published by the *News* on 28 July, MacGahan wrote: 'I think I came in a fair and impartial frame of mind ... I fear I am no longer impartial, and I am certainly no longer cool...'. His most telling account was from the village of Batak. Despite his own remarks about impartiality, it is a model of how the controlled reporting of facts, rather than emotions, is the most effective form of journalism:

> The hillsides were covered with little fields of wheat and rye that were golden with ripeness. But although the harvest was ripe, and over ripe ... there were no sign of reapers trying to save them. The fields were as deserted as the little valley, and the harvest was rotting in the soil.

... At last we came to a little plateau on the hillside ... We rode toward this, with the intention of crossing it, but all suddenly drew rein with an exclamation of horror, for right before us, almost beneath our horses' feet, was a sight that made us shudder. It was a heap of skulls intermingled with bones from all parts of the human body, skeletons, nearly entire, rotting clothing, human hair, and putrid flesh lying there in one foul heap, around which the grass was growing luxuriantly.

... In the midst of this heap I could distinguish one slight skeleton form still enclosed in a chemise, the skull wrapped about with a coloured handkerchief, and the bony ankles encased in the embroidered footless stockings worn by the Bulgarian girls.

... On the other side of the way were the skeletons of two children lying side by side partly covered with stones, and with frightful sabre cuts in their little skulls... As we approached the middle of the town, bones, skeletons, and skulls became more numerous. There was not a house beneath the ruins of which we did not perceive human remains, and the street besides was strewn with them... The church was not a very large one, and it was surrounded by a low stone wall, enclosing a small churchyard about fifty yards wide by seventy-five long. At first we perceive nothing in particular,... but upon inspection we discover that what appeared to be a mass of stones and rubbish was in reality an immense heap of human bodies covered over with a thin layer of stones.

... We were told there were three thousand people lying here in this little churchyard alone ... There were little curly heads there in that festering mass, crushed down by heavy stones; little feet not as long as your finger on which the flesh was dried hard by the ardent heat before it had time to decompose; little baby hands stretched out as if for help; babes that had died wondering at the bright gleam of sabres and the red hands of the fierce-eyed men who wielded them; children who had died shrinking with fright and terror; young girls who had died weeping and sobbing and begging for mercy; mothers who died trying to shield their little ones with their own weak bodies, all lying there together, festering in one horrid mass.

They were silent enough now. There are no tears nor cries, no weeping, no shrieks of terror, nor prayers for mercy. The harvests are rotting in the fields, and the reapers are rotting here in the churchyard.

MacGahan's reports (which were reprinted across the world and later published as a booklet in many languages) instantly detonated a chain reaction of enormous proportions. Amid the worldwide indignation that followed, the British government was forced to concede the truth, pressure for military intervention built up and, in the spring of 1877, Russia launched a war against Turkey.

80 correspondents arrived to cover the Russian side but such were the rigours of the campaign that by its end less than a year later, only four of the original reporters were still in the field. MacGahan, of course, was among them. He had gone off to war with one foot in plaster, after injuring it in a fall.

He ignored this and two further accidents which seriously crippled him, and carried on reporting, watching the fighting from a gun carriage. Six months and two treaties later, the nations of Bulgaria, Serbia, Montenegro and Romania had come into being, Russia was enlarged and the British had Cyprus.

MacGahan, however, was not alive to report it. A few weeks after the end of the war he went to Constantinople to nurse his friend, Francis Greene, through typhoid fever. Greene survived, but MacGahan caught it himself and on 9 June 18 he died, aged 34. The Bulgarians, who had already christened him 'The Liberator', buried him in Pera, masses were said for his soul in St. Petersburg and he was mourned in London, Paris and America. In Sofia a statue was erected to him and for years afterwards his death was commemorated with an annual requiem at Tirnova.

Five years later his body was brought by an American warship to New York, where it lay in state in City Hall, and thence was taken to its final resting place in New Lexington, Ohio. His wife, who had been the Russian correspondent of the *New York Herald,* crossed the ocean with her husband's body and became the American correspondent for the Moscow paper, *Russkaya Viedmosti.* Later that year an official inquiry confirmed, in the cool calm of hindsight, everything that MacGahan had written from the chaotic killing fields of Bulgaria. Universal journalism is nothing new.

Skill in Specialisation

The news is the timely report of events, facts, and opinions and interests a significant number of people. It is a new piece of information about a significant and recent event that affects the audience and is of interest to them. The definition of a news item is dependent on :

(a) the size of the community,

(b) the periodicity of the publication,

(c) the social character and economic base of the community,

(d) the focus of attention of community.

Jhon Bogart pointed out that unusual events fall under the purview of the news. Later, Joseph Pulitzer, publisher of New York World defined news as "original, distinctive, dramatic, romantic, thrilling, unique, curious, quaint, humorous, odd and apt-to-be-talked about". Walter William, the founder of the first school of Journalism, defined news as, "News in its broadest sense, is that which is of interest to the readers-the public....."

The former-managing editor of the New York Times said that the news was "..... anything you can find out today that you didn't know before."

Thus, the news is Perishable; of interest to a large number of people; of unusual events and happenings; what is new to the public; an event put forward by a reporter.

Hard News and Soft News : These are the two main categories in which the news is mainly divided.

Hard News is mostly event-centered. It is a narration of an event. The Hard news items are centered on, "what, when, where and why".

No doubt, the major thrust of a daily newspaper is the hard news. The main task of the dailies is to provide information to the readers. Mere accounts of events however do not satisfy the readers. They would like to enter beneath the upper crust of hard news. This type of news is called soft news. Thus, soft news goes beyond what has happened. It analyses, interprets and draws logical conclusions. It is becoming a very important segment of the daily newspaper.

The Matter

Timeliness : News must be timely and new. It loses interest if it is already known.

Nearness : People are more interested in what happens under their nose. They are more concerned in the occurrence of an immediate impact on them.

Conflict : People gather in a street if and when there is a fight. Conflicts of all kinds are part of life and make good copy.

Prominence : What happens to important persons makes news. The value of the news increases with the prominence of the person involved. What the prominent people say, is also grist for a reporter's mill, particularly if they make some announcements which have an impact on the common people.

Government Action : The passing of a law or other orders concerning general people, cabinet meetings, parliament and assembly sessions, notifications about new rules and regulations are news worthy.

Development Projects and Issues : This is not news about government action, activities, though sometimes it will also qualify to be covered. The intention of a high yield variety rice and its success in changing the life-style of a community will be of interest to people who will financially benefit from it.

Weather and Sports : Both the weather and sports have great news value. Also entire page is devoted to sports in many newspapers.

Follow-up : The news item become very interesting for the general public when the issues are followed and updated. It is important to remember that follow-up of news events will keep the interest of the readers alive.

News Values : News values differ from community to community, country to country. News values are also different for developing and developed countries. For the industrialized and individualised societies of developed countries, communally provocative speeches and incidents may be reported word for word, blow by blow. But the same treatment would be suicidal in a developing country. One should take all possible care in reporting such developments keeping in mind the volatile nature of the audience and the reach of one's publication. One must follow some journalistic ethics and at times some self-censorship. Freedom of the press is not a licence to damage or destroy any one's reputation.

Fundamental Qualities

Accuracy : Accuracy is basic to any news item. When you fail in accuracy, you lose credibility. Cross check your facts and information. Check figures, names and facts. Make sure that the meaning is not changed and the statements are not quoted out of context. Exclude rumours or gossip from your report.

Balance : To be balanced in reporting, is as important as being accurate. While writing about a controversy, both sides of the story should be given. A story may appear to be 'imbalanced' and thus biased, if it has too much of government views, or tends to give too much of foreign news which has little relevance to readers.

Objectivity : Your opinion should not be mixed in the story. Report only facts and other peoples opinions. You should be a disinterested observer, reporting events without taking sides.

Clarity : Your introductory sentence should be short and in active voice to the maximum extent possible. The ideal length of each para may be 3-4 lines containing one-to-three small sentences to facilitate easy comprehension.

Impact : Whenever you do a news report, consider the impact your story should have. Will it induce some changes somewhere for the better? Develop a "nose for news", particularly news that will make an impact.

News Sources : A reporter, to be successful, should have a variety of reliable and highly placed contacts. There are some of the useful 'sources' for his information. Among the news sources, some are available to all reporters, such as public meetings, monitoring of radio and television programmes, press conferences, news briefing, seminars and other functions. But the contacts are sources of exclusive information for the reporter. They may be in the government, public or private sector business or just anywhere. Some of the contacts may like to be quoted for the story as it gives them publicity. In case of a critical story, they may not risk their neck. In that case, the story may have to be distributed to 'sources' only. It is the responsibility of a reporter to ensure the truthfulness of a report. In such cases, it will be advisable to keep some documents or audio tape to prove your story.

In the business of collecting the news, particularly of critical and investigative nature confrontation with the government is inevitable. A journalist chronicles daily events, places facts before the public, and tries to communicate that he considers truth. This may not suit the politician all the time, hence confrontation may occur. In case, a confrontation becomes inevitable, a reporter should face it. He should also treat his sources as 'sacred'. There may be pressure on the journalist from the government and the judiciary at times to disclose the sources. Protecting one's source is a cardinal principle of journalism.

News Reporting : Here is a description about news reporting and the main components of a news report-the body and the lead.

The Lead : The lead should contain the essence of the story. It should give the reader an idea of what the story is about and help the copy desk to pick a suitable headline for the story. A good lead should arouse the reader's curiosity and force him on to read the rest of the story. It should be precise and made up of short, simple sentences. The lead should answer the five W's-Who, What, Where, When and why and How.

The Body : While the lead should arouse the reader's interest, the body should sustain it. The body should flow smoothly and logically from the lead. The body should be as complete and as tight as possible and should provide all the relevant information within the shortest space possible.

The essence of good journalistic writing is brevity and simplicity. Do not use a complex or long word where a short word would do.

Various Types

Objective Reporting : A reporter is essentially a short story teller and he should tell the story in an objective and truthful manner, without lacing it with personal opinions or subjective comments. He should be fair and impartial and present both sides of the story. Complete objectivity is a mere concept. The reporter is a human being and he has certain ideas, feelings, attitudes, opinions and prejudices. However, a good reporter should try to rise above them and tell the facts as he has collected them in his search for truth. Objective reporting is, of course, not synonymous with dullness. It means fair and impartial reporting that is free from personal bias or prejudice.

Interpretative Reporting : It combines facts with interpretation. It delves into reasons and meanings of a development. His the interpretative reporter's task to give the information along with an interpretation of its significance. In doing so he uses his knowledge and experience to give the reader an idea of the background of an event and explain the consequences it could led to. Besides his own knowledge and research in the subject, he often has to rely on the opinions of specialists to do a good job. Interpretative reporting goes behind the news, brings out the hidden significance of an event and separates truth from falsehood.

Investigative Reporting : It is difficult to define the term 'investigative' journalism. In one way, of course, investigative journalism is a redundant concept, since all stories require some kind of investigation on the part of the reporter. However, the investigative reporter is expected to dig deeply beyond the facts stated in the hard news. Though we may face difficulty in defining the term, we can not ignore the concept of investigative journalism. Investigative reporting has made great leaps in western countries. In India, it is still in its infancy. Attempts at investigative reporting, to quote one eminent Indian editor, arc like drilling for oil. A fair amount of wastage of effort has to be taken for granted. But when the oil is discovered and becomes marketable, the sense of achievement is usually more than in any other sector of journalistic enterprise. In India, investigative reporting started making a mark after the end of internal emergency in 1977. With governments becoming increasingly secretive and corruption spreading its tentacles far and wide, the need for investigative reporting can not be over emphasized.

Investigative reporting requires hard and sustained work. The investigative reporter should be combination of a crusader, super detective and blood bound and should have the necessary time and finance to carry out his work. The best thing of Investigative Reporting is that which keeps the public interest in mind. It may highlight an injustice, expose corrupt practices or unmask dishonest politicians and bureaucrats.

But experience shows that unless an investigative reporter or a crusading reporter gets the support of the judiciary, the executive or the legislative, can not bring his reports to logical ends.

Crime Reporting : There is tremendous public interest in crime stories and no newspaper can afford to ignore them without damage to its circulation and credibility. Crime is a part of life and it is newspaper's duty to inform the readers of what crimes are going on in their city, state or country.

Crime reporting is a highly responsible and specialised job. The reporter should not only have the ability to shift the grain from the chaff, and the truth from lies, he should also have good contacts in the police and other departments of the administration as well as working knowledge of the penal codes and law on libel and other relevant matters. Besides, he must observe a code of honour. He should not suppress news of public interest. Nor should he seek to settle personal scores with police officers or lawyers or judges. And he must be careful that in the course of this work, he doesn't necessarily invade a citizen's privacy. The crime reporter must never violate standards of decency and good taste.

Crime as News : There are several types of crime news-murders, fires, accidents, burglaries, fraud, blackmail, kidnapping etc.

Fires : The reporter must get his facts correct about the essential elements of a fire story-the number of persons killed or injured, the extent of damage, to property, the loss of valuables. He should question eye-witnesses about any act of bravery or cowardice. All these are essential ingredients of a fire story.

Homicides : In cases of a major murder, the reporter should rush to the scene as soon as possible and gather all the relevant facts. Their dependence on police information often hampers their search for truth.

In reporting dowry deaths or alleged dowry deaths, the reporter should refrain from levelling uncorroborated statements by one party or the other.

Accidents : Most accidents are reported on the basis of police bulletins or information supplied by police spokesmen. However, wherever possible the crime reporter must rush to the scene of a major accident to give authenticity to his story.

The Qualities : A journalist must possess and uphold certain noble qualities in order to be professional. Integrity of character, commitment to the truth and a reasoning power of mind are essential to any reporter. These qualities also contribute to the credibility of the reporting organization. Besides, a journalist has to be truly responsible. A journalist is responsible to the audience as much as to the news organization. Again a journalist is always responsible to the sources who reveal information. A reporter must also have a healthy respect for news values.

The Responsibilities : It is said that a reporter is both eyes and ears of a news organization. It is not possible to strictly prescribe qualifications which a good reporter must possess. However, novice reporters must train themselves informally for the job so that they would be able to discharge their responsibilities with confidence, courage and competence. To be a successful reporter and to accomplish your job competently, you must be able to perceive, predict, calculate and plan your action appropriately in anticipation of a news event.

Important Factors

A Nose for News : The reporter is the most important functionary of a newspaper. So one must know what constitutes news in order to be able to gather news. A reporter's job of discovering the news has been simplified in one, way and rendered difficult in another sense, in this age of information. While there are the usual press notes on which news reports can be based, there are other sources of information on a variety-of news event. But quite often, most of the material before a news reporter may just be a publicity matter. Therefore, as a reporter, one must check the material and squeeze the news that would interest one's reader. A sharp sense of observation may also help one to gather amusing sidelights of interest to one's readers. This alertness will help one to discover contradictions and problems.

Outgoing Nature : Professional journalists are never arm chair writers. Introverts normally make poor reporters. Reporters have to move about meeting people, making their acquaintance and winning their confidence. This would help them to establish contacts, which in turn helps in writing well-investigated reports. This is the era of investigative reporting and readers are keenly interested to know what is going on behind the scenes. To get that kind of stories, one has no alternative but to be outgoing. One has to develop an affable temperament and an easygoing nature.

Ability to Establish Contacts and Develop Sources : An outgoing nature is the basic quality to establish contact and develop sources. You must have the ability to win the confidence and respect of those who may be potential sources of news. During the course of your regular duties, people may voluntarily offer you information.

Alternatively, this might not be the case when you are working on an investigative story. People may hesitate to talk on sensitive matters. They may like to reveal, yet are afraid to in case it were to affect them adversely. It may be quite difficult to win their trust. While you are establishing contact, there may be some among them who may want to plant information on you to serve their vested interests. Such information may consist of half-truths and even lies. So, you must have other independent contacts through whom you can verify the information. What matters is the alertness and ability to pursue your sources to get the right lead.

Ability to be an Unprejudiced Observer : The reporter must be an unprejudiced observer of events, one who presents the facts to the reader in a balanced, objective manner. It has been said that reporters mix comment with fact and so their reports are quite subjective. The reporters should not allow personal opinions at any place in the copy. One must be able to throw light on unclear aspects if any, of the news event. At the same time, the news reporter must endeavour to write a report which is only a statement of facts.

Thus, the first thing is to source your copy properly, to assure the reader that what you are passing on as news, is not your opinion. Even when you are not able to quote the sources, you must ensure that the story is balanced, by giving adequate coverage to all the sides of the subject. You should also ensure that the information you are presenting is true, which can be done by counter checking.

But remaining an unprejudiced observer does not mean adopting what is known in American journalistic parlance as 'man from the Mars' stance, i.e., seeing each event afresh, unconnected to any previous expectations or future possibilities and passing them on untouched by interpretation. In many cases, this would mean an irresponsible attitude, a refusal to make the reader understand the event in its proper context and realise its significance.

Clarity of Expression : Your command, as a reporter, over the language must be such that you can explain even the most complicated issues in simple terms to any general reader. In addition to specialised subjects such as science and technology, even government press notes are written in complicated language, burying the news point. You must be able to simplify it and bring out the news point.

Team Spirit : Except for routine coverages which can be handled by one person, many investigative stories have to be handled by a team. You must be able to work as a member of such a team. And you must pool your talents, sources and contacts into the team and work under a leader. In the course of time, you may rise to head such a team. Working under a team discipline will certainly be of help to you later.

Ability to Cope with Pressure : With investigative journalism seeking to bring out scandals and exposures, there is bound to be pressure on journalists to keep someone's wrong doings hidden from public view. The 'pressure' on journalists is exerted in the hope of preventing exposure. The concerned journalist may also be bribed with attractive favours in return for silence on the matter.

The pressure could be used to make you change the news or 'kill' a story. This constitutes censorship. Pressure could also be applied with the hope of inducing journalist to volunteer the change or omission which is then equal to self-censorship.

There are three ways of coping with pressure: fighting it, giving in or anticipating the pressure and taking preventive measures.

Preventive measures to fight pressure could be legal steps, like seeking a court stay on any law or ordinance that could affect the freedom of the press.

Other Responsibilities **:** The reporting profession is unlike any other profession. At times, some slight carelessness in doing one's duty, can cause incalculable harmful repercussions, both for the news organization and society. A slight laziness in cross checking certain facts could endanger the credibility of the news organization.

Responsibility towards the News Organization **:** As a reporter, you have to follow the character, style and policy of your newspaper or magazine or news agency. There are conservative papers which may prefer to stick to routine coverage, not bothering about investigation of scandals. In such papers, you have to stick to their policy even if it cramps your style. But in a news organization with a more dynamic approach to news, you must develop the skills of an investigator. Whatever you do as a reporter will affect the newspaper and its reputation. So you must take pains to ensure accuracy and objectivity in your stories.

Responsibility towards the Sources **:** Your sources are sacred. Your credibility in their eyes could be a major factor in your performance as a newsperson. There are sources with whom you will have to take great pains to establish your credibility to make them open up towards you. You will have to assure them that no harm will come to them, and if they so desire, you must keep their identity a secret.

Responsibility towards the Reader and Society **:** As a news reporter, you have a duty to provide accurate, unbiased and objective information to the reader. Every effort must be made to ensure that the news is accurate, free from prejudices and that all sides of the news event are presented fairly.

To maintain your credibility with the reader you have a duty not to accept things or favours or pursue any activity that might compromise your integrity.

However, in these days, publicity seekers including those in private business, organize press conferences and conduct tours with attractive gifts and other incentives. While private firms depend mainly on advertising for publicity, they sometimes want their activities to be carried as news items since news carries greater credibility than advertisements. News reports are written by newspapers who are supposed to be independent and objective.

Interviewing Skills : A very authentic way of gathering facts, figures and opinions on various issues is to interview the persons concerned. The interview is a very useful input for all the media-print and electronic. It depends on how one would like to use an interview. It may be used as a programme to make the audience/reader get information/facts from the source directly. The interview can form the basis of an article, a feature or a commentary.

How to Prepare for an Interview : The most important part of the interview is to know your subject as completely as possible. It is imperative for you to not only fully research the information you want from your subject, but also the person behind it. You should also have all the essential background information on the interviewee which will help you to build an instant rapport with the interviewee.

Research : It is most important to research your subject matter. It could be a subject in which you neither have any interest nor adequate knowledge. But once you are fully armed with the basic and important information acquired through books, newspapers, journals or magazines articles, you will be much more comfortable and should be successful in your venture.

You must know your subject matter as well as the person whom you intend to talk to about the subject matter.

Editing Interviews for Use : Two fundamental factors are to be remembered by all journalists-First, all interviews are subject to editing. So there is no harm in culling more information than you can use. The information that you need to buttress an argument or to refuse another or to make a point, can be used at the appropriate place. The rest can be stored for use in future.

Second, no statement made in the interview is allowed to be used out of context. If the authority interviewed does not generalise it, the reporter or, sub-editor is debarred from generalising it.

Strategy : It is important to establish contact with the interviewee much in advance of the interview. More often than not, where important interviewees are concerned, there is a channel you will have to go through. It could be the private secretary or the members of the family referred to as the "protector of the interviewee".

So, the first thing to do is to establish a rapport with the protector. To get to your subject-matter or the person, you must be able to play to the gallery to defeat all the obstacles imposed by the "protectors".

What You Want from the Interview : If the first thing is to establish contact and to build up a rapport, the most important part of the preparation is to decide what you want to get out of the interview. May be you want substantiation of a fact you have discussed; or the refutation of something; or may be you want the interviewer's views on some, proposition you or someone else is making.

It is vital for an interviewer to decide what he wants out of the interview. It is not a fishing expedition in which you net whatever you get. It is a hunt where you go after a target and get it.

Also one has to keep his senses on full alert and the antenna unfurled to each nuggets of news which have a knack of falling from the lips of the interviewee at the most unexpected moments.

Preparing Yourself : It is important and essential to make a deep study of the individual you plan to interview. Paying attention to his minute, apparently insignificant, matters really helps in conducing the interview smoothly. You must build a personal rapport to begin with, so you may start the interview comfortably.

Physical Preparation : If it is a television interview, then you need the cameraman, sound recordist, lighting technician and sound technician.

The other way in which the interview is to be held in a studio, then arrangements should be made accordingly in the studio. For the radio studio interview, a good recording machine is required, a lip microphone is used which prevents extraneous sound from getting injected into the microphone.

How to Get an Interview : Getting an interview can often be difficult, because the interviewer is generally viewed with suspicion. The interviewer labours between two competing factors. One, the public has the right to know and you are the tool employed to gather the information. Two, from the legal point of view nobody can be forced into talking hence, the job can be tiresome and at times, very frustrating.

It is very important that one's own participation in the interview is secondary. One must let the interviewee do most of the talking. To make this happen smoothly, a number of skills have to be deployed like :

(a) There is the direct approach-to telephone and tell the interviewee what you want.

(b) *The End Round:* A secretary in a business or government office will generally try, and give you the 'brush off'. The attempt of the interviewer should be to try and make the secretary one's friend.

(c) When faced with repeated failure, find out the person's hide-out and with an overdose of apology, just barge in.

(d) *Sit in:* It pays to just 'sit and wait' till the subject of interview shows up in spite of secretaries saying that 'the boss has no time to see you'.

(e) *The Appeal:* As soon as you get the glimpse of the reluctant interviewee, make your appeal as quickly and strongly as possible.

(f) *Be Courteous and Polite:* Tell the interviewee that there are two sides to every story, and we want to know yours. Thus, you arouse the interviewee's curiosity and attention. In many cases, it pays to tell the interviewee of the other side.

Do's and Dont's for an Interview

(a) Be operational on time for the interview. This is very important. It shows the importance of the interviewee and that he has not been taken for granted. In a nut shell, you must be ready right on time to start the interview.

(b) Outline your reasons for being there, unless you are working on something very sensitive.

(c) Start the interview with a broad question. This helps you to size up the person and also collect your thoughts. It also helps to receive information you may not have anticipated.

(d) Do not interrupt until the interviewee has relaxed. Avoid making the interviewee uncomfortable at the outset. It would be of little value.

(e) Let him speak at length on his favourite topic/ achievement/feat. You will get nuggets of information. The irrelevant facts can always be edited out.

(f) Grunt and chuckle occasionally.

(g) Stick to your subject.

(h) Avoid commenting except to egg him on to top more. Let the interviewee do most of the talking.

(i) Do not end the interview till you have the basics-how does he spell his name, official title, age etc. Preferably get the details in advance from his staff and then get it confirmed by him.

(j) Be understanding. Do not be insensitive. Make the interviewee feel important. Keep the interviewee at ease.

Interviewing Skills : Advance preparation for the interview by way of well-thought out questions and a thorough consideration of approach is very helpful. One need not fear that the final outcome will sound stilted with no natural spontaneity. Usually the reverse is true.

Taking Notes : Taking notes is an essential part of interviewing. Some take down everything, even irrelevant and redundant remarks. Take down only what is important. People sometimes stop talking when you start writing and so taking down only the important remarks may not be possible. And you don't always know what is relevant until you have written it all down and reviewed it.

(i) Write as fast as you can.

(ii) Keep hand and mind together, listen to key phrases. A tape recorder helps you to review the interview *in toto*. It is a must for a question and answer story.

Conducting An Interview : Know your subject. Read the person's eyes and mannerisms since these offer a reliable clue on how an interview is to be handled. Since the interview rarely goes as planned, therefore the interviewer requires a lot of instinct.

How to Establish Rapport with the Interviewee

(a) In many small and big ways, try to make your interviewee feel nice, cheerful and important.

(b) Outline your reasons for being there. Bring the interviewee up-to-date on what you are looking for.

(c) Start with a broad question. This helps you to see the person and collect your thoughts. It also gives you an opportunity to receive information which you may not have anticipated.

(d) Stick to the subject. Do not ramble or chit-chat. Neither is it advisable to beat around the bush. So go ahead and simply ask your questions straight-away.

(e) Doodling or writing down a lot of useless matter in your notebook can be helpful. Those who have important information to transmit, like to feel they are being recorded. You might be asked to show what you have taken down. For all that, jotting down points helps you to prepare the transcription of the interview-session for publication.

(f) Listen. Listen. Listen. Not only does this make the interviewee feel good and wise, but it also helps you to control the interview. An interviewer might start speaking with good intentions and slowly digress. You can bring him back to point. "You were saying something about the time you were in college, prison, etc. When was that?" And you are back on the track.

(g) Be understanding. Nobody likes insensibility. The interviewee is often quite nervous while discussing his/her wrong doings, sin or tragedy. Help him/her to relax. If your mind goes blank, just say, "Excuse me. I forgot where we were and what I need to ask".

2

Reporting News

In the third stage, when the message reaches the receiving end, that is, the media organisation, the decision-makers there begin their selection. The message goes through the 'gatekeeper'. Kurt Lewin was the first to introduce the term 'gatekeeper' in 1947 with reference to the people in a news organisation who watched the flow of news. David Manning White and Warren Breed popularised the idea. According to Breed, the policy of a publisher gets translated into action by the 'gatekeepers'. Manning found that the 'gatekeepers' had the power to decide if an item would have to be changed before it was transmitted. At this stage, major decisions are made regarding the selection of stories for the day's issue the decision-makers go through the stories selected by reporters and judge wire service news stories. The decisions are usually made at the afternoon editorial conference where each section editor brings in what he has chosen for inclusion in the next issue. As Lippmann observed, there are no written rules on decision-making, only conventions.

Some scholars have given more importance to the decision-making process at the first step, namely, the news gathering stage. For example, Bass considers the news gatherers' decision more important than the news processors' decision. The news gatherers, according to him, consist of the writers, reporters, bureau chiefs, and city editors; the news processors include editors, copy readers and translators. But this does not deal with the organisational and sociological imperatives exerting influence on the climate of the news gathering and selection process. For an understanding of this influence, we have to refer to some other studies based on the content of news media.

In their classic study of a demonstration against the Vietnam War, Halloran and others showed how events were selected for news reporting in terms of their fit or consonance with pre-existing images. In other words, the news of the demonstration confirmed earlier ideas. Their conclusion was:

> The more nuclear the news item and the more uncertain or doubtful the newsman is how to report it, the more likely it is to be reported within a general framework that has already been established.

Four other factors were cited by Halloran based on the findings of Galtung and Ruge as vital components of news value: reference to elite persons; references to elite states; personalisation or personification; and negativism. Do media select top people and top nations more frequently than others? Is news reporting person-centered? Are negative events preferred to positive ones?

Another important finding of Halloran and associates was that despite the outward differences among various newspapers, all of them showed a fundamental similarity in the presentation of factors which made events news. They found little variation in the approach of the various newspapers to the demonstration against the Vietnam War.

Viewers and readers were not presented with various interpretations focusing on different aspects of the same events, but basically the same interpretation which focused on the same limited aspects-the issue of violence.... Events were not so much deliberately distorted or otherwise falsified by presentation, as selected and interpreted for their relevance to the basic and predetermined news issue. The simple negative image built up for the demonstration story was the only image made widely available to the public by press the television news.

It is in the function of selection and interpretation that the news producers exercise their value judgements. This function is performed with reference to a framework of ideas and symbols considered important not only to the communicators but the 'communicatees'.

Stuart Hall's comment on the process of interpretation in broadcast media is relevant to that in the mass circulated press as well:

> Every news event is already, completely, assigned to a context which explains it. The broadcaster, or his reporter and cameraman in the field, must already have such a context in mind in order to know what to film, which to select and send back to the editor, which to include in the broadcast.

If we accept this premise, we have to concede that in the process of news selection. Agenda setting is unavoidable because the recipients of communication should be provided with certain stories presented in a certain way for contextualisation. For many years, researchers have been trying (and they are still trying) to find relationships between media usage and attitude change. Agenda setting is a trend discernible in the mass media and it is resorted to by the media owners to bring about a symbiotic relationship between their priorities and their audience's supposed priorities.

The ultimate aim is to find that perfect fit or consonance between the communicators and the audience which is essential to maximise sales of media products and hence profits. Through agenda setting, the media fare will synchronise, it is hoped, with 'what the public wants', on a daily basis. People exposed to the mass media do learn from them and form opinions based on that learning. Can the press steer the course of their thinking or influence their thinking process? According to Shaw and McCombs, the two researchers who studied this issue empirically, the press presents to the people should be concerned about. It may be argued that enlightened people will have their own independent judgement on all such issues: but research has shown that the press through the agenda setting process provides issues and event to think about, if not opinions to hold. The concept is defined as 'the ability of the media to influence the salience of events in the public mind'. It has been derived from two important pronouncements made half a century apart-one by Walter Lippmann in 1922 and the other by Theodore White in 1972. Lippmann spoke about the power of the press in creating pictures of the world in the minds of the readers. White spoke about the press setting the agenda of public discussion.

Through the process of selection, as already explained, the media transit to the audience those national and international issues which they consider newsworthy and hence worthy of the audience's attention. Shaw and McCombs have shown that people form their individual political cognitions based on what the mass media present as salient. The agenda-setting function of the press is put into practice through the following steps:

The Audience : We are now in the fourth selection stage, namely, the audience of media fare. There have been many studies of the audience of all types of news including foreign news; but most of the studies have concentrated on how to effect behaviour modification through appropriate messages to the audience. Since a study of the effects of messages on the audience is not our aim, it is enough to mention that members of the audience select messages depending on their particular needs and interests. Newspapers are aware of their audience's selection of messages, and they hope to reach messages they consider important for the readers by placing them in special positions or displaying them distinctly. The placement of messages and their display is allied to the concepts of selection and agenda setting. Since agenda setting is linked to the fourth selection stage in the communications model, some details of that concept are worth examining.

The press, as Walter Lippmann said in his classic work, Public Opinion, fills in our unseen environment, and helps us to form our mental picture of the world.

1. daily selection of news events and issues by the wire service reporters and editors;
2. daily selection from the wire service news and issues by the newspapers' editors (gatekeepers); and
3. placement of the news and views in the newspaper by the new editor.

Placement in the broadcast media is achieved by the numerical order in which the news and views are presented. Whichever is announced first is the leading news story of the hour. In the newspaper, what the news editor considers to be more important news events will be placed on the front page. These will not only be placed on the front page, but discussed in the editorial and opposite-editorial pages. Among the important stories on the front page, the most important will be presented in large size types, with bold letter synopsis, 'boxing', etc. Sometimes pictures are incorporated to heighten the importance of the event.

Items placed on the let hand corner catch the readers' attention first since people's eyes move linearly from left to right, except in those countries where they read from right to left. What the media emphasise through selection, placement and display go down in the audience's consciousness as salient. According to Shaw and McCombs, the agenda setting power of the press may be thought of as, a process of consensus building between those who have access to the press or whom the press regularly covers with news, the press itself, and the audience or society at large. Agenda setting represents social learning.

The above discussion shows that reporters and news editors or the maker of news have the power to select events and topics. They exercise this power on a daily basis and what the audience gets is the product of their selection. We move on now, to some more conceptual matters relating to news selection and newsmaking.

The Access : Access to the press is supposed to be the corner-stone of democracy since it ensures open debate on public issues. The freedom of the press is ultimately people's freedom to express their views even when those views are against the prevailing authoritarian forces. But, can every citizen be guaranteed access to the media? Is the modern, well-established, high technology press small enough to be accessible to the ordinary citizen?

Technological progress has changed the structure of media organisations and the very nature of mass communication. The trend towards centralisation of the technology and ownership of the mass media has been referred to already. Big newspapers force the smaller ones out of business and multimedia conglomerates dominate the communication scene. The concentration of the media in the hands of a powerful elite minority is not conductive to citizens' access and to the freedom of the press. In the United States, newspaper monopoly exists in 95 per cent of the cities. In India, there are thousands of small towns and villages which do not have any newspaper circulation at all. Lack of access leads not only to the loss of vital information but also to the stifling of dissenting views and to a lack of diversity. Despite the argument that it is impossible for any newspaper to publish everything that comes to it, it should be recognised that the only way to ensure access is to multiply media voices through alternative media, if necessary. If the media of communication continue to depend on centralised, capital-intensive, high technology, they will remain inaccessible to the average citizen's points of view.

The Continuity **:** This is a quality often stressed by newsmen. It is closely linked to completeness, but since newspapers are mainly in the business of bringing the latest news, and not that of completing an already broached story with additional facts and figures for the edification and education of the readers, continuity is not often adhered to as an inviolable news principle. A big story of yesterday will be discontinued or inadequately treated today in order to play up today's big story which in turn will be replaced by another story tomorrow. Do various newspapers follow a pattern of omission or inadequate treatment of an already broken-in story? Are there reasons for this other than the desire to bring the latest 'big story and action news' to the readers? Are there organisational pressures or governmental pressures? By discontinuing stories or reporting incompletely, especially news about other countries and cultures and national minorities, will not occur distortion in news treatment? These are questions that have been answered to some extent by Gans and Tuchman who, like Gans, studied the newsmaking process as a participant observer accomplished in a void, and so a second theme is that professionalism serves organisational interests by reaffirming the institutional processes in which newswork is embedded.

Construction of Reality **:** Tuchman gathered, over a period of ten years, relevant data on the process of newsmaking in two television stations and three newspapers. She also interviewed several news-related organisations and workers. Her main theme is that act of making news is the act of constructing reality itself rather than a picture of reality Newswork transforms occurrences into news events. It draws on aspects of everyday life to tell stories, and it presents us to ourselves. By accomplishing this second task, it serves us as a basis for social action. But the process of making news is not accomplished in a void, and so a second theme is that professionalism serves organisational processes in which newswork is embedded.

According to Tuchman, bureaucratic chains of command

are developed in the newspaper organisation to keep track of daily occurrences out of which particular stories are woven into news and in this process, 'newsworthiness' is bestowed on selected occurrences. Reporters and editors create a 'web of facticity' for the sake of news credibility, and this web legitimates the status quo. Newsmen identify some sources and institutions as the appropriate location of facts and dismisses others. When legitimate leaders are unavailable, news organisations bestow authenticity to news into hard news, soft news, spot news and developing news. They also call some news items 'continuing news'.

But in their pursuit of more important news every day, they leave out the concept of continuity, although they may claim that a 'fair amount of coverage' is given to all stories. Perhaps certain news events are covered more frequently than certain others depending upon the importance the news organisation bestows on them.

Affirmative Sides

Connected with selection, continuity and access, is the idea of objectivity. Some newsmen consider their papers to present 'objective news' and take great pride in it. Objectivity is, no doubt, an ideal worth striving for. In it are included other ideals such as impartiality, fairness, truthfulness, reality, and total detachment of the newsmen from their sources and their news. Objectivity is not an ideal that can be achieved easily or frequently. In practice, subjectivity is involved in the selection and presentation of news. Even definitions of news are subjectively derived and not scientifically or objectively tenable. At any given moment, what is newsworthy depends on the decision-makers' socio-economic and cultural background, and the political climate that prevails in his country. As members of a social group, newsmen have certain symbols embedded in their consciousness which they use to interpret reality. Very often these symbols help in the perpetuation of the existing order and systems rather than in replacing them with something different or hitherto untried.

Objectivity is usually considered attainable by reporting opposing points of view. In fact, searching for the opposite side has almost become a ritual with newsmen. But there are a thousand shades of opinion between the two sides. On specific issues, many hundreds of people do not take any rigid view based on party affiliations. Since the newsmen's objectivity is limited in scope, the differences they try to bring out from opposing camps are not real differences but artificial ones couched in terms used by opposing camps. This can create a semblance of objectivity. The average citizens are sometimes misled by the artificial objectivity in news reports. Even in the first selection stage itself, subjectivity determines what news items and which news sources should be let into the news framework. Once newsmen realise and recognise the process of selection that goes on in their day-to-day work, they will not be as vehement in their protestations of objectivity.

An argument put forward by Tuchman is particularly relevant here. She believes that although it is wrong to accuse newsworkers of bias, and though it is difficult to define objective truth, it is valuable to identify news as an artificial accomplishment attuned to specific understanding of social reality. Those understandings, constituted in specific work processes and practices, legitimate the status quo.

A newspaper does not hold up a mirror to nature or to events because its reflecting scope is limited. News cannot be comprehensive because of the very nature of newsmaking. The 'reality' constructed by newsmen is not, or need not be, the actual reality or the whole reality. It is only aspects of reality which they produce and present to the public. Berger and Luckmann have discussed the concept of 'construct reality' elaborately in their work. That concept is applicable to the newspaper because, irrespective of the nature of external reality, journalists see it only through their own constructs. As far back as 1953, Kuart and Gladys Lang had shown that events covered were themselves journalistic constructs of related phenomena.

The *'medium is not the message'*, since the message depends on the men who utilise the medium. Communicators work in a national culture constructed out for several sub-cultures but very much under the powerful influence of the dominant group that holds economic, political and military power. This is why Gans calls news among other things, the exercise of power over the interpretation of reality.

Similar views are expressed by Tuchman who believes that the work of the media should be evaluated in terms of the sociology of knowledge. Since knowledge is power and communication is part of the knowledge industry, those who run the media are doubly capable of strengthening their network of power over society. They, in fact, start from an already powerful position for reasons of conglomeration with other forms of production. Readers and viewers are not totally helpless if alternative media choices are possible, and if journalists try to maintain news credibility and reliability; but as Manning has said, the media's views ultimately prevail because they have the final say on what gets into the channels and hence on access and availability.

In the interpretation of reality, the news media use certain techniques for attracting the audience, the most important of which is the technique of dramatisation. This is especially true of television news as confirmed by Epstein who studied the news manufacturing process in the three major networks of the United States. There is no doubt that the newspapers are now compelled to imitate television practices to survive the fierce competition from the electronic industry in technologically advanced countries and also in some developing countries where television is gaining strength. Most news stories open with a dramatic lead. The element of fiction in news stories is also not negligible. These news practices will continue because newsmen in the print media listen to the radio and television news bulletins broadcast early morning for lead stories in their afternoon editions, and the bulletins of the evening broadcast for their morning editions.

Newsmen's preoccupation with personalities and their tendency to personalise news are also allied to the technique of dramatisation. It is easier to dramatise an event if colourful and controversial personalities are involved in the news story. Pictures will heighten the dramatic aspects of a news event. Selection of news is influenced by picture possibility as well as opportunity to dramatise the event through well-known personalities. But who are the personalities who usually appear in the news?

After studying a six-month sample of stories appearing in alternate months during 1967, 1971 and 1975, Gans found that most of the news was about affluent people; the main actors inmost stories were people in the top 1-5 per cent income bracket, although most were distinguished by their geographical, racial, ethnic and religious background far more often than by their economic background. The magazines were found to universalise upper middle class practices as if they were shared by all Americans. Gans concluded that news story selection was based on availability and suitability of news and that it was the economically and politically powerful people whom journalists sought out for news stories. But drama and colour may not be the only considerations by newsmen since most often, those dramatic events and colourful personalities are chosen, who fit the socio-economic and political environment in which the media operate.

Under the influence of the electronic media, newspapers have changed the format of their pages, increasing the picture content and visual appeal of every page. One of the editors interviewed by this researcher said that he had standing instructions to use at least three pictures on the front page-one big and two small, and one picture on each inside page besides advertisement pictures. News items with picture possibilities and readily available pictures naturally find a place on the front or inside page much more easily than those without a picture. Thus, questions of immediacy, objectivity, completeness, continuity, and other values usually held in high esteem by newsworkers, are affected by the actual process of newsmaking.

The foregoing discussion should convince us that it is essential to look at the newspaper as a product of the efforts of a professional group of people who have identical interests and who belong to more or less the same socio-economic, political, and cultural systems. The newspaper is not just a picture of constructed reality, but constructed reality itself to those who produce it. It serves socio-economic, political, surveillance, cultural and entertainment functions news does not simply happen. There are occurrences in everyday life in every part of the world out *of* which news events are woven with due attention to factual correctness, balanced judgement as far as the selected facts are concerned, relevance to the audience, clarity, contextuality, completeness as far as the chosen facts are concerned, authentic references to news sources specially selected for the purpose, the reliability of the facts selected and presented. One of the substantive considerations among newsmen and newspaper organisations is that domestic news is more important than foreign news; however, when national interests abroad are threatened, foreign news relating to those interests becomes as important as, if not more important than, domestic news. In the study planned here, foreign news presentation occupies the major position and hence a detailed discussion of foreign news selection is necessary. Newspapers and all mass media disseminate information not only about events happening in their own countries but in other countries as well. The selection of foreign news is stricter for several reasons, some of which are discussed here.

The Space : Normally, only about one-third of the total space in a commercially successful and profitable newspaper is devoted to news. The rest of the paper is taken up by advertisement matter of one kind or another. And the bulk of the area devoted to news (called newshole) goes for metropolitan, state capital, large town or newspaper town and suburban news. A sizeable portion is cut out for regional and national news. It is the remaining space that is devoted to events occurring in other countries. Completeness, continuity, objectivity, access, authenticity, and other qualities expected in domestic news presentation will suffer heavily in the case of foreign news because of the pressure on space.

In an investigation of the reasons why newspapers rejected most of the foreign news that flowed into them through the wire services, Casey and Copeland found that 20 per cent of foreign news copies were rejected by American newspapers for 'lack of space', 35 per cent for lack of appeal or interest to readers, lack of news value and significance, 16 per cent because of loss of timeliness and 27 per cent for various technical reasons. They also found that large metropolitan papers allotted proportionately more space to foreign news than did non-metropolitan papers. The International Press Institute study of 93 US newspapers during four separate weeks between October 1952 and January 1953 during the Korean war concluded that the average proportion of foreign news material to text space was little more than 8 per cent.

Economic and Political Reasons : Sunwoo Nam hypothesised that the flow of news reflected the power configuration of world politics and depended on the political alliance and functional proximity of the reported country, rather than on geographical proximity or any other factor. He also expressed the view that the bulk of foreign news is not meant for the general public, but to help specialised audiences, decision-makers and foreign affairs experts in the functions of surveillance. According to his argument, the press in developing countries reports more foreign news because the press in these countries is elitist. Markham and Hart expressed similar views in their studies of the South American press.

Smith indicated that the growth of a country's interest in international communications is directly proportional to its military, economic and political interests in international areas. Gerbner has indicated that the modern mass media are the cultural arm of modern industry and business. A study by

Onyisi under Gerbner's supervision concluded that the southern part of the African continent received the most attention in the United States media because the multinational corporations with headquarters in the country had strong economic interests concentrated in that region of Africa. This relationship had already been studied more elaborately by Schiller in the case of the United States and he concluded that the American mass media were part of an American industrial and military complex. Abu-Lughod found that the degree of international coverage in a country's media depended on that country's dependence on other countries. He also hypothesised that the United States received a disproportionate amount of 'big power' coverage because several countries depended on it.

Lent has pointed out that 'national interests, crisis reporting, foreign censors, and a shrinking corp of correspondents' constrain international coverage in the US media. Gerbner and Marvanyi have graphically represented the many worlds of the world's press after making a multinational comparative study of foreign news coverage, confirming that coverage depends on the big power configuration that dominates the modern world.

But Elliott and Golding have pointed out that foreign news like domestic news is developed by the media, organisers as a marketable commodity throughout the world. According to them:

> "the culture to which news, and other aspects of the international system contribute, is not related to any single society or social structure so much as to that network of economic interests and organisations that is international corporate capitalism. Increasingly the growth of the international media system enables the news media to play broadly the same ideological role at an international level as is already apparent nationally in particular developed countries. The international media system is one mechanism by which

> developing countries are brought within the common cultural hegemony of western capitalism."

World Press Agencies : Heavy dependence on the global wire services has been cited by some as a determining factor in the selection and quantity of news from other countries. The IPI study, already referred to, found that the news agencies were the paramount source of international news and that the coverage by the news agencies centered heavily on the major countries of the world. To Hachten, the flow of news concerning less developed countries seemed to be more closely related to the use of a world news agency than to geographical proximities or language similarities.

Most newspapers of the developing countries do not have the economic capability of stationing their own correspondents in foreign countries. In developing as well as developed countries, it is the big chains and conglomerates that have their own wire services staff and special correspondents in other countries. All the rest depend on the big news agencies of the world. This leads to verbatim reproduction of news agency reports, sometimes including spelling and other errors.

Foreign news in most countries' newspapers is likely to have more or less the same content as far as a particular news story is concerned. There may be differences in the stories selected, but not much variety in the presentation of individual stories. The history of the development of the news agencies have a great impact on the process of foreign news selection and reporting. This leads us to the fourth factor that influences the selection, presentation and quantity of foreign news.

The history of colonialism had an equal impact on the growth of the international news media. Towards the end of the nineteenth century, the newly established European news agencies concluded a series of cartel agreements by means of which they divided the world between the, according to the prevailing imperial spheres of influence. These first links in the international media system set a precedent for much that was to follow as the media in developed and developing societies alike became progressively more involved in corporate capitalist economy.

Colonial news agencies are still strong in erstwhile colonies, and several of their reports could reflect the national interests of the countries in which those agencies originated. They reflect their national ethnocentrism which paves the way toward cultural imperialism.. The reporting of an event in a developing country may be influenced by the world's leading wire services, all of which are headquartered in the developed countries. The wire services' reports, thus, could lead to distortion and omission of vital aspects of the events, since they tend to interpret the event from their own national and global economic interests.

Foreign Policy Considerations : As mentioned earlier, domestic news becomes foreign news depending on the foreign policy actions of a country. When millions of refugees from East Pakistan fled to West Bengal and Bihar, their plight was first considered a foreign problem, but the stern action taken by India against Pakistan made it domestic news in India. Similarly, news about a country's nationals in other countries, although strictly news of foreign origin, becomes domestic news because of special domestic links with the nationals residing abroad. With the deep involvement of the United States in Vietnam, the latter country became domestic news in the US media. Afghanistan has now become well-known in the US and the USSR after the latter's troops marched into that country. The conflict in the Falkland Islands became national news in the British news media. Thus, foreign news is not wholly foreign; it is in a way domestic news extended to a foreign country.

Several researchers have found that three types of countries dominate foreign news in a country's newspapers: its closest or most powerful allies; its chief foes and their allies; and the rest of the world when something extraordinary occurs there. Gans, for example, fund that most foreign news in newspapers in the USA was about England, France, West Germany, Italy,

Japan, Israel, Egypt, the Soviet Union and mainland China. He observed that:

> Foreign news deals either with stories thought relevant to Americans or American interests; with the same themes and topics as domestic news; or when the topics are distinctive, with interpretations that apply American values... often limit themselves only to the most dramatic overseas events. In addition they tend to follow American foreign policy, even if not, lavishly Foreign news adheres less strictly to objectivity than domestic news; but... the values it applies are not very different from those that appear, less explicably, in domestic news.

This observation, is not only applicable to the US, but to India and other countries as well. In fact, major newspapers of all countries toe the official foreign policy line most of the time.

Issues of nationalism and patriotism might motivate the media to conform to their national government's foreign policy. It is difficult to find consistently favourable reports about socialist countries in capitalist countries newspapers (unless there is a very special relationship between them) and vice versa. Similarly, it is difficult to find reports, not to mention favourable reports, about enemy countries in a nation's news media unless the government itself wants certain information to be passed on to the people in order to alert them.

Since foreign policy is a major determinant of foreign news selection, most economic and political developments are seen in terms of the East-West ideological conflict or of the Cold War. Smaller countries are usually ignored unless news about them has some relevance to the newspaper's country. Some major countries are seen as allies or foes. Favourable reports about allies appear in the country's newspapers despite the existence of some very grave threats to human rights in those allied countries.

Reports about Latin American countries in newspapers of the US are examples of this. Every foreign news event is likely to be interpreted in relation to either the US or the Soviet Union by most newspapers of the world. 'The daily task of constructing the segment of international reality takes place in a particular kind of setting, both institutional and social', says Cohen. His views about the selection of foreign news are relevant to our discussion:

> Effective decisions are made... at a number of different points, although the general news editor and the telegraph editor, who preside over the bank of news tickers, together with whatever assistants they might have, make the major decisions involving selection and layout. These men do not, of course, start the editorial process anew each day; they approach the task with an experience and a perspective that have both long and short term components. Over the long term, particular classes of stories prompt the leading news spaces economic reform, war, international political competition... In the short run, the editors carry in their heads the knowledge of what the news has been over recent days and weeks. Hence, they come to their tasks every day with half-formed and unarticulated notions of what the news is apt to be like.

Cohen agrees that no newspaper can 'shovel out to its readers as news the total stock of information and stories that it receives,' but he points out that :

> "priorities and not absolutes determine the amount of... foreign affairs news. Foreign news has to compete with other types of news for getting into the paper. Space allocations are not made every day, but as part of a long term policy, which will be changed only by the top personnel. The selection of all types of news is done by editors on the basis of prior decisions on what the readers will buy".

However, it is not always the sales angle that determines the selection and presentation of foreign news. Political or ideological considerations, global economic interests, military strategies, patriotism, national security interests-all these exert a decisive influence on the selection of foreign countries and themes for presentation to the newspaper readers. Journalists often willingly cooperate with government when national security is threatened. As Cohen observes, 'personal friendships between government officials and newsmen are common, extending right up to the Presidential level'.

There may arise an occasional conflict between senior government officials in charge of foreign policy and some journalists who go wrong in their facts. But by and large, there develops a symbiotic relationship between the foreign news correspondent and his country's local embassy officials and this leads to reporting of events from the official point of view.

Sometimes, conditions ripe for revolution in a far-off country, or the true facts of a revolutionary movement may miss the attention of the correspondent who hastily accepts embassy hand-outs for transmission to the newspaper's headquarters. The newspaper organisations are willing to cooperate with the government by resorting to self-censorship on matters of national security or safety of citizens abroad.

Several instances can be cited from the reporting of the Vietnam war or the Indo-Pakistan war where journalists as citizens cooperated with the government. Gans even goes to the extent of saying that journalists occasionally report news from distant countries based on slender evidence.

The intimate cooperation between journalists and government has been discussed by Cohen:

> Stories about foreign aid, Christmas food packages, disaster relief packages, etc., illustrate how the press as a system of communication has become an integral part of the battery of instruments by means of which American foreign policy makers try to

> influence the expectations and the behaviors of other peoples and governments-friends and allies as well as potential enemies and countries with wandering affections.

The mass media's supply of international news is an important factor in everyone's picture of the world. But foreign policy influence on the press affects the public's attitude towards, and image of, the people in other nations. According to Petersons, there is a correspondence between public opinion and official attitudes with regard to foreign policy.

Major Features

In the formation of national images of international events and personalities, the transnational news agencies play a dominant role. They also play a role in educating the people of poor countries about rich life-styles. There is a view among researchers that after constant exposure to media fare from rich, technologically advanced countries with multinational economic interests, people of the poor, developing countries learn to identify whatever news they receive over the international news agency channels as relevant to their own circumstances. Himmelstrand and Headman believe that 'in the long run, people's definition of news will become the same as the supply of news, as they will demand the information they are used to receiving from the news agencies. One might say the news agencies create their own demand'.

It must be stressed that the multinational agencies are under the strong influence of their own national government's foreign policy when they report foreign countries.

How newspapers change their attitudes to countries on the basis of changes in their own countries' foreign policy has been documented by Sahin, Kreisberg, and by Lynch and Effendi. These three studies were based on the pattern of reporting in the New York Times over long periods of time. Very little news, for example, appeared about China in the US papers during the two decades following the Chinese revolution. But once President Richard Nixon broke the ice, the newspapers began to turn more frequently to China for news.

There is some merit in the argument that foreign news is meant primarily for the benefit of foreign policy formulators and top echelons of government, and that the average citizen is not deeply interested in foreign affairs. Much of the foreign news published may not be read by ordinary citizens. Some theoretical support to this view has been derived from the oft-quoted 'nature of news' theory of Schramm's.

The Body : While the lead should arouse the reader's interest, the body should sustain it. The body should flow smoothly and logically from the lead. It should expand each of the points mentioned in the lead and, as far as possible, in the same order. The body should be as complete and as tight as possible. It should provide all the relevant information within the shortest space possible. The essence of good journalistic writing is brevity and simplicity. Do not use two words where one word would do. And do not use a complex or long word where a short word would do. Eventually, you should reach the point at which, choosing the story structure becomes second nature to you. This will, of course, come with experience and practice. You will then begin concentrating on the more creative and experimental aspects of writing.

A good reporter will spend a great deal of his time not sitting in the office but visiting places and meeting people who are potential sources of news. He should always keep his ears and eyes open. He should know where to go for the facts he needs for the story, recognise news when he encounters it, select the vital points for inclusion in his story and discard the inconsequential details.

Kinds of Reporting : Let us now turn to different types of reporting such as objective, interpretative investigative and crime reporting.

Objective Reporting: Reporting of news, unlike editorial writing, is often described as a coldly impersonal job. A reporter is essentially a story teller and he should tell the story in an objective and truthful manner, without lacing it with personal opinions or subjective comments. He should be fair and impartial and present both sides of the story.

Complete objectivity is a mere concept. The reporter is a human being, not a robot, and he has certain ideas, feelings, attitudes, opinions and prejudices. However, a good reporter should try to rise above them and tell the facts as he has collected them in his search for truth.

No responsible reporter would behave like the notorious American journalist, Janet Cooke, who won the prestigious Pulitzer prize in 1980 for a story about drugs which was later proved to be fictional and fictitious. The journalist committed a deliberate fraud by dramatising a fake scene in which an eight year-old boy is injected with heroin supplied by the lover of the boy's mother.

Nearer home, the story of "mass rape" at a students function in a Madhya Pradesh town, published in a national newspaper was found to be baseless. When the report appeared on the front page of the newspaper it caused a sensation. The Editor asked a reporter to investigate. On arriving in the town the reporter first questioned the reporter of the news item, who insisted that the mass rape did take place. By way of corroboration he produced a number of eye-witnesses. However when they were cross-examined and asked specifically to reveal only what they had seen, and not what they had heard, the investigator soon realised that the reporter had written the story on the basis of a bazar gossip and filed it without verifying the facts. All that had happened was that during a function to celebrate the annual day of a local college, a portion of the shamiana came down, the electricity got cut off and a few students entered the women's enclosure and molested some of the girls.

There is this apocryphal story of a cub reporter, who, on his first day at work wrote a piece with a cocksureness which was misplaced. On reading the piece, the editor advised him to be cautious and a little circumspect when writing about sensitive issues. The press, the editor reminded him, must not ordinarily violate the various laws on the statute book concerning libel, national security and parliamentary privileges.

The next day the cub reporter submitted a story which ran as follows:

> "Mrs. Gulab Paniwala, alleged wife of Mr. Rakesh Paniwala, who claims to be the mayor of Shangrila, gave a cocktail party at her house in Model Town on Monday to bid farewell to Mrs. Jyoti Jariwala, reported to be the wife of the well-known industrialist, Samar Jariwala. Among those present at the party were Mrs. Romi Puriwala, said to be the widow of the late Hansraj Puriwala, a former cabinet minister, along with her alleged offspring, Jani Puriwala..." and so it went on.

The reporter had quite clearly gone to the other extreme in writing this report which was quickly consigned to the waste paper basket.

In reporting news, you must remember that facts are sacred. You must check and cross-check the facts from different sources until you are absolutely sure of them. Only then should you write your story. The golden rule is: tell the truth.

Objective reporting is, of course, not synonymous with dullness. It means fair and impartial reporting that is free from personal bias or prejudice.

Reporting Speeches: Speeches are a major source of news and every day many news items that appear in the newspapers can be traced back to some speech or the other. Sometimes several speeches from part of one report. This happens in reports of seminars, symposia and legislatures. In such situations the most important speech, normally from the most important speaker, gets prominence.

While covering political party conferences and international conferences on various subjects, one has to deal with several speeches in a row. Depending on the content and the speaker a reporter has to decide who should come first. Effort should also be made to generalise observations if possible and then mention who said what. In such cases the most important things said by different speakers should be mentioned and there should be no repetition of ideas. If there are contrary opinions expressed by different speakers they should be mentioned and then supporters of different schools of thoughts should be quoted. Here again repetition of ideas should be avoided.

The importance of speeches and speakers varies from occasion to occasion and relative importance of other speakers. A reporter must evaluate various factors and use judgment while writing the story. For example, if many ministers speak in a party their speeches are important and what they say will be important according to the content of the speech. But if the prime minister speaks and he touches upon points which have been covered by other ministers already and adds something to it, he will get the maximum space and the rest of the ministers will be mentioned in the story with very little of what they said.

If in a special debate in a house of parliament the speech of a minister of state gets prominence in case the cabinet minister of the same department does not speak. If the cabinet minister also speaks then the state minister is normally pushed out of intro. If the prime minister intervenes during the debate and says something on the subject even the cabinet minister is pushed below in the body of the story. So while reporting multiple speeches the reporter must evaluate all these factors.

"There are occasions when copies of a speech may be supplied in advance. Sometimes the story prepared is based on the advance copy and a reporter goes to the site when the speech is made-just to check whether the speech was made and if so whether it followed the advance copy. The advance story is subject to an embargo which is released automatically at the time up to which it is embargoed (should not be used before/ should be used on or after...). A reporter or sub-editor who writes the story from such a speech has enough time to his disposal and should read the speech carefully and write the story on the top of which 'not to be used before...on...' as mentioned in the embargo should be typed. Normally, this embargo time is the time of the event where the speech is to be made. News agencies sometimes creed the embargoed story in advance. It should be used only after the embargo is lifted."

Where advance copy is not made available the reporter must reach the place where speech is to be delivered and check from the organisers if they are supplying a copy of the speech. If the copy is supplied before the speech then the reporter should start working on it immediately. He should go through it carefully and mark what he considers as important points.

He should also mark the order of their importance so that he loses no time when he has to type or dictate his story. He should carefully check the copy when the speech is made and see if there are any major deviations from the text supplied. Sometimes what is said by the speaker outside the supplied text is more newsworthy than all what is given in the text. Such departures from the prepared text should find place in the intro or body depending on their news value.

Many a time a speaker does not read the prepared speech and says that the speech be taken as read while what he says is in addition to that in that case the reporter is supposed to listen to the speaker carefully and read the text also before writing the story.

If the organisers promise that the copy of the speech will be supplied but it is not distributed when the speech begins, the reporter should start taking notes from the beginning of the speech imagining that the copy is not available. Many such promises of the organisers prove false and if the reporter does not take notes or record the speech when it is delivered, he will be in difficulty. Moreover he will miss any departures from the text.

A reporter should make use of the copy if he gets it within a few minutes after the event, otherwise he should rely on his notes and do the story. The copy can be used for quotations from the speech.

But there are occasions when the copy of the speech is not supplied. This happens in seminars and almost all the public meetings of political parties. A reporter can record them on a tape recorder. He must take care to take down important points in his notebook. In this way he can do the story quickly, for he will not have enough time to replay the full speech and then write. A tape recorder is useful because it helps the reporter in reproducing exactly what the speaker might have said,on a controversial or important issue.

A speech can sometimes yield more than one story. In certain circumstances a reporter can add colour to the story by describing the atmosphere or some sidelights. Such opportunities should not be missed.

It is interesting to see how the same speech is covered by different newspapers. Following is the address by the President of India to Parliament (February 20, 1986):

Honourable Members

1. It gives me great pleasure to welcome you to this first session of Parliament in 1986. I felicitate the new members.
2. The year has seen Parliament transact its business in a purposeful manner and in an atmosphere of cooperation. I extend to you all my best wishes for the successful completion of the budgetary and legislative business that lies ahead.
3. In July, 1985, the Government took a major initiative

to resolve the complex and difficult problems in Punjab. Our prime concern was to strengthen the forces of unity and integrity. Policy was governed by the perspective of serving the highest national interest. The democratic process triumphed over terrorism. The peaceful elections in Punjab testified to the desire of the overwhelming majority of the people for peace and normalcy in the State.

4. A great responsibility rest on those who have secured the mandate of the people. The supreme task is to isolate those who are resorting to violence to disturb communal harmony and peace. In this task they will have the support of all political forces committed to the unity and integrity of India. There cannot be and must not be, any compromise with the forces of disintegration. It is imperative that all secular and democratic forces join hands in a mass campaign to safeguard the values enshrined in our constitution-nationalism, secularism, democracy and socialism-the bedrock of India's unity.
5. The Assam settlement was followed by elections to the Legislative Assembly and the Lok Sabha. A new Government has taken office.
6. Government are committed to the fullest implementation of the Punjab and Assam Accords.
7. Government express their deepest sympathy with the families of all those who lost their lives, or were injured, or suffered loss of property in violent incidents in different parts of the country. Violence in public life is the very antithesis of the ethos of our civilization. The frequent resort to violence to settle what are perceived as grievances of one group or another should deeply disturb those who uphold democratic values. While governments must firmly put down violence wherever it may occur, it is essential that political parties committed to democratic values should deal with the

root causes of violence through purposive and sustained work among the people. The temptation to seek short-term advantages from communal and other types of violence must be eschewed.

8. Communalism continues to pose a serious threat to national unity. It is being reinforced by religious fundamentalism and fanaticism. These trends represent a reactionary social outlook, directed against the struggle of the poor and the underprivileged against the vested interest. The reconstituted National Integration Council will have to act decisively and systematically to strengthen secularism.

9. In my Address on January 17, 1985, I had outlined the major policies and programmes of the Government. I recapitulate the main points:
   (i) Commitment of a clean public life;
   (ii) Administrative reforms;
   (iii) Judicial reforms;
   (iv) A new national education policy;
   (v) A new national programme for women;
   (vi) Participation of youth in programmes for promoting national integration and achieving excellence;
   (vii) Establishment of a Wasteland Development Board;
   (viii) Formation of a Central Ganga Authority.
   (ix) A new textile policy; and
   (x) Thorough examination of safety measures for industrial establishments.

10. My government have fulfilled in substantial measure the tasks they had set for themselves for the past year.

11. The anti-defection Act is now in the statute book contributions to political parties by the companies have been permitted by law. Government have endeavoured to set a new tone in public life. This has strengthned

national confidence. A strong sense of involvement in public affairs among all sense of involvement in public affairs among all sections of the people and a buoyant spirit have characterised the year that has gone by. We have to build on these assets to raise the standards of public life.

12. Vigorous steps have been taken to combat corruption and to improve the performance of the public services. Strong emphasis has been laid on sound personnel management and training of personnel at all levels. Machinery for redressal of public grievances is in place. Its results are being continuously evaluated. A new Ministry has been set up to monitor the implementation of various programmes. All Departments of Government have been directed to formulate detailed action plans for the coming financial year, against which their progress will be judged. Administrative reform is a continuous process. Detailed exercises are underway to reorient the system to speedier decision-making and better implementation.

13. Government are determined to eliminate delays in dispensation of justice. The experiment of Lok Adalats has proved that an innovative approach is required to cure this malady. The establishment of Administrative Tribunals will also lighten the burden of the courts, enabling them to devote more time to the liquidation of arrears. However, these are just the first steps in tackling the basic problem of making justice inexpensive and easily accessible to the poor. Drastic changes are needed. Government have entrusted to the Law Commission the task of recommending such changes.

14. Government published in August 1985, a status paper entitled "The Challenge of Education", This was intended to stimulate wide and intensive national debate on issues and alternatives. Government note with satisfaction that the debate has involved all sections

of the people and many useful ideas and approaches have emerged. A draft of the new Education Policy will be presented shortly to Parliament.

15. Government have set up a new department to look after the development of women. A comprehensive national programme for women is being worked out. It will aim at enabling women to play their full Part in developing a strong and modern nation.
16. Programmes for youth development have made considerable headway but much more has to be done in this area taken to ensure full and efficient implementation of the policy.
17. The Wasteland Development Board has been set up and has started work on an ambitious's programme of afforestation. In a recent meeting, all the State Governments endorsed an integrated approach to a National Land Use Policy as well as the strategies and policies for wasteland development.
18. The Central Ganga Authority has come into existence. With the cooperation of the concerned State Governments, work has started in full swing on stopping the population of the Ganga.
19. A new textile policy was announced in June 1985. It aims at production of cheaper cloth for the people. An equally important objective of the policy is to protect the interests of handloom weavers. It is envisaged that in the Seventh Plan the entire production of 700 million sq. metres of controlled and janta cloth will be transferred to be handlloom sector. The Handlooms Act, 1985 has been passed to strengthen this vital sector which provides livelihood to millions.
20. Government have completed examination of issues relating to industrial safety and management of hazardous substances and legislation will be introduced in this session of Parliament.

21. Government will establish seven zonal cultural centres-three have already been set up-to promote a sense of cultural cohesion. These centers, cutting across territorial and linguistic boundaries, would project the rich diversity of regional cultural traditions and their underlying unity. They would take the best of our culture to the masses, harmonising it with their lives and struggles. Their essential thrust would be to break the artificial barriers created during the colonial era between the masses and the living tradition of India's age-old culture in all its forms. The centres will also aim at revitalising folk art which has enriched the country's cultural life.
22. I would now refer to the major trends in our economy.
23. The seventh Five Year Plan was approved by the national Development Council. The basic strategy of the Plan is cast in a longer term perspective of eradication of poverty and building a strong, self-reliant and modern economy. The plan sharpens the focus on the anti-poverty programmes which will have an expanded coverage. It also envisages adequate investments in the core sectors to strengthen the growth potential of the national economy.
24. The fulfillment of the Plan required total commitment and determination to mobilise adequate resources for investment. To translate the vision of a strong, prosperous, self-reliant India into reality requires unremitting to and capacity to sacrifice and to bear hardship. Adequate savings have to be mobilised to pursue a non-inflationary path of development. More importantly, these savings have to be used effectively. The challenge has to be met. There are no short cuts to development, no alternatives to hard work.
25. Vigorous implementations of anti-poverty programmes yielded significant results. The Sixth Five Year Plan aimed at assisting 15 million families under the

integrated Rural Development Programme; 16.6 million families were actually covered, of which 6.4 million belonged to the Scheduled Castes and Scheduled Tribes. These programmes are being strengthened and surplus foodgrains stocks will be used in 1986-87 to expand the National Rural Employment Programme and the Rural Landless Employment Guarantee Programme to cover one million additional families. An amount of Rs. 100 crores has been provided annually during the Seventh Five Year Plan for the construction of housing for the Scheduled Castes/Scheduled Tribes and freed bonded labour.

26. By the end of March, 1985, of a total of 2.31 lakh problem villages lacking safe drinking water supply, 1.92 lakh villages had been provided with at least one source of water supply. During 1985-86 the programme was further accelerated.

27. In 1985-86 agriculture continued to make steady progress. In November 1985, foodgrains stocks with Government were higher by nearly 15% over 1984. This has enabled Government to launch a scheme for distributing wheat and rice at specially subsidised rates in tribal areas and to other vulnerable sections, especially the Scheduled Castes, expectant mothers, children, etc. A comprehensive crop insurance scheme has been introduced in specified areas for the kharif crop. Government are considering further expansion of such schemes.

28. During the first seven months of 1985-86, industrial production grew at the rate of 6.3%. The policy initiatives of Government have created a buoyant investment climate. The infrastructural industries have performed well. Compared with the first nine months of the last year, power generation was up by 8.2%; saleable steel production by 12.9%; fertilizer production by more than 10%. Our ports handled 13.2% more

cargo and the railways created an all time record in freight traffic movement.

29. In 1985-86 the Central Plan outlays were stepped up by 15% over 1984-85, especially on anti-poverty programmes human resource development and infrastructure. There was considerable increase in the outlays of State Plans. Government will have spent in 1985-86 Rs. 1,650 crores on food subsidy and Rs. 2,050 crores on fertilizer subsidy. Public distribution system was strengthened and prudent management of supplies prevented shortages. It is gratifying that a significant increase in public investment was achieved.

30. Tax collections have been buoyant belying gloomy forebodings. The collection of direct taxes is up by about 23% compared to the corresponding period last year indirect tax collection has increased by 22%. Total tax collections have increased by 22% which is the highest in the last decade. An effective drive was launched against tax evaders, smugglers and blackmarketeers. Action has also been taken against personnel found guilty of colluding with economic offenders. Government are determined to cleanse the economic life and to fight the evil of black money.

31. For the first time, a long-term fiscal policy co-terminous with the Five Year Plan has been announced. A long-term direction to economic policy has been provided. Government are confident that the policy will ensure economic growth and speedier expansion of productive investment and employment opportunities.

32. It is necessary to focus attention on the structural problems of the economy to further our basic objective of growth with social justice. India's development depends upon steadily rising levels of public investment. How are these investments to be financed? Massive investments made in the previous Plans must yield adequate returns. Costs of production have to be

reduced. Every Rupee of national savings has to be put to the most productive use. Otherwise it will be difficult to find real resources for the larger and larger investments required for maintaining the tempo of self-reliant growth, for enlarging our antipoverty programmes and for preserving our economic independence. Sooner or later, sooner rather than later, we have to face the realities of the situation. No one should be under the delusion that growth, social justice, price stability and self-reliance are achievable without efficiency, discipline and sharing of burdens. Contemporary history warns us of such pitfalls.

33. We must reduce the costs of our inputs and prices of final products and services. We cannot afford the luxury of pricing ourselves out of both the domestic and the export markets. A modern industrial society cannot rise on the basis of continuing low levels of productivity and high costs of production. New jobs cannot be 'created if existing enterprises incur losses year after year. Operational inefficiency increases the cost of production and is inevitably reflected in increased prices which are a burden on the people. It raises costs all round, reducing real investment.

34. The future of the planning process depends on our capacity to face up to difficult questions and to take hard decisions, decisions that may involve sacrifices but without which forward movement will not be possible. Growth is absolutely vital to raise the standards of living of the poor. Can we evade decisions that protect and strengthen this development process? Nations are built by generations that sacrifice for a better tomorrow.

35. The balance of payments position poses a similar challenge. Our exports have remained sluggish in 1985-86 but our imports have increased. The imports of petroleum products and edible oils are well above the

limits the country can afford. The question basically is whether we want to stand on our own feet or not if we do, there is no question that we have to curb the growth of consumption of petroleum products and we have to be self-sufficient in oilseeds. We also have to have a fresh look at our imports of capital goods. We do not want to shut out new technology because that will harm us, but we have to make sure that such technology meets the rigorous criteria of essentiality. External financial flows are needed but Government are determined that India is never at the mercy of foreign banks and institutions. Economic independence and self-reliance are central to our philosophy of development. We shall pay whatever price is required to maintain our economic independence.

36. The primary objectives of our foreign policy continue to be the promotion of non-alignment, advocacy of peace and nuclear disarmament, enlarging the area of friendship and cooperation and building of a just world order.

37. We welcome the resumption of high level dialogue between the Russian Federation and USA. It is imperative to take urgent steps to bring about a freeze in the nuclear arms race and a comprehensive nuclear weapon test ban treaty. The six-nation initiative has called for these measures. The Delhi Declaration of January, 1985 had a good impact on public opinion throughout the world. The leaders of the six countries are in touch with one another about further steps.

38. During the last one year the atmosphere in the subcontinent has distinctly improved. We have succeeded in making progress with our neighbours in many fields. But we remain concerned about the ethnic situation in Sri Lanka and Pakistan's continued pursuit of a nuclear weapon capability. We remain convinced that the situation in Sri Lanka can be settled only

through political means; attempts to seek a military solution will fall and will only result in the loss of a large number of innocent lives.

39. The Government welcome the establishment of South Asian Association for Regional Collaboration launched in Dhaka in December, 1985. We expect that it will help strengthen forces of friendship and cooperation in our region.

40. The Government have made untiring efforts towards the resolution of the major areas of tension. At the Commonwealth meeting in the Bahamas in October, in which the Prime Minister participated, our delegation played a leading role in the adoption of the Commonwealth Accord on South Africa. We continue to demand comprehensive mandatory sanctions against the racist regime in South Africa. If the authorities there, and other Governments in a position to influence South Africa, do not act in time, violence on a large scale will become unavoidable.

41. The Prime Minister also attended the 40th anniversary of the United Nations. The Nassau Declaration on World Order adopted by Commonwealth leaders, contained a strong plea for adherence to international norms and principles and the strengthening of the United Nations. Support for the United Nations system is one of the corner-stones of our foreign policy. We are concerned at the growing threat to the multilateral institutions and the increasing tendency to resort to unilateral action. Government support international efforts to combat international terrorism, while recognising the rights to people under colonial occupation to use all means to attain their just objectives.

42. The Government deplore the fact that the Palestinian people continue to be denied their inalienable rights, including the right to an independent homeland of

there own. Until this problem is tackled, West Asia will not see a basic lasting peace.

43. The Prime Minister paid official visits to the Russia, Egypt, France. Algeria, the USA, Bhutan, the UK, Cuba, the Netherlands, Vietnam, Japan, Oman and Maldives. Our traditionally close and friendly relations with the USSR have been further strengthened following the Prime Minister's discussions with Soviet leaders in Moscow. The visit to USA has significantly, enlarged the content of our bilateral relations with the USA. The Prime Minister visited Dhaka to express our solidarity with the people of Bangladesh during the cyclone disaster and participated in the meeting of Heads of State and Government for launching the South Asian Association for regional Collaboration. The Prime Minister addressed the UNESCO during his visit to France. He addressed the annual conference of the I.L.O. in Geneva. We had the privilege to host visits by the Kings of Nepal and Bhutan, the Queen of the Netherlands, the Presidents of Mexico, Maldives, Sri Lanka, Tanzania, Indonesia and Pakistan, the Chairman of PLO, the Head of State of Ethiopia, and the Prime Ministers of Poland, Yugoslavia, Mauritius, Britain, New Zealand, People's Democratic Republic of Yemen and Trinidad and Tobago. The Crown Prince and Princess of Norway and the Pope also visited India.

44. Let me now outline some priority areas for 1986-87 and beyond.

45. The need of the hour is to enable the poor to better their lives. Science and technology have to support this fundamental objective. To this end, government are mounting technology missions in the following areas:

    (i) Drinking water for all villages;

    (ii) Eradication of illiteracy;

    (iii) Vaccination and immunisation of children;

(iv) Production of oilseeds and manufacture of edible oils;

(v) Improved communications.

46. In the course of the year more thrust areas will be identified with the object of using technology for improving productivity in industry and agriculture in selected areas science and technology missions will endeavour to place India in the front rank of scientific activity.

47. A comprehensive agriculture policy will be formulated to promote an optimal cropping pattern, to improve water and soil management, to increase productivity of all crops to enhance the incomes of small and marginal farmers and to enlarge our hard-won self-sufficiency in foodgrains through production of oilseeds and pulses. A time-bound action plan will be drawn up to take the green revolution to the eastern region.

48. It is gratifying that a national consensus has emerged on treating water as a national resource. Government attach high priority to the evolution of a national water policy which would optimise the use of water for agricultural, industrial and other social needs.

49. Government have carried out an indepth analysis of our family planning programmes. Profiting from the experience of the past, an effective strategy for family planning is being worked out and will be announced shortly.

50. The focus on anti-poverty programmes will be sharpened. A new programme, which builds on the success achieved by the revised 20-Point Programme, is being formulated and will be announced soon, it will bring together all the elements, policies and programmes for a major national effort to tackle the problem of mass poverty in all its manifestations, specifically the problems of Scheduled Castes and Scheduled Tribes. Programme for the social economic

educational and cultural development for the Scheduled castes, Scheduled Tribes and other weaker sections will be vigorously implemented. The implementation of the 15-Point Programme for thus development of minorities, with special emphasis on increasing economic opportunities will be closely monitored.

51. To rapidly increase employment to stimulate development in backward areas and to enhance the efficiency by Indian industry to serve the masses better, a more comprehensive framework of industrial policy is required. Many changes have already been made in our industrial policy which now reflects the new thrust for modernisation, absorption of new technologies and promotion of indigenous technologies. High cost and inefficient industry hurts the poor, because it absorbs resources that are needed to create new jobs for them. A vast increase in the production of goods and services for the masses in rural and urban areas is central to our strategy for the removal of poverty. This necessitates a fresh look at policies governing the scale of production, capacity utilisation, the role of indigenous technology, labour productivity, the detailed regulatory mechanism, thus future perspectives for small and medium industry and the existing administrative and management apparatus. Industry must serve the large masses.

52. To meet the challenge of maintaining a viable balance of payments position, a major thrust for promotion of exports and tourism is called for. Any slackening of progress on this front will jeopardise our overall development strategy. Government will take new initiatives in this critical area.

53. It is imperative to effect changes in our administrative system to bring it in tune with the objective of growth with social justice. Management in Government has to be imbued with a new social outlook, it is not a question of imposing something from above. The impetus to

reform must come from within. The national community as a whole must debate issues affecting the working of the administrative system. A concrete agenda of action will thus emerge for implementation. Our watchwords must be improvement of efficiency and enforcement of accountability.

54. To safeguard the health and vitality of our basic political institutions, changes will be needed in our electoral and other laws. Government will hold wide-ranging consultations with the leaders of political parts with a view to formulating concrete proposals to ensure cleaner public life.

55. The vision of a mighty Indian will be realised only in the actual lives of men and women who have strength of character, tenacity of purpose and commitment to excellence. Government's strategy for human resource development aims at developing these qualities in our national life. The new education policy will be an integral part of this strategy. It will aim at the physical, intellectual, cultural and moral development of society in a harmonious fashion.

56. It is not enough to state objectives. A national mobilisation is essential to ensure that the resources required to implement the education policy are forthcoming. Even more important is the involvement of the youth, students, teachers, the intelligentsia, workers and farmers in giving a new direction to the national effort in this area. Education has to be transformed from an activity in the classroom to a social process for building the India of our dreams. It has to be integrated more closely both with production and our commitment to conserve and enhance our cultural heritage to make us proud to be Indian.

57. The years ahead are years of challenge. Government have taken a number of measures to accelerate growth, to modernise the economy and to give new content to

our programmes for achieving social justice. It is imperative to impart a sense of urgency to the task of implementation.

58. Much has been achieved this past year, and the hopes and expectations of our people are high. As their representatives, you have the onerous duty to fulfill their aspirations. Above all, people's representatives and organisations of all political persuasions should work together to strengthen the secular and democratic foundations of our society. The forces of violence and fanaticism have to be fought. The economic capabilities we have built up since independence have brought us to a point where determined and concerted efforts to take us forward and to remove poverty are feasible. Now is the time it ensure greater political cohesion so that the battle against poverty and backwardness can be won. I wish you all success in the tasks ahead—*Jai hind*

Now let us examine how this address is covered by newsmen. The copy of this speech was made available to all correspondents when the President began to read it. Given is the report of the speech published in the Times of India, New Delhi.

Opposition Boycotts Address

Isolate terrorists, says President

The times of India news service New Delhi, February 20. The President in his traditional address to the joint session of Parliament outlining the agenda of the government today pointed to the "inevitability of hard decisions without which forward movement will be possible."

The address promised a comprehensive agriculture plan to promote an optimal cropping pattern, a more effective strategy for family planning and sharpening of the anti-poverty programme.

Technology missions will be mounted to ensure drinking water for all villages, eradication of illiteracy, immunisation, oil-seeds production and improved communications.

New initiatives will be made for promotion of exports and tourism with a view to maintaining a viable balance of payments position.

There will be wide ranging discussions to formulate concrete proposals for changing electoral and other laws. Administrative reforms to improve efficiency and enforce accountability will be introduced. The joint session, with its usual ceremonial, was still shorn off the excitement and rapture which featured in the function only a year ago. Most non-Congress groups stayed away as announced leaving gaps in rows.

Not since 1973 have so many groups joined in such a boycott. Even Congress members did not find any cause to cheer during the entire reading of the address. They thumped the desks only at the end as the president resumed his seat.

There was a moment so suspense when the President paused at the beginning. It was then noticed he was looking for his reading glass.

At the same time, the President address made it plain that hard decisions were inevitable in the pursuit of self-reliance, economic independence and eradication of poverty.

Sooner or later we have to face the realities of the situation. No one should be under the delusion that growth, social justice, price stability and self-reliance, are achievable without efficiency, discipline and sharing of burdens," Mr. Zail Singh said.

The President began his speech with a reference to the "triumph of democratic process over terrorism in Punjab" and held that the supreme task now was to isolate those resorting to violence.

He reiterated the government commitment to the fullest implementation of the Punjab and Assam accord.

3

Reporting, with Purpose

Highlighting Events : Development reporting is somewhat different from routine reporting from court, legislatures, crime, science and technology or sports. However, it may involve writing our programmes and policies resulting in economic change, social programmes and community feelings and reactions to programme and change.

Ever since India adopted a process of planned development through the five year plans in 1951, rapid transformation have taken place in all walks of life in the country. Some of these changes have been welcomed by people, but many have been opposed also. Also, as development takes place, numerous new issues are thrown up. As a development reporter, you will be required to help in creating awareness about these developmental issues. You will also be required to create an atmosphere of understanding the objectives of these schemes and ultimately mobilizing people in seeking their willing participation in development programmes. Development Reporting needs some special skills, preparations and qualities to be imbibed by reporters of print or electronic media. To be able to do this job successfully, a reporter has to collect information on different development programmes.

Various Aspects

Styles of Development Reporting : Development has led to some disastrous results such as widespread pollution of air, water and soil, besides deforestation. This resulted in a rethinking on what constitutes development. It has also increased the responsibility of the development journalists. Therefore, a journalist reporting on developmental issues should organize and arrange his report logically.

— He has to collect data on the area which is being developed.

— In wrıting development stories, you have to be equipped with factual information which is generally not easily available.

— You will have to develop your own outlook which is more important than styles and techniques.

— Your language must be as simple as possible. While mentioning the figures of development, round up these instead of using fractions.

The Development Process : The process of development is generally slow, because people are slow in adopting novel idea. The process of development also requires people's participation and acceptance. It is here that the development reporter explains to the people the rationale behind building roads, schools and hospitals, use of high yielding resistant varieties, and other such matters. But the process of development has become very complex and in many parts of the world; the people are opposing large development programmes, almost to the extent of attaining an anti-development attitude. Billions of rupees have been spent on different development programmes but not much has been achieved in terms of returns. All these issues need to be presented to the people and the authorities. Development reporter in all mass media can help a great deal in this direction.

The Development Story : There are areas of development news and ideas which are only casually or rarely covered in the media. There are thousands of development stories lying buried under realms of paper but never come out for the general public.

To be a successful development reporter one has to be mobile and meet people who are involved in researches, attend seminars and conferences, ask questions, try to keep up with the latest trends in the world of science and human endeavour.

Also, keen habit of reading will sharpen your knowledge and technique. You will never be short of ideas.

***Tasks of Development Reporting*:** Roughly, a development reporter has three tasks to perform—inform, interpret and promote. If properly executed, a development reporter's job is more exacting than that of mere news reporters. A development report must be included with a noble motive of supporting, crusading or promoting a cause. A sincere development writer's role in the overall progress of the country is as vital as that of a person working with his own hands. As a development journalist you will have to develop a sixth sense to smell the rot before it envelops you. Avoid '*mouthpiece writing*' at any cost. Also, the reporter must be honest to highlight the achievements and laurels won by the people executing the schemes.

To be a successful development reporter, one must inculcate certain characteristics:

(a) Fostering a wide range of contacts.

(b) Contacts with International Organizations.

(c) Keep a desk diary.

(d) Maintain your own reference material.

***Specialised Skills Required* :** Development Reporting encompasses a number of areas and every field needs and demands special skills to report on that particular area fully and competently.

As a communicator, you have a very formidable task of collecting information, transforming it into a right format and passing it on to the users. Avoid technical jargon and approach directly in a simple language. Tap every source of information.

As a development reporter, you have a prodigious task before you. You can choose any programme and monitor its progress in a regular column in your medium. You can help in mobilising people's participation in these programmes.

Development Reporting for Press : As a development reporter, you will be required to process and present facts in an intelligible form to the reader/viewer/listener. There are more than 1500 daily newspapers published in all the 18 national and other languages. Several newspaper devote full pages to development news. Development stories are best done in the form of a feature article.

Photo features on development projects can also be presented effectively. Interviews with the recipients of the benefits of the projects already completed can also help evaluate their impact on the masses.

An imaginative development writer can do free-lancing for the press, radio and television. A development reporter has a challenging job and requires hard work, commitment and dedication.

Development Reporting for Radio : In India, radio has proved its utility as a potent audio medium for creating awareness among people. It helps in promoting an instinctive urge for development, by broadcasting programmes designed to help people diagnose their problems and clarify their objectives so that they may be able to make their decisions more wisely.

From 6 radio stations in 1947, All India Radio has grown to nearly 200 radio stations. Rural Radio Forums were started in 149 stations. Each forum consisted of 10 to 20 villages. Increase in knowledge in the forum villages was spectacular, whereas in the non-forum villages it was negligible.

As a development reporter for radio, there is plenty of

scope to write scripts, to devise special programmes and also the work in the capacity as a free lancer to do development field stories.

While reporting development for radio, you must remember that you are talking to the people. You shouldn't appear as if you are reading. For this purpose, you must write your script in simple language. When you want to reach people who can not read or write, or the people who live in remote villages, and when you want to teach people speedily, the radio is the answer. The 'development' is actually meant for these people. You use the radio to inform, alert, suggest, direct, interest, stimulate and motivate people.

Development Reporting for Television : Television was first started in India in a small way in 1959. As a development reporter, you can use television to spread know-how, to as many people as within the reach of television centre. However, to be effective, your development programme must be field-based. Television is a visual medium and if visuals are missing or if you fail to focus on the relevant visuals, then the television's impact will be completely lost. For making a good television programme with a view to motivate people for development require a lot of effort, research and commitment. For writing a good television script, fewer words and more visuals are needed. Much more is communicated through visuals. Never make only studio based development programme for television. Go to the spots. Visit the remote areas. A well made television programme can help you expose the loopholes in our planning and implementation of the developmental plans.

Reporting on Sustainable Development : The term 'sustainable development' was popularized by the report of the World Commission Environment and Development (WCED). To some, sustainable development is a long awaited call for political recognition of global environmental decay, economic injustice and limits to material growth. The decline in environmental quality has however underlined the need for harmonizing the logic of economics with that of ecology.

The sustainable development, represents an opportunity for humanity to correct a historical error and develop a gentle, more balanced, and stable relationship with the natural world.

A total reorientation is required in development reporting in India. When writing about any development project, you must ask questions like how it will improve the quality of life of the people without damaging the quality of air, water and soil and also without eroding the moral and social values.

Sports Reporting : Sports writing and reporting is as specialized an area as any other. It calls for both technical know how and a good writing style. As a sports reporter, you will have to be conversant with the tactics, rules and scoring patterns of various sports and games. You will also have to be knowledgeable about the lives of top players in the sport or game.

The art of successful sports reporting and writing, and any other special work, is the art of fully knowing the various popular games and sports. You must endeavour to write a news item or feature on any game with the objectives of making it appealing to a particular class of readers interested in those games.

Even as all sports and games are competitive, so too are the areas of sports writing and reporting. In such a scenario, as a sports writer, you need to structure your story around the reader's interest. You need to be thorough with your facts and capable of churning out a report under pressure of meeting a deadline.

How to Begin : Renowned sports journalists are known to have formed the habit of jotting down every idea or scrap of information that comes their way. Thus, to be a successful sports journalist you should first of all cultivate a habit of keeping notebook and pen with you all the time to record ideas. It is also rewarding to prepare notes on the end pages of the books you read. And it is essential to preserve the material that you have collected.

Clippings Collection : While reading paper or magazines, you should mark those articles and news reports which particularly interest you. Cut them and date those marked articles and file them under the appropriate subject. You will find that from the material so collected you can obtain information about your subject and may be some views of a handful of experts. Also, you will be able to refer to these clippings for facts and figures that you may quote in your own article or report. Facts are vital to analysis and comment.

In Search of Ideas in Sports : You have to develop your own powers of observation. Keep an eye open for any interesting out of the ordinary themes that you can write an article about. It is part of training to learn to look at life with a journalist's eye. You will then not only be knowledgeable but also will broaden your outlook. A good sports journalist has not only to be conversant with important person in sports but also has to be equally proficient with the technicalities of sports.

The Ignition Point in Idea-finding : The ignition point in idea-finding is not automatic, nor does it come readily. You have to devote enough and more time and effort to become proficient in finding an idea. Be watchful, patient and gather as much experience as you can. Thereafter, you can be sure to locate and identify ideas.

Putting Ideas in Writing : Think and think clearly before you start writing down your thoughts. In case you have not formed the habit of clear, constructive thinking, your story will reflect the confusion of your thoughts. Clear thinking will help you to write a thought provoking piece in lucid style. And also generates a flow in your ideas.

There is no better way to learn than self-analysis.

Style in Sports Writing : In order to write well, you must develop an easy, conversational style and tone that enables you to gain and hold the attention of the readers. You must learn to write simple sentences and use simple words instead of resorting to high-sounding words. Learn to write in a simple style.

Importance of a New Angle : Every sports reporter is faced with the task of discovering a new angle to a sporting event. You would probably be up against this kind of difficulty in the beginning of your career as a sports journalist. If you take the right and professional approach, you will find that the readers will read your entire report through.

Keep Your Eyes and Ears Open : Howsoever good your writing abilities, your network of contacts or even the sphere of your influence as a sports reporter, you can not escape the rigours of painstaking research, so necessary for any news item. You must keep your ears and eyes on the alert. Sometimes, even an innocuous meeting or drab cocktail party may provide a clue, or a lead for a sensational exclusive story, known as a 'scoop' in the newspaper world.

The Professional Approach : You must write for the people who were not lucky enough to be present at the site of the match. When you write a sports report, you must first consider which point you would like to highlight in your lead. Your report will be natural or original only when you lend a fresh perspective on the sporting event. You must give your best to the report that you have written. If you develop this kind of attitude, you will find that you will neither let yourself down.

Writing to Length : The most important aspect of sports journalism is precis-writing. The more precise you are, the more you will impress your readers. Readers are generally very busy, they do not have the time to read lengthy and vague news items.

Your have to possess enough knowledge, have information at your finger tips in order to write sports news. Space is allotted on the basis of relative importance of the news topics. It is better for you to revise your own copy thoroughly before you submit it at the sports desk.

How to Write ? When you report sports events and issues, you must know how to find the news and write the report. The most important thing is that a reporter wanting to make a mark in the profession must inspire confidence. You should, therefore, know landmarks in the history of the game, its rules, terms etc. The background information and achievements of players should be on your finger tips.

The readers are interested in the prospects of the individual players and of the team as on the day of the match, also all possible information about the event and finally, a post-mortem of the contest.

Good sports writing is good news writing. Sports news reporting is slightly different from general reporting because a sports reporter enjoys great freedom of self-expression.

One should rely on accurate and objective writing, stressing simplicity and clarity while avoiding unfamiliar terminology. Avoid writing vague reports when writing about stars and professional players, choose your words with care. The profession is quite hazardous. Do not make indiscreet comments.

Need for Specialisation : The arena of sporting activities is indeed a vast one. As a sports reporter, you have to know something about every sport, at least the salient features, rules and regulations. Also specialise in one or two disciplines (games). Much depends upon your interest and inclination.

Specialization, however, comes much later in one's career graph. You must train yourself to write on a variety of topics. At the same time your must also specialize in style that is both refreshingly different and illuminating to the general reader. To succeed in this, all that is required is accuracy of reportage and an original style of writing.

Facts for the Advance News Story : You have to depend upon the concerned officials, coaches and managers to get details for an advance copy. In the face of a defeat, an official may yet be willing to speak to you provided the two of you enjoy a good equation. The temperament and psychology of the players are equally important, if not more important than technique and skill. Finally, a sports reporter has to exercise tact and perhaps persistence when seeking information from officials. You have to study the situation well before you ask questions.

Covering the Game : You must learn to take notes systematically. Remember all the important incidents and happenings including the major moves or strategies that had a bearing on the outcome. When you write your copy, tell the story immediately. Avoid showing off your vocabulary. Report the action of the sport or game in as much detail as the word limit permits. While there is no rigid formula for a sports reporter, there are some conventional rules about the structure of the sports story. These are listed below:

Lead : Who won where, where, why and how.

Major Details : Star players, breaks and weather, if necessary

Minor Details : Other players, other plays and the behaviour of spectators

Other Details : Statistics, line-ups and substitutions.

Tips for Sports Reporter

— Study the rules of the game in question.

— Study their history.

— Cultivate friendly relations with officials of various clubs and associations.

— To specialise in reporting a particular sport, you must first acquaint yourself with every aspect of the sport.

— Read the journals pertaining to your particular sport.

— Try not to have confrontation with players and officials.

— There is no sports reporter who does not err. Accept the lapse instead to defend the indefensible.

— Have a positive outlook and think constructive.

Science Reporting : The laws of Nature are revealed to human beings through science. Technology involves the application of science to invent, innovate and improvise newer machines, products and services.

Must for A Science Reporter

Recapitulate School and College Science Studies : Recapitulation here means going over again and again, or revising the main points. All science reporters must have a basic knowledge of the elementary principles of science. A knowledge of scientific vocabulary is necessary.

That does not mean only science graduates can report happenings in science. Science education at school is broad-based and can be built upon.

Tips on Science Communication Awareness : Communication is sharing of information. As a science reporter, one must have the curiosity to know the latest happenings in the field one is covering. The moment one has learnt about a particular happening, must write a report for publication.

The best way to develop science communication awareness is by reading good science books and journals and by watching popular science programmes.

Checking Facts through Reference : There is no scope for factual errors, half-truths, exaggeration and hoax in Science. So also in science reporting. Scientific truths and technological facts are verifiable. It is always safe to check the facts with the source of the news or from other sources. A reporter who verifies facts as a matter of habit will earn the reputation of being credible.

Verification through Interviewing : Always keep a list of scientists and technologists of merit, living in the city or town where you are functioning as a reporter, so that the scientific facts and principles can be verified. It is important for the reporter to go ahead and cultivate an acquaintance with these scientists and technologists.

Personal Glossary : A science reporter, like all reporters is hard-pressed for time. They have deadlines to keep. As a science reporter, one will often be faced with technical terms. Scientists and technologists and indeed all specialists, are used to speaking in their own technical language. While taking down notes, one may not be able to translate these into common language. Therefore, prepare and keep the glossary of commonly used technical terms, arranged in alphabetical order. And should always be kept updating.

Institutions of Research and Development : As a reporter covering science and technology in India, you must have a comprehensive knowledge of the institutions of research and development in the country. India has built up one of the world's largest network of R&D facilities. They will be a major source of science-technology news.

The Department of Science & Technology of the Government of India looks after the policy planning and administrative details of the largest chain of national laboratories. These come under the council of Scientific & Industrial Research (CSIR). There are about 40 major research laboratories under CSIR. Atomic Energy and Space are two of the areas where India can boast of frontier research and development. Technical departments under other control ministries too have their research programmes.

Science-Technology Induced Development : In modern times, much is said and written about the human environment, both physical and social. The print and electronic media put out almost a daily dose of news and features about the environment. A science reporter must have a deeper understanding of the environment. The deeper the understanding of the environment, the higher would be the scientific temper.

One basic principle of mass communication is that you should not clutter up your news reporting with too many, facts. Also, you must not talk or write in complex terms. That way, people with different levels of understanding will not be able to grasp your meaning.

Language in Science-Technology Reporting for Popular Appeal: Journalistic writing must be a precise form of communication. Science reporting calls for even greater precision. Science deals with laws of nature. Ideas and images in science communication should flow in logical progression. The skill of good writing improves with usage. As a reporter you have deadlines to keep and so may not have time for re-writing. Good science technology reporting needs language that communicates clearly and here comes the matter of grammar and usage. One has to follow the grammatical practices that make the writing orderly for others to follow.

The English language is today considered as the window to the science-technology information of the world.

Words, Sentences and Readability **:** Words denote images. There are tested patterns of constructing newspaper stories. The opening sentence must say the most important point of the news. The first two to three sentences should give the gist of the story. The paragraphs must be small. The story must move on from sentence to sentence and paragraph to paragraph.

Report Structure **:** A good beginning has the more important news point at the top of the story, and the lesser ones mentioned, as you go down. All the five Ws and H need to be cluttered in the introduction. Nothing is ever printed without being edited. Science-technology news reports are almost never rewritten, because nobody wants to be accused of having tampered with its precision.

Human Interest **:** People are interested in reading something which concerns them directly. If your science-technology story says something which people are interested in, just make it feel. Seek to be the best source of information for your reader, the consumer. Make the readers feel that you are their monitor and reporter.

Avoid Exaggeration and Sensationalism : Science-technology facts simply can not hold exaggerations. If a discovery, invention, or improvisation has an element of sensation, you should not be inhibited in including some of the sensation in your story. Do not make an invention look like something the world has been waiting for, when it is just an improvement on something that already existed.

Sensationalism and exaggeration can only do harm to the publication and to the credibility of a reporter. Just like the scientist, a science reporter also should be a seeker of truth. Like a technologist, a technology reporter too should be one who believes in precision and in updating knowledge.

The Importance of Rewriting : A sentence, a paragraph or a piece of writing can never be perfect. Only when a reporter makes sense to the largest section of readers does he or she qualify to be a professional writer. The first draft of any writer may need a lot of tightening up, chipping and polishing. So rewrite whenever your first effort is unsatisfactory for the reader's sake.

Place the important points at the precise junctures of your story. One needs to revise the copy and make it crisp.

Legislature Reporting : Legislature Reporting, an essential part of mass media function, is a significant feature of Parliamentary democracy. Both people and the government are benefitted by legislature reporting. Parliament or state legislature, Vidhan Sabha and Vidhan Parishad, is called 'legislature' and reporting the day-to-day proceedings of these bodies is called legislature reporting.

Reporting the proceedings of a legislature is a highly responsible job, for which an experienced reporter is sent to cover the proceedings. The reporting job includes the complex process of legislature, debates on subjects of public importance, writing for the media about several other features that go to make Parliamentary proceedings.

Parliament Structure : The constitution of India provides for a bicameral Parliament consisting of the President and the two houses-Lok Sabha (House of People) and Rajya Sabha (Council of States).

The Lok Sabha is composed of representatives of the people chosen by direct election. Unless sooner dissolved, it continues for five years from the date of its first meeting. The maximum strength of Lok Sabha is 552 members. 525 are from states, 20 from Union Territory and 2 nominated by President from Anglo-Indians.

In Rajya Sabha, 12 members out of 250 are nominated by President for their special knowledge and the remaining seats are allocated to the various states and Union Territory.

Like Parliament, there are some states which have a bicameral legislature-assembly and the council-i.e., Vidhan Sabha and Vidhan Parishad. But there are also states which have only the Vidhan Sabha and no Vidhan Parishad.

Parliament and State legislatures become great sources of news when in session. The government makes all the major announcements in Parliament. There are moves and counter-moves by ruling and opposition parties which are grist to the news person's mill.

As a reporter covering parliament, you should know the rules and procedures of legislatures. By and large, these are the same for both the parliament and the state legislatures.

Essentials of Parliamentary Proceedings : The various features essential for the parliamentary proceedings (on a normal day) can be listed as:

(1) Question Hour

(2) Papers to be laid on the table of the house

(3) Zero Hour

(4) Legislative Business

Question Hour : The first hour of every legislature sitting is normally devoted to questions. Questions are of three types:

Starred Questions : A "starred question" is the one to which a member desires an oral answer in the House. Other members can ask supplementary questions which are relevant to the main question. Generally, the answer to the main question which is listed, is in written form with explanatory statement. But supplementaries will have to be answered orally by the minister concerned.

Unstarred Questions : An "unstarred question" is one to which an oral answer is not called for in the house and on which no supplementary questions can be asked. To such a question, a written answer is deemed to have been laid on the *'Table of the House'* after the question hour by the minister to whom it is addressed.

Short Notice Questions : It is related to a matter of urgent public importance and can be asked with the consent of the minister concerned, at a shorter notice than the period of the notice prescribed for an ordinary questions. While 20 questions can be listed for oral answer on a day, as many as 230 questions can be listed for written answers. And it is through questions in Parliament, that the government remains in touch with the people. Questions bring to the notice of the ministers many an abuse which otherwise would have gone unnoticed. Sometimes questions may lead to the appointment of a commission, a court of enquiry or even legislation. Therefore, seasoned parliamentary correspondents are generally entrusted with the task of covering the "question hour". The reporter should remain alert when the minister answers or tries to answer probing questions by members on matters of national importance.

Thus, Parliament questions cover all the ministries and give authentic information. They should be kept by the correspondent for future use as they may provide leads to other stories.

Papers Laid on Table : After the Question Hour is over, the House will take up papers to be laid on the table. These are official documents relating to various ministries and departments and are tabled by ministers concerned. These papers often yield good stories. As a reporter in-charge of papers laid on the table, one should carefully read the agenda paper of the House.

Zero Hour : The zero hour which follows immediately is the most challenging for a young reporter. For, this is the time when members belonging to various parties spring on their feet and try to draw the attention of the chair to the issues they think important and need the government's response. It becomes very difficult to pick up the words of the members as many speak at the same time. All your attention should be centered on what is happening and must note down as quickly as possible what the members say.

The reporter, with his notes and a fair background knowledge of the issues raised, will be able to write a good copy. It is also important for the reporter to be thorough with the morning newspapers, at least with the stories likely to figure in parliament in the day.

Legislative Business : Legislative business consists of introduction, consideration and passing of government bills. After a bill is passed in both Houses, it goes for the Presidential assent, following which it becomes an act of Parliament. The stages through which a bill, which is a legislative proposal, has to pass are :

Introduction of the Bill : The bill can be introduced in either house by a minister in-charge of the subject of the bill. Once the House, that is the majority of members, gives leave to the minister for introduction, the bill is deemed to have been introduced.

General Discussion : At the second stage, a general discussion takes place on the bill as a whole followed by a clause consideration of the bill. At this stage it is open to the House to decide to refer the bill to a select committee of the House or a joint committee of the two Houses.

Voting **:** When all the clauses and schedules of the bill have been considered and voted upon by the house, the minister in-charge moves that the bill is passed.

Call Attention Motion **:** Essentially an Indian procedural innovation enables a member to draw the attention of the government to development of public importance and to elicit government views there on.

Adjournment Motion **:** This is a motion by any member to demand the adjournment of all other business in the house to discuss the issue he may raise. To raise a discussion on the issue, the member must ensure that his motion is supported by the majority of members present.

No Confidence Motion **:** The motion is at times brought by the opposition to express its lack of confidence in the government. After the motion is allowed, a detailed discussion takes place. After the discussion, voting may take place.

Privileges of Parliament **:** The concept of privileges of Parliament rests on the principle that a sovereign legislature should be able to perform its legislative and deliberative functions independently and effectively. For this it should possess certain inherent or conferred powers to punish for breach of such privileges. Articles 105(3) and 194(3) of the constitution empower Parliament and State Legislatures respectively to enact laws codifying their privileges. However, neither parliament nor any of the legislatures of the states has so far done so. Breach of privilege of either House of central or state legislature is usually known as 'contempt of parliament' like the contempt of courts.

A journalist or editor can be punished with imprisonment or administered a warning, admonition or reprimand for the breach of privilege of the House. He can be asked to publish an apology. However, no fines are imposed.

Contempt has a wider sweep than breach of privilege. Contempt can be committed by an act or utterance which undermines the dignity of the House even without violating any particular privilege of the legislature.

But, it is not a breach of privilege to publish without malice a substantially true report of the proceedings of the house even if it is defamatory, seditious or obscene in nature. The legislature in India has not enacted any law codifying its privileges, mainly because any such law will be subject to a judicial review in respect of the citizens' fundamental rights. The Press has been rightly demanding that the privileges of parliament should be codified so that it knows the scope and limits of its freedom vis-a-vis the legislature.

Breach of Privilege : Article 361-A of the Constitution of India protects publication of proceedings of Parliament and state legislatures from any civil and criminal action. No person commits any civil or criminal offence, if he publishes substantially true reports of the proceedings of a House. However, if the publication has been done with malice, the protection conferred by Article 361-A does not apply. Publication of the expourgeal portion of the proceedings of a House, is a breach of its privilege. Article 361-A was inserted in the constitution in 1977.

The House is the custodian of its own privilege and is empowered to take action against a reporter, if his conduct or writing is in breach of its privileges. Since the scope of parliamentary privilege has not been codified, the reporter has to use abundant caution in reporting the proceedings.

Deliberate, distortion of speeches, aspersions cast on a members behaviour in the House, and imputation of motives to him for his speech or behaviour in the House are serious transgression of the privileges of the members. It is one of the privileges of the Parliament and State legislatures to exclude any stranger, including press reporters, from the sittings of the House and from the press gallery.

Reporting the legislature's proceedings by the media is extremely useful for the common people in a democratic setup. Journalists have to be on the constant look out for publishing important decisions taken or not taken in these houses as it is the day-to-day reporting of the legislature's activities that electorates perceive as to what these elected representatives are doing in Parliament and other legislatures. But in doing so the journalists are sometimes likely to err on the wrong side of the law. Thus, a number of laws have been provided to ensure that media do not cast aspersions on their conduct or adversely comment on their report in a House. These laws govern the powers and privileges of legislatures in so far as these common journalist's work may interfere with the right to the freedom of the press or reporters.

The representative of the press are generally provided facilities to cover the proceedings of legislature from the press gallery by issuing an accreditation card to press persons. The reporters should however study parliamentary privileges and Article 361-A of the Constitution of India to safeguard themselves against any default that may occur in reporting proceedings of a legislature.

Court Reporting : Here we shall discuss five different areas of reporting-Court Reporting, Legislature, Science & Technology, Sports Reporting and Development Reporting.

Who are Court Reporters : There are too many courts, and newspapers have neither the time nor the space to cover everything that happens in the court. Papers cover only those stories in which their readers are interested.

There are only a few big newspapers in India who have full time correspondents exclusively for their court beat. These correspondents generally have adequate legal background. Other newspapers mostly hire stringers to cover court stories. A newspaper which does not have a full time law reporter may send its regular staff correspondent to cover an important court story.

Must for a New Law Reporter : One would expect the Law Reporter to be knowledgeable about legal matters. The range and nature of information one must have at one's finger tips are following :

Knowledge of Court Jurisdictions, Procedures and Hierarchy : A trainee journalist aiming to be a future court reporter must at first acquire some understanding of the court jurisdiction, its procedures and its hierarchy. If a reporter is acquainted with the jurisdiction of different courts, then one can easily locate the specific court for a particular matter. Similarly if one is familiar with the hierarchy in the courts, one can easily guess where the appeal would be filed.

Some Legal Terms : For a court reporter, some basic knowledge of some of the most frequently used legal terms is a must.

Professional journalistic practice requires each technical term to be briefly explained when it is used in a story for the first time. A legal term, not used in the story, confuses the reader.

The English knowledge is predominantly used in the higher courts of India. Therefore for a reporter of a non-English daily, some knowledge of English language always helps.

News Sources : Much of a reporter's success in the coverage of the courts depends on one's contacts and sources, and one's ability to gain access quickly to records. For a reporter the key person in the court is the clerk of the court. A court clerk prepares and keeps the records. Court reporting involves diligent checking of records. The judge who presides a trial is seldom one's source. A court reporter should also have good contacts with the lawyers working on a case and with the respective parties.

Trial Coverage : While taking notes in a trial coverage the reporter needs to have a sixth sense. Guided by this news sense, one could begin to take notes of important dates. When a reporter misses an important testimony, one can always regain lost ground during the recess by consulting one's colleagues in the court, or the court stenographer.

Writing with Quotes : In trial proceedings, wherever possible, the reporters must learn to quote the questions and answers or comments and remarks that arise in the course of court's sittings. A story with quotes makes fascinating reading though sometimes, due to paucity of space; Many comments may not be quoted in the news item.

Precautions in Writing Court Stories : While writing stories one must be cautious in avoiding any contempt of court. Sometimes, a reporter files the court story without comments and sometimes with one's own or someone else's comments.

Contempt of Court : The law relating to contempt of court can be braced from the Contempt of Court Act, 1971 and from various case laws. A contempt can be civil or criminal offence.

Civil Contempt : It means wilful disobedience to any judgement, decree, direction, order to other process of a court, or wilful breach of an undertaking given by a person to a court. There will be no civil contempt where there is ignorance of the order of a court leading to unintentional breach.

Criminal Contempt : It mainly means publication of any matter, or the doing of any other act, which :

(i) Scandalises the authority of any court; or

(ii) Prejudices or interferes with the due course of judicial proceedings.

Scandalising the Court : Under the law, publication of matter which creates doubts about the ability or fairness of a judge of a court is prohibited. A newspaper should not impute of improper motives to a judge. Casting defamatory allegations against a judge or judges, with or without reference to particular case, is contempt because it creates distrust in the popular mind and shatters confidence of the people in the judiciary. However, the Contempt of Court Act 1971, is basically designed to protect the judiciary from unwarranted allegations, and not to safeguard corrupt judges.

Prejudicing Fair Trial **:** Court reporting prejudicing fair trial may be of various forms. It is contempt-

(a) If a newspaper report deters a person from giving witness in a court;

(b) If the report offers threats or is written in abusive language compelling a party to discontinue the court proceedings;

(c) If the report discusses the merits of a case pending in court.

The Precautions **:** According to Section 5 of the Contempt of Court Act, 1971, a person shall not be guilty of Contempt of Court for publishing any 'fair comment' on the merits of any case, which has been 'heard and finally decided'.

What is Fair Comment? There is no single formula to decide the fairness of a comment. The matter depends on the facts and circumstances of each case. To comment on the correctness of a judicial decision is not contempt. Similarly, to point out inequality of sentences in two different cases of the same nature, is also not contempt. However, while commenting on the merits of a case if improper motives are imputed to the judge, then the comment ceases to be fair. Similarly, to express that the judgement was arbitrary or the judge was incompetent is also contempt.

Heard and Finally Decided **:** A fair comment on the merits of a ease be made when it is heard and finally decided. A case can not be said to have finally decided until the period of limitation for filing appeal has expired. Where an appeal or revision has been filed the comments on the merits of the case should not be published until the appeal is finally decided.

Ignorance of Pendency **:** If a court story interferes with the course of justice, but its reports had no reasonable ground to assume that the proceedings were pending, then one will not be guilty of contempt of court. Prior to the enactment of Contempt of Court Act, 1971, ignorance of pendency was not a defence or excuse.

Fair and Accurate Report : According to Section 4 of the Contempt of Court Act, 1971, fair and accurate report of the court proceedings is lawful.

However, a report will be contemptuous if it has been prohibited by the court or is forbidden by any law.

Truth No Defence : Though truthfulness of a statement is a good defence in an action for libel, it is no defence when it comes to contempt of court.

Academic Writings : Academic writings or a report written academically on a point, of law is not a contempt of court, just on the ground that the law discussed is at issue in a court.

Punishment : The maximum punishment for contempt of court is simple imprisonment of six months, or fine of two thousand rupees or both. If the accused apologies, the person, may be discharged by the court without punishment. It is for the court to decide whether the apology is acceptable. Generally, an apology, to be acceptable by the court, should be sincere, unconditional and without delay.

Reporting and Reviewing

There are as many definitions of 'depth reporting' as there are reporters. Or almost Editors are often heard to remark that there is so little of depth reporting in their papers that they feel the news they provide is incomplete. What is depth reporting?

The Perception : Here are a few answers:

> Depth reporting is what makes readers aware of all aspects of a given subject by giving them all possible information, including, background and atmosphere.

Depth reporting treats a story with a kind of thoroughness of detail and background that a 300-word story cannot. It tells the reader not only what happened but why it happened.

Depth reporting means giving the reader the entire story,

an exhaustive, balanced and well-organized way with full backgrounding.

Depth reporting is simply good reporting with an eye for accuracy and detail.

Depth reporting is the explanatory story that accompanies or follows a breaking news story.

Depth reporting means going into a news development and explaining its significance with the possible accompaniment of photos that help illustrate the story.

Depth reporting is sound planning in anticipation of news and vigorous execution while the news is fresh.

Depth reporting is not a one-man job but is the product of teamwork, allowing for maximum flexibility.

Depth reporting deals in explanatory facts and not explanatory opinion.

Depth reporting is that which leaves no occassion for more questions to be asked by the reader.

Depth reporting is not just presentation of facts as they appear at first, but which delves into the origins, the logic, the pressures and the interests involved, making the reader understand not merely who and what, but how, and more importantly, why.

Depth reporting is digging beneath the surface and coming up. With facts that aren't immediately visible, but which nevertheless contribute to an understanding of the story.

No matter how it is defined, in-depth reporting, in the final analysis should tell us the whole, unvarnished story as it is.

His a mistaken notion to think that an in-depth story should necessarily be long, though *New Yorker* reports which are magnificent examples of in-depth reporting run into several thousand: words. Length has nothing to do with depth. And, while obviously it is not always easy to cram many facts in a short piece, a perceptive reporter should be able to provide the maximum information in the fewest necessary words. Wordiness is not wisdom and padding is usually seen for what it is.

Often the best in-depth reporting is done by a team, especially if one has to consider the time factor. While the total number of man hours put in pursuing the facts and writing the story may be about the same if the piece was written by just one reporter, team writing has the additional advantage of bringing the thinking of several men to the final story and should generally be preferable.

The line dividing an in-depth from a feature article or an investigative report is pretty thin indeed and one can often be confused for the other. The presumption usually is that in an investigative report the object is to ferret out important secret information which somebody is determined to keep secret. But there is no hard and fast rule which says that a writer of a feature article should not reveal secret information or that in-depth reports should confine themselves strictly to presenting background information in detail. The *Indian Express* in late April and early May 1979 ran a series on what it is like to be in a jail by one of its reporters Ashwini Sarin. Sarin got himself arrested and provided some excellent inside information about life in Tihar Central Jail, Delhi. The four-part serial was part in-depth reportage, part feature and part investigative reporting at its best.

Investigative Reporting: Ever since Woodward and Bernstein of the *Washington Post* broke the Watergate story and followed it up to the point where President Nixon finally had to resign, investigative reporting has received a fillip out of proportion to their real contribution to journalism. For the fact is that much of what the two reporters put out was based on FBI reports that were passed on to them by sources that had their own axes to grind.

And while this is not to minimize what Woodward and Bernstein had done, it is well to remember that investigative journalism is more than rephrasing leaks. At its best, investigative reporting is master detective work. It is a *way* of reporting that makes it a tool of the in-depth writer. Also, it is *situation reporting* rather than *event reporting*, although events may be involved.

An investigative reporter starts with the hunch that there is more than meets the eye in something of which he had heard. But he can only function best if he is assured of strong editorial direction and backing. Without that the most perceptive reporter would be wasting his time and the paper's money.

This means that the investigative reporter will have to clear his assignment with the editor and function with the knowledge and-consent of his seniors, if only because no investigation can be successful without the time to do a decent job. A City Editor of-the Detroit *Free Press* is quoted as giving the following suggestions to the prospective investigative reporter:

> Don't overlook a tip from any source. Some of the best leads may come from the tips that don't look promising. Many-perhaps most-won't pan out. But don't overlook any possibilities.

Stay within the law. Don't attempt to open safes or burgla Tise offices for 'evidence'. Don't be a policeman.

Make plans from the start. Don't leap into it. Check the evidence and keep checking as you go along. Keep up your lines of communication with those working in the field.

Keep going. The investigative way is hard, but don't stop if you think you have something. If your curiosity is burning you as it should, you won't.

'The curiosity of Ashwini Sarin of the *Express News Service* got the better of him in wanting to know what conditions in

Tihar Central Jail, Delhi, were. One-fifth of India's Jails were built in the 19th century. Another two-thirds were built 60 to 80 years ago. But concerned citizens eager to help improve conditions in jail were repeatedly denied access to them. Sarin volunteered to get himself arrested on a minor charge and file a first-hand report-on conditions in Tihar Central Jail. Following is an extract from part one of his four-part report, a good example of investigative reporting:

> New Delhi: I still shudder to recall the experience. "Never again." I prayed as I stepped into the waiting taxi on the night of April 20 (10.30 p.m. to be precise) after my release from Delhi's Tihar Central Jail. I had been lodged there two days earlier charged with disorderly behaviour in a public place under the influence of alcohol.

"A day more here and I would have turned mad" I told' B.M. Sinha, my chief reporter who came to take me home from an assignment which turned out to be something I had not bargained for.

The idea was to know at first hand what exactly it means to be an under-trial in Tihar Jail. Our earlier efforts to penetrate the secrecy behind the high walls through official and other sources had failed.

I was to get myself arrested on a trumped up charge and then, refuse bail.

My first effort to create an unruly scene, without consuming liquor, at the Delhi Haryana border on April 17 was futile. A burly police sub-Inspector gave me a long lecture on cultivating good habits. "You seem to come from a good family" he said. "Care for their honour if not your own." He hailed a taxi and put me in with instructions to the driver to "unload" me safely at my house.

I left the taxi at Kalkaji, tipped the driver and took a bus home.

The next day, April 18. I left home after a hearty breakfast of boiled eggs and toast. "Have your fill because there will belittle to eat for the next three days," Mr. Sinha cautioned me. About 11.30 a.m. we took a taxi and headed towards Badarpur. The arrangement was that Sinha would shadow me after my arrest.

This time I choose a spot very near the Badarpur police station. I abùsed a shopkeeper with an empty beer bottle in one hand and using the other to stop the traffic trying to enter the old Badarpur settlement from the historic Agra Gate side. My torn faded jeans and the ageing check-shirt with the upper two buttons missing suited my role nicely.

The word soon reached the police station and within minutes I was dragged into it. The old lanky Sub-Inspector and the baton-wielding constables were not too rough. Sinha was watching from a distance.

They put me under arrest. Within half an hour the papers charging me under Section 93 and 97 of the Delhi Police Act were ready. A police pick-up took me to the Patiala House Court and I was produced before the Magistrate who remanded me to jail custody till Monday, April 23, if I failed to produce a bail bond. The court allowed my application that I be allowed to take Rs. 25 to jail.

Outside, some touts offered to get me out on bail. "This is a very minor offence. Why are you spending five days in jail? I will get you bail for 20 rupees" one said. I thanked him as the cops took me to the lock-up room in Patiala House. I was already in low spirits. This was going to be no fun.

In the succeeding three parts Sarin gave a vivid account of what it was like to be in a jail with professional criminals. And whether, in the end, the revelations achieved anything is beside the point. What is relevant is that the four-part series was a professsionally, competent one.

Investigative stories may be written in a variety of ways.

When the subject matter is familiar and little explanation is called for, the story can be written as straight news. But if the investigation deals with complicated issues, then a good deal of interpretative material will become necessary. The important thing to remember is that the writer must remain calm, restrained and detached if he is to make any meaningful impact on his reader. The hystorical I-am-a-detective who-dug-it-all style is unbecoming and could even be counterproductive.

Serious Coverage : In a sense all good editors are crusaders for a cause or causes.

In the early thirties and forties, till indeed India became free, journalism in our country was largely crusading journalism where the national press was concerned. And the crusade, understand ably, was for freedom. *The Free Press Journal* in its early days ran strong stories supporting the cause of Indian shipping.

A crusade implies not merely a cause to be fought for but steadiness and constancy, a stout heart and an unflagging interest. A crusade is not fought by writting one editorial or one news story. Perseverance, often against entrenched hostility from the powers that be, is the hallmark of a crusade. Bal Gangadhar Tilak was a crusader; so was Mahatma Gandhi. At the turn of the century, Lovat Fraser, then editor of the *Times of India* ran a crusade exposing the inhuman working conditions in Bombay's textile mills where men worked 12 hours a day. Fraser ran a tearing campaign :starting with an article entitled "Bombay's Slaves" which was to result in a succession of Factory Acts that brought the Indian industrial system in line with world practice.

A crusade can be for any good cause: against child marriage, in favour of prohibition, for ushering in linguistic states...several are the causes that the Indian press has fought for over the years. The obvious characteristic of a crusade is that it is concerned with the public good as seen by the editor. In conducting a crusade, the editor may bring all the ammunition he has to the battle: editorials, depth-reporting, investigative reporting, even cartoons. It was Joseph Pulitzer who first established the crusade as a way of life for American newspapers by setting up a prize for such kind of journalism. He himself ran crusades against predatory financial interests, bad housing, the white slave traffic to mention only a few causes that he strenuously espoused. Today, in the United States, the Pulitzer Prize remains a major incentive for journalists to carry on with the Pulitzer tradition.

It may be mentioned in passing, however, that neither in the United States nor in any other country, India included, is a crusade necessarily inducted in the public interest. It does happen all too often that a crusade is just one more gimmick to raise the paper's circulation. Not that this is necessarily wrong; if the public interest coincides with the paper's interest, that is no reason why eyebrows should be raised. But nevertheless it is just as well to remember that what shines for public weal may turn out to be another way to augment private profit.

In itself, a crusading newspaper is neither good nor bad. That depends, as a distinguished American publicist, Robert J. Blakely pointed out in his Don R. Mellett Memorial lecture, in large part upon its motivations. There are newspapers that 'crusade' for ulterior reasons-to build up circulation or to grind an axe rather than to sharpen the sword of justice. These are contemptible.

They injure the innocent. They rarely accomplish beneficial results that endure, always stopping short when the cream of sensationalism has been skimmed and never pressing to where they touch the really powerful and dangerous elements of the community.... But to me the free press reaches its zenith in a good newspaper looking for a fight in a good causein its own avenues and alleys. Few personal satisfactions can match the knowledge that one is making one's community a better place in which to live".

The value of a true crusade is that it quickly endears itself to the reader. And the newspaper which shows that it is unafraid or the powerful is quickly recognized as a trustworthy watchdog. More, once the public realises that the local newspaper is interested in exposing scandals it will come forth with a surprising amount of information. Trust begets trust.

A crusade can be most productive when the situation is ripe for action. A little corruption does not invite much attention. Large scale corruption does. Mr. Amitabh Chowdhury won an award while assistant editor of *Jugantar* by exposing graft in Calcutta. The graft was of such a kind that it could not go unrecognized. During his years as editor of *The Times of India*, Mr. Frank Moraes ran a crusade against prohibition. It took courage to buck the Establishment of that time. Mr. Moraes had to pay for it. An editor who runs an unsuccessful crusade *pari passu* runs the risk of losing his job.

Feature Writing : The standard English dictionary defines the word 'feature' as follows:

1. part of the face. The nose, mouth, chin and forehead are features,
2. features the face,
3. distinct part or quality; thing that stands out and attracts attention,
4. a long motion picture,
5. a special article, comic strip etc. in a newspaper.

To say that a newspaper feature is a "special article" does not say much about the nature of that article. What, then, is a feature article? Too many newspapermen think vaguely of features as something of a timeless nature-a story that can be pushed in when there is not much news, or a story that reads well on a Sunday in the magazine section. In fact one thinks of features strictly in terms of magazine reading.

What is there about a feature that makes it attractive to readers? Contrary to some belief, it is its *timeliness.* A feature to be read and appreciated, must have immediate reference to what the reader knows only sketchily. A feature, in the circumstances, must fill in the reader with new information of which he has been hitherto ignorant. It must provide him with all that he wanted to know but had no time to inquire about.

A feature can be written on any subject. Think of all the features that have appeared, for example, in *The Illustrated Weekly of India.*

News Item: Dr. K. Shivarama Karanth has been awarded the Jnanpith Award for 1978.

Feature Story: Who is Dr. Karanth? Why was the Jnanpith Award given to him? What is the source of his greatness as a writer? A discussion of the quality and content of some of his books with, possibly, an interview with the award winner.

News Story: A child is born conceived in the laboratory, a miracle of modern science.

Feature Story: What is the ballyhoo about a "test-tube" baby all about? Who are the scientists who made the birth of the first test-tube baby possible? What techniques did they use? What are the lessons to be learnt from them?

News Item: On September 9, 1978, the Soviet Union celebrated the 150th birth anniversary of Count Leo Tolstoy.

Feature Story: What is the relevance of Tolstoy to India? What are his links with India? What was the nature of the correspondence between him and Mahatma Gandhi?

News Item: On August 17,1978, three Americans landed their giant helium-filled balloon in France to become the first aviators to balloon across the Atlantic.

Feature Story: When was the last attempt at crossing the Atlantic by balloon made? What is the history of ballooning?

How many attempts have been made at all? Where? With what success? At what cost?

News Item: The Government of India has placed a ban on foreign film units making a documentary of the Rajneesh Ashram.

Feature Story: What kind of ashram is run by Bhagwan Rajneesh? What are his antecedents? What is his philosophy? Why is he so controversial? News item: The site of the Mathura Refinery has been chosen on the basis of techno-economic studies, but without going into the problem of pollution.

News Item: A proposal has been made by Mr. George Fernandes, Minister for Industry for the nationalization of the steel, aluminium and automobile industries.

Feature Story: Are the three concerned industries really in bad shape? What motivated the Minister to call for the nationalization of manifestly profit-making units? What does the Minister have to say in defence of his proposal? What do the stalwarts of the industries themselves have to say in defence of the private sector?

It will be noticed that every feature arises out of a news item; the news does not tell the whole story; it is left to the feature writer to fill in the blanks. The feature becomes attractive in direct proportion to the element of curiosity stirred by the news item.

In fact, there is a direct co-relation between a news item and a feature and the writer who is quick to grasp it can be the first in the market to sell it to a magazine or a journal. A feature is saleable to the extent that it strikes reader interest when the news is still "hot."

Though Some magazines have a regular feature editor, more often than not it is the free lance writer who provides the features. The topics for the features literally suggest themselves to the perceptive free-lancer or professional writer. A film actress commits suicide. That is the news. Topic for a feature: how many people commit suicide in a year? Who are more prone to commit suicide: men or women? In India which state has the highest rate of suicides?

Which country in the world has, similarly, the highest rate of suicide? Why do people commit suicide? What can be done to prevent them from killing themselves?

Or again: Mr. Zulfikar Ali Bhutto is hanged. Topic for a feature: Is Mr. Bhutto the first political leader to be hanged for alleged crimes committed while in power? Who other have met a similar fate? Is hanging desirable?

When it was reported that there had been a sudden spurt in cases of jaundice in Bombay city, *The Illustrated Weekly of India* commissioned a distinguished medical practitioner to write about why and how jaundice strikes and what remedial measures could be taken to prevent its occurrence. It was a sell-out issue.

A feature is expected to give the background to the news, which includes analysis, explanation and discussion. It should document facts, possibly anticipate developments. Perception is a great gift for a feature writer who wants to make his mark as a knowledgeable person. In fact the more of a specialist he is, the better are the feature writer's chances of selling his product.

A feature can be based on a news item. It is a news feature.

A feature can be based on sports. It is a sports feature.

A feature can be based on adventure (mountain-climbing, hunting). It is an adventure feature.

A feature can be on science. It is a science feature... and so on. A feature becomes attractive to editors if it is (a) timely (b) written by an authority, (c) illustrated suitably. Magazines, especially, prefer features that can be richly illustrated.

But there are other kinds of features as well. A cartoon strip is a feature. A personal diary is a feature; a column is a feature. A '"middle" is a feature. So are book reviews, film criticism, art and, theatre criticisms-all features in their own right. Feature writing, in the circumstances, is an art that is best handled by an expert-or specialist in his field.

A personal diary is something intensely intimate. It records the impressions of the writer in subjective terms-the 'I' predominating. President Franklin D. Roosevelt's wife Eleanor wrote a personal column for many years and it was widely read because of the position she held as the President's wife. Mrs. Roosevelt was also, controversial as any good personal columnist should be in a healthy way and often readable as well.

Among the more distinguished personal diarists in India was Pothan Joseph whose column "Over A Cup of Tea" which he began during his days at the *Bombay Chronicle* and continued to his last years on the *Deccan Herald* was one of the most widely-read in India. He wrote in snippets. Below are examples:

> "The consequences of abolishing Guindy races would be the sacrifice of our horses" writes a Khadi-clad sportsman mournfully. Aswamedha represented supreme attainment, you ass. Become a member of the Turf Club, support "Government policy, do your betting elsewhere, vote for the liquidation of properties, see to the sale of land at high prices, take your share of the :proceeds, and go home, singing in the rain.

Pandit Nehru warns us about, the possibility of Englishmen (before they quit) of "wreaking damage on our minds and hearts and producing a dangerous ulcer." Not to mention an Ulster.

"There is no room for goondas in any religion" says Mahatma Gandhi. Scarcity of accommodation in the cities is largely responsible for their being underground.

A new member of a certain Government bureau made life miserable for his associates by pretending absolute infallibility.

One, day, however, he startled his co-workers by admitting that 'once" he had been wrong. "You wrong?" exclaimed one of them, "Impossible!" "Yes," replied the infallible one, "once I thought I was wrong, when I wasn't."

General Manager T.A. Joseph says that Janata trains are not popular in South India. The South Indian is a born democrat and likes the higgledy-piggledy form of travel, mob-style, that keeps him in athletic fitness. With bodies normally bare as Mother Nature meant it, airconditioning interferes with his perspiration,.. and with music freely rendered by mendicants, he can do without artificial luxuries offered by the coaching department.

Jawaharlal is sorry to hear of the Andhra Kesari's passing, but President Prasad has been more liberal in his eulogy. When Sikandar Hyat Khan died, Jinnah was in Delhi, rather cross about the unenthusiastic views on partition entertained by the Punjab Premier. A statement was requested of the Quaid-e-Azam by the present writer. The tribute expected for record on a long sheet of paper ran: "I am sorry to hear Sikandar is dead." There it ended, like a knife-clasp.

In a newspaper, the columnist is something of a privileged person. He can venture into fields that are forbidden territory to reporters. He can say his piece with little fear of being called on the coals by the editor. But, as with Pothan Joseph or M. Chalapathi Rao, an editor may both write an editorial and a column as well. In fact many editors have their special columns. In his time, Frank Moraes wrote a column for the Sunday *Times of India,* M. V. Kamath wrote a gossip column for the *Free Press Bulletin* and Chalapathi Rao himself wrote a column called *Off the Record:* under the pseudonym Magnus.

Although the word "column" might indicate that the contents run to the conventional 1,000 words or so of the usual newspaper column measurement, the length of a column varies. Some columnists may turn out the full 1,000 words, some would be satisfied with much less and D.F. Karaka, writing for the defunct *Bombay-Chronicle* wrote a "half-column" under the pseudonym Dim that was often less than half a column in length. And fans of the celebrated American humourist Will Rogers will attest to the fact that he wrote a famous column which averaged but one paragraph!

There are, in a manner of speaking, several popular types of columns:

(1) The signed editorial column: Here we find what resembles an editorial in form, but an editorial so palpably personal that it is a cross between an editorial and a column. When an editor writes a piece under his own name he is trying to lay his prestige on the line, Frank Moraes used to write front-page editorials for emphasis. This kind of column is resorted to but rarely by editors.

(2) The standard column: This type of column handles editorial subjects of lesser importance and deals with each in a paragraph or two. A good example is "Current Topics" in *The Times of India.* These are primarily backgrounders and not really opinion pieces. They are unsigned and are frequently the work of two or more members of the editorial staff. Outstanding columns in this category are "Topics of the Times" in the *New York Times.*

(3) The hodge-podge column: Here the columnist presents to his reader a hodge podge of stuff of little or no consequence on the principle that variety is not only the spice of life but a sure formula to catch reader interest. Pothan Joseph's *Over a Cup of Tea*-very nearly approximates to this description.

(4) The middle: The "middle" is so-called because it occupies a position on the editorial page between the main article and the standard column, Current Topics in the case of *The Times of India.*

    The middle's sole purpose is to lighten what could

otherwise be serious reading which an editorial page normally is and is expected to be. It is generally humourous and in any event it should be entertaining and is usually written in a lighter vein. In length it is about 500 words and the more off-beat it is, the better.

(5) The essay column: This type of column is rare today. Students of English literature will recognize the essay columns of Joseph Addison, Charles Lamb, Oliver Goldsmith, G.K. Chesterton and A.A. Milne. As an essay, it has style. Its range is unlimited but it must stick to one rigid rule-it must never be didactic or dull.

Consider this piece on C.K. Nayudu by Chalapathi Rao (Magnus):

> C.K. Nayudu was too alive for long to have become entirely a legend. It is difficult to bury him, as other great cricketers are buried, under a mound of metaphors, though the language of cricket is rich in them. He combined Spartan physical strength with an artist's grace. To think of him mainly in terms of his sixes is poor appreciation, like his Padma Bhushan which was poor recognition. His sixes were only the sparks of his scientific hitting. Nor is it adequate to recall Neville Card us with his poetic phrases borrowed from the language of music, because Cardus had only a glimpse of Nayudu's greatness.

Nayudu could be said to be the father of modern Indian cricket, the man who stamped the age with his strength of character. He is often compared to Jessop, to Trumper, to MaCartney, or to Woolley; with similar grace and freedom from care, Woolley was probably the closest to him. In Indian terms, Nayudu's place was by the side of Ranji, Duleep and Pataudi. Ranji was remote to the modern generation. Dulip with his tulip's delicacy gave of his best in England's green fields. Pataudi was not the success he had been at Oxford when transplanted. Nayudu was wholly indigenous, almost self-taught and self-schooled. Like others, he had to suffer from the imposition of princes in the privilege-ridden days of cricket. Nayudu was a commoner, but a commoner who was king.

It would be ceremonial piety to say that his death is a loss to cricket. He lived a life of achievement, more than that, of fulfilment, and his death is a loss in the sense that a magnificent personality, a magnificent presence, has been withdrawn from a greying landscape. His qualities as a cricketer have been described by many, from Hobbs to Miller, and by a variety of writers using a rich vocabulary.

But for those who saw him at his best, no mere tribute to his technique is ever adequate. He was a Greek or a Roman at the wicket; every stroke spoke of power and thinking, the merest gesture was an expression of a powerful personality. The way he used his athlete's physique enabled him to use his springy wrists and supple footwork to impart a rare strength to his strokes.

It was an attitude of mind, an attitude of adventure and daring. There was security about his centuries but there was a dignity even about his ducks. Statistics tell nothing and it was ill luck that he was passing his prime when India entered Test cricket, and even then he showed without doubt what he could have done in the age of statistics.

Even Wisden speaks of his promise, not of fulfilment. He had stature and grace; if strength is added to grace, it results in grandeur. He was an all-rounder who did not cease to be a front-rank batsman. As a bowler, he could be as wily as Odysseus. To see him field was to see a panther at work. But it was as captain that he was at his best and his character was fully expressed. He was a leader of men, alert, stern, encouraging, forbidding, and bringing out the best in them. It was as a captain of India and as a captain of Holkar that his personality found full play, and cricket politics, which prevented him from presenting fully his wisdom to the generations which grew under his shadow, withered in his presence. As leader, he was a maker of men, some of them princes among men, like Mushtaq Ali.

(6) The gossip column: No daily newspaper carries a gossip column and its natural habitat is the film magazine which flourishes on gossip, some malicious, some harmless but unquestionably titillating. *Stardust* sells largely on the strength of its gossip column Neeta's Natter which is about film stars and their doings. The columnist is fed with juicy tit-bits sometimes by the actors and actresses themselves and sometimes by their PR men on the principle that the more they ate talked about, the greater the chances of their successes at the box office. Few, if any, of these show biz people are known to resent the gossip written about them though there are no reports lacking of actors punching the gossip-columnist on the nose for exceeding the bounds of decency.

Consider this sample from *Stardust:*

> It may not be the only one, but definitely the *main* reason why Rishi is marrying Neetu Singh is because his papa (Raj Kapoor) advised him that it is the right thing to do and the right stage (image-wise) to do it. Which means that Raj is once again playing favourites with his sons. Remember how vehement he had been when Daboo had wanted to marry Babita? He had given his consent only at the twenty-third hour and that too when he realized that Daboo intended marrying Babs anyway.

Reena Roy refuses to let anyone call her by her original 'Surname-Rai! Because, according to her, "It sounds so middle class." Web, it's easy enough for a person to change a name. Isn't it a pity that one can't do the same to a face?

After the release of "Baton Baton Mein" everyone criticised Basu ("he is a fluke director") and Tina ("she can't act for nuts") and the only guy who got away with the applause was Dhruv. A very close friend of his (no, not Shabana) confided that he was playing his real life role. Now I wonder if Ms Azmi would agree to that!

Ex-Mrs. Bedi, Protima, happily played *kabab mein haddi* between Kabir and Susan and sportingly smiled away the moment') when Kabir, suddenly overcome with love for his new wife, would peck her tenderly.

(7) The Question and Answer column: The Question and Answer column comes in various colours. It could be a medical column in which a qualified doctor answers queries on health. It could be a sobsister column in which readers ask questions about their personal problems and get appropriate answers depending on whether the questions are plain, plain silly or serious. Filmfare ran a column in which I.S. Johar, the well-known film actor replied to questions the best of which were awarded cash prizes. Filmfare still runs such a column with Johar's scintillating replies. Sample:

In our films, when somebody is about to die, the earthen lamp starts to flicker. When the flame dies, the person dies. Why not take more care of the lamp, and put more oil in it?

A.K. Das Gupta, New Delhi.

This letter won a prize of Rs. 50.

In more serious magazines, the column could be run to elicit, serious replies. Thus, *Science Today* runs a Question and Answer column. The questions apparently are from readers-it is not specifically stated-but the answers are from experts. The questions are somewhat on the following lines: Why do waves break? What is a mirage? Why is the sky blue?

(8) The Sports Column: There was a time when some leading Indian newspapers had their daily sports column, but this is getting to be rarer these days. Among the distinguished sports columnists is A.F.S.

> Talyarkhan, who, indeed, is the doyen of sports columnists and whose column *Take It From Ale* was once read avidly by sports fans. Presently he writes a column for *Blitz* under the title *Knock-Out!* Take this example:

Very recently, going through some old clippings of my scriblings, came across an article on the need to go back to three day Tests before boredom sets in. That was written about fifteen years ago and if this is raked up here it is because there are clear signs that too much, over too long a period, inevitably causes reflection:

> The just-concluded limited overs competition sponsored by Wills is why am stressing today that the answer to many problems afflicting the Cricket Championship (call it Ranji Trophy if you prefer) is largely due to the want of attraction where the lover of the game is concerned.

If some one was to work out the figures, am almost sure that ninety five per cent of the preliminary rounds of the Championship are decided on the result of the first innings:

> So much so that reporter after reporter writes about a team gaining the VITAL LEAD, quite rightly, too, because it is only to get the lead on the first-innings of a three day (never to be completed) match that the State teams battle for. No, not battle, struggle is the better term. You never await a report or a broadcast of an outright win, it is always the vital lead on the first innings of a pure farcical three-day Ranji Trophy match that counts. On most Indian wickets, and at the time of the year we choose to play much of our big cricket, conditions are more or less static so that it is solely the first innings lead that a team, strives to achieve thus claiming "victory" and the right to progress further in the tournament.

This being established fact, the answer seems to be to change the early rounds of the Championship matches to limited over matches thus retaining the magic "vital" first innings lead, but changing the tempo of the cricket which will make for more dynamism among players and keenness among followers of cricket.

Thus the present farce of deciding a three-day first-class match on the result of the first innings will remain but since there is a limit to the: overs to be bowled, the striving for the precious "lead" and "victory" will yet be there but there will be purposeful cricket all the way.

The purist will not like this much-I do not-but what's to do when in truth the Championship has been transformed into a positive force by deciding on the result of the first innings lead.

So, since we cannot decide a so-called three-day Championship fixture in the allotted period of three days, and know fully well that all that counts is the "vital lead" on the first innings, why not stick-to this formula and make the cricket trebly exciting and competitive by switching to limited overs matches? The Board might care to give this a thought for they cannot deny that as things are, the Ranji Trophy matches-the vast majority-are decided on the first innings. So make the innings lead a specified fight.

A columnist who signs his wares may express himself with the utmost freedom so long as he steers clear of libel and obscenity. Newspaper publishers who take on columnists often give full freedom to them to air views contrary to those editorially held. This is particularly true of American newspapers which may give hospitality to columnists of various political shades of opinion. Indian newspapers haven't yet come to that stage fully, partly because Indian cities have more than one newspaper while most American cities have only one newspaper and it cannot appear to stifle contrary opinion.

The columnist is generally a specialist, like Talyarkhan whose knowledge of sports in unchallenged. But there could be generalists like Khwaja Ahmed Abbas whose *Last Page* originally a feature of the Sunday *Bombay Chronicle* (now defunct) has been transferred to *Blitz*.

Whether he is a specialist or a generalist, a columnist who is reasonably aware of his limitations and does not stray beyond what is permissible, considering his talent has no difficulty being accepted. The criticism against columnists is that, once they are established, they tend to consider themselves as specialists one very thing in the heaven above, on the earth beneath and in the waters around. Publishers sometimes are reluctant to let them off their pages and they develop inflated egos and traits of omniscience. Westbrook Pegler, no mean columnist himself, once commented on this tribe with unusual candour:

> Of all the fantastic fog shapes that have arisen off the swamp of confusion since the big war, the most futile and at the same time, the most pretentious, is the deep-thinking, hair-trigger columnist or commentator who knows all the answers just off hand and can settle great affairs with absolute finality three days or even six days a week.

What causes us? Well, as nearly as I can figure it out, this trade began as a sort of journalistic vaudeville intended to entertain the customers and exert a little circulation pull of a slightly higher tone that of comics.

(9) The humorous column: Morning papers in India still fight shy of having a regular daily humorous column, but an evening paper in Bombay carries a column by one of its staff men under the pseudonym Busybee. Busybee's column *Round and About* is one of the best-known columns in Bombay. Here is a sample.

According to a report in the morning papers, jawans serving at high altitude will be given coffee, tea, milk and dry fruits instead of rum, once total prohibition is introduced. Which does not concern me. But what does concern me is hostesses doing the same at cocktail parties in Bombay. I visualize the follow*ing* situation:

> Wife and I arrive at a cocktail party and the hostess greets us and says: "So glad you could make it. Now what will you have, coffee, tea or milk?"

"Coffee to start with" I say.

The wife whispers in my ear:

> "I thought you had promised not to touch a drop of coffee and restrict yourself to milk."

A waiter serves me coffee and dry fruits and, as I am sipping it, the host comes up and says: "Come on, drink it up. There's plenty more where that comes from."

The wife tells the host: "He has not been feeling well all this week and has decided to go easy on coffee. Just one cup should be enough for him."

A guest at the party who in the pre-prohibition days enjoyed getting everybody slightly drunk at parties, pushes another cup of coffee in my hands and says: "If you don't drink, then the party just won't start rolling."

I have two more cups of coffee and a third one when the wife is busy talking to some guest. After that I am feeling a little sick, though only very little.

The hostess says: "Here, eat some dry fruits, you will feel better." By this time the party is really swinging. Some of the men have consumed pots and pots of coffee, others have finished' equal quantities of tea. Most of the women have been drinking milk. And, as it happens at such parties, the dry fruits ran out.

Late in the night, after one last coffee for the road, we leave the party. And, on the way home, the wife says: "You have' started getting as tight on coffee as you used to on rum."

In a sense all these, in essence, are opinion pieces, as are editorials, theatre, film, art and music criticisms. It is not every reporter who can aspire to be a humorous columnist, an art critic or a sports commentator. From each a certain amount of expertise is called for; the critic, in the first place, must have credibility. In other words, he must be knowledgeable in his chosen field of comment. But above and beyond expertise, he must have a wider knowledge of life and letters. The narrow specialist may have credibility but it is the specialist generalist who will have the audience.

To review any piece of creative work, the reviewer must not only be aware of the artist's own past work but must be able to judge it in the context of other works of the same genre either of his contemporaries or his predecessors or preferably both. In others words, the reviewer must judge against a comparable background. While a review is primarily a subjective piece of writing-the reviewer, after all, can only write in terms of his own knowledge and understanding-it would be a mistake to think that opinion, howsoever well-based, is all.

Critical Mindset

To project too much of the critic's own viewpoint or to criticise a work for the sake of criticism or even worse, to set off a controversy, is to misunderstand the nature and function of criticism. A-critic must *describe* a work as faithfully as possible, assess it as *fairly* as possible and suggest improvements as *comprehensively* as possible, taking care to see that he will not write anything that he-could not defend before a jury of experts or will be ashamed to tell the artist to his face. The critic must remember that the reader will quickly see through bias or hasty judgements and that, inasmuch as the critic judges the artist, the reader will judge the critic.

A critic must be an ornament to his profession. He must be a father figure to artists, criticising them when criticism will do good, cajoling them when cajoling will help, praising them when praise is called for and encouraging them when necessary. A critic is the watchdog of good taste. A well-informed critic is a nation builder in that he helps push the creative talent in the land to greater and greater heights. In the repertoire of a good critic, there can be no malice or ill-will.

Expertise involves study in depth. It is not enough to see plays to be a drama critic any more than it is enough to see films to be a film critic. It helps to read up on theatre and films, to be in constant touch with playwrights and dramatists, actors and actresses, directors and cameramen, musicians and stage hands. In other words, there must be total involvement on the part of the critic to be effective as a critic. The ivory tower critic remains what he is a man far removed from reality.

Some of the best advice on how to review a play was given by Alexander Woollcott, himself a distinguished play-reviewer and essayist.

"The review of a play" he wrote, "as it appears in the morning papers, is addressed not to the actors nor to the playwrights, but to the potential playgoer. The dramatic critic's function is some what akin to that of an attendant at some Florentine court whose uneasy business it was to taste each dish before it was fed to anyone that mattered. He is an ink-stained wretch, invited to each play and expected in the little hour that is left after the fall of the curtain, to transmit something of the play's flavour, to write with whatever fond tribute, sharp invective or amiable badinage will best express it, a description of the play as performed, in terms of the impression it made upon himself.... If he be skillful at his task, the interested playgoer ought to be able to guess pretty shrewdly from his report whether or not the new play in town is of the kind he or she would enjoy.

Woollcott himself was great at giving what he called the play's "'flavour." To him the quality of *Cradle Song,* the lovely drama of a founding baby girl left on the steps of a convent was "like the-chime of bells on a clear frosty night." Woollcott could also be :sharp but perhaps not as sharp as the late A.B. Walkley of *The Times* of London who showed a mastery of succinct as well as sharp inventive when he described a play entitled *A Dreadful Evening* in just one word: "Exactly!" Below are a few examples of good criticism that are worth noticing:

Theatre: The World Turned Upside Down: Cottesloe

The Times, London

In his book *The World Turned Upside Down,* Christopher Hill gave the lie to those who define history as the propaganda of victors. A study of the long-submerged radical movements that flourished in England in the decade, after the Civil War, it is a lasting memorial to the Socialist Britain that might have been, but for the factor which Cromwell's contemporaries termed "sin."

Some of Hill's heroes have already made a theatrical return in plays like John McGrath's *Comrade Jacob* and Caryl Churchill's *A Light Shining in Buckimghamshire,* but the idea of a piece claimed as an "adaptation" of Hill's book, with its hydra-headed sectarian factions confusedly evolving political doctrines out of a world of religious magic, strikes one in advance as an impossibility.

What Keith Dewhurst has done in his play for the Cottesloe is to limit the action to a bare 18 months from the execution of the King to the dispersal of Winstanley's Digger settlement at Cob ham and to admit only the Diggers, Levellers and Ranters as radical spokesmen. It is a sign of our times that throughout this treatment of one of the most fervently God-fearing episodes in our history, there should be no scene of radicalism from the pulpit.

For Bill Bryden and Sebastian Graham-Jones production, the interior of the Cottesloe has been remodelled by William

Dudley into a timber-floored traverse, bounded at one end by huge emblems of state power and at the other end by a towering liberty tree; boundaries that determine the entrances of the royalist and Cromwellian top brass and of the common people or mutineers arriving for trial and execution.

The setting has a Handelian clarity, lending itself to civic processions, marching songs (musically this is a splendid occasion), and enactments of ritual death. It also lends itself to confrontation debates and to elaborate spectacle, such as a prolonged display of musket drill by a firing squad, or an orgiastic love-feast for the Ranters who wind up skipping in the nude.

But despite its severe editorial restrictions, the play does not convey a clear account of the hopes and disillusionment of those who welcomed Charles execution as the planting of the liberty tree the production operates by means of rapid synaptic leaps into particular situations, briefly evoking the Lockyer rebellion or the dispersal of Winstanley's followers, and leaving you to develop an interest in the connecting historic threads.

On those terms, the production is dazzlingly successful. Unlike some of is forerunners, this is not a romantically left-wing occasion, and no false climaxes are introduced to drive home the message Instead there is a crack ensemble accommodating a great variety of dramatic colours and stylistic changes.

Western Music: Allegri Ensemble: Wigmore

The Times, London

Since demand for tickets for the Allegri-Robles Ensemble on Tuesday again exceeded supply, as at Christa Ludwig's recital on Saturday, Wigmore Hall's new chamber music festival seems to be meeting a real need. With harp, flutes and clarinet at hand as well as string quartet, the programme was ideal for a summer night.

The first half went to Mozart, with the clarinet quintet as *piece de resistance.* That brought first-rate teamwork with Jack Brymer's clarinet never dominating, but beautifully intertwined with the light texture of the Allegri team. His own nuances in cantible and the liquidity of his appeggio flourishes were a delight.

The D major flute quartet, K 285, represents a less mature Wolfgang, and we know from published correspondence how severely Leopold Mozart chastised his son for not trying hard enough with this particular commission. Its brief slow movement is a minor miracle, all the same. Christopher Hyde-Smith's phrasing here was a little unyielding, but he made amends in a sparkling finale.

Whether the unremarkable set of variations included by Marisa Roblesin the first half were composed by Mozart remains a moot point. She played them boldly; but inevitably more the spellbinder we remember of old, in terms of magical sonority, in Bax's one-movement Elegaic Trio of flute, viola and harp (a feast of nostalgia) and Ravel's still more seductively scored *Introduction and Allegro* which united all seven artists. At first it seemed as if the attack of out-of-tuneness that had marred Schubert's *Quartettsatz* from the Allegri team might bedevil the Ravel, too. But once the introduction was passed, those players found their form. The *Allegro* was subtly balanced, coloured, and phrased, with smouldering embers bursting into flame at the climax of the development in preparation for the harp cadenza beautifully weighed and measured by Miss Robles.

INDIAN MUSIC: DUET BY SALAMAT AND NAZAKAT

The Times of India, Bombay

The vocal duets of Salamat Ali and Nazakat Ali, who gave a three hour performance under the auspices of Arun Sangeetalaya at Khar Saturday might have been the subject of much animated discussion in the musical milieu of Bombay ever since the two Pakistani artistes made their first appearance in the city four years ago. After having heard them at several concerts during their first visit to the city, this reviewer had a feeling that the controversy touched off by the music of Salamat and Nizakat was not so much a measure of the aesthetic awareness or capacity of the average connosieur to understand and appreciate the subtle refinements or traditional music.

If anything it was rather indicative of this era of mass-culture values-where the box office takings come to determine the greatness of an artiste! Indeed, Salam at and Nizakat-the latter, by the way, is more or less a sleeping partner in the team-work-possess talent in ample measure. They have a winsome command of technique and an acute sense of rhythm. They are, above all, quite novel and unconventional in their singing. But that is not all. Their singing, on the contrary, does not have a refined sense of design and proportion. It is unimaginative.

Saturday night's concert only served to confirm my earlier impressions. The artistes chose for their fare the ragas *Malkouns, Darbari* and *Adāna.* In between they rendered two lighter pieces in *Mishra Pahadi* and *Multani Kafi.* The concert started an hour behind schedule. The popular sarangi player, Ram Narain, who was to accompany the principal performers did not show up at all. Then there was the erratic behaviour of the microphone which posed a great problem throughout the concert.

The presentation of the opening item in *Malkauns,* which Salamat and Nazakat rendered in *vilambit, drut,* in *jhaptaal* and then in *tritaal,* to be followed again by a *tarana,* lasted well over an hour and a half. It gave the impression that while the technical virtuosity of the artistes was unquestioned, their main obsession was to display their tonal facility, vocal gyrnnastics and grasp of the intricacies of their melodic theme instead of to employ them for a really aesthetic presentation of their art. Added to this was the reckless fondness for ornamentation and catchy, theatrical improvisations in *sargams* that carried but momentary appeal. Frankly, the rendering was overdone. The exposition in *Darbari* which the artistes rendered in *viambit, drut* and *tarana,* was decidedly the best item of the concert. It was marked by a better sense of purpose and clearer sense of direction. Theitem that followed, namely, *raga adana* in *jhaptaal, tritaal* followed by a chaturanga-like piece, could have been equally good if it were not beset with out-of-tune patterns every now and then. The tabla wizard Alla Rakha, and the vocalists also engaged in a race of melody and rhythm and the entire performance degenerated into unmusical acrobatics. As for the two lighter pieces, there was nothing much to say. They were sung light-heartedly.

The newer technique of musical expression sought to be popularised by Sahmat and Nazakat is something of hectic experimentation at achieving something new that is trying hard to take root in the soil. A good many people have called them prodigies. Some call them gate-crashers and to many others the artistes seem to be a musical enigma. It may, therefore, be hazardous to suggest that these musicians disappointed the audience. After all, most of the listener; did get what they wanted the acrobatics and pyrotechnics of music and not necessarily the aesthetics of it!

Book Review: Reviewing a book is as much an art as putting a-chair together or doing heart surgery. To review a book calls for considerable knowledge not only of the subject covered by the book, but of the author, his previous works, his expertise as measured against his compeers and of its relevance. Nothing is more degrading in journalism than to assume that *anybody* can review a book.

A competent book review-especially of fiction-reports to the reader on the following lines:

(1) It gives an understanding of the nature, but not the surprises of the plot.

(2) It tells of its type or class-historical novel, psychological novel, mystery story etc.

(3) It indicates the locale in which the story moves.

(4) It gives a hint of the book's tang and flavour through short quotes.

(5) It introduces the chief characters.

(6) It expresses an opinion as to how the author has handled his material.

Book reviews can be short, of medium length or longish, in the style of the *New York Review of Books.* Where space is lacking some books are dismissed in one para notices that just mention the 'name of the book, the name of the author, the name and full address of the publisher, the number of pages and the price, as well as the year of publication.

And no matter whether the review is short or long, this is the basic information that must necessarily be provided. It is the first courtesy due to the publisher who sends a book to an editor for review.

It is often customary to first outline what the book is about to acquaint the reader what to expect in it. The critic will then assess its merits, literary, stylistic, technical or otherwise. Is it a scholarly' piece of work? Does it stand up to scrutiny? Is it socially relevant? How does it compare with works of like nature? In this the critic will bring to bear on his own writing a measure of scholarship worthy of the book.

Consider this review of a Bengali novel that appeared in *The Book Review;*

Ami Anupam (I, Anupama Bengali novel) by Nabaneeta Deb. Sen; Ishan Publishers, Calcutta, 1978; pages 180; Rs. 8. Reviewed by Meenakshi Mukherjee.

This is the first novel of a writer who has so far been well known to Bengali readers as a poet. But her novel is not poetic in the usual sense of the term.

In a style that is cerebral as well as graceful, Nabaneeta Deb Sen writes of a situation uneasily familiar to most of us-the conflict between integrity and expediency. This is done not in terms of a simple statement, but is concretized in a situation that has all the unedited and unexpurgated complexity of real life.

Contrary to current expectations, her protagonist is neither a common man nor anti-hero, but a brilliant academic who has succeeded in everything he has done so far. Anupam Roy at the height of his career is a national figure whose weekly broadcast and newspaper column of poetical analysis influences public opinion and sparks off controversies. He is respected not only for his intellect and fearless views, but also because he has refused many lucrative high level jobs in order to maintain his, intellectual independence.

In his personal relationships also Anupam is impeccable. Although he does not believe in extremism in politics, he loves many of the extremists personally, and gives shelter to Naxalite young men at home. He helps the Legal Aid Committee for justice to political prisoners. To his old mother and less successful younger brother, he is tender and dutiful. If women find him, irresistible he cannot help it, and is human enough to recognise his occasional need but he lets women enter his life only for as long as they do not threaten his freedom.

Summarised thus, the portrait of Anupam Roy seems to be a broad brush-stroke job, but actually in this novel, *Ami Anupam,* nothing is stated-the details are gradually and subtly revealed through action and conversation, specially conversation between Nabaneeta Deb Sen-excels in catching accurately the subtle nuances of speech. Only when the image of Anupam Roy is established well, the layers can be peeled off effectively to show what lies within.

The gap between the public image and the private self is seen to be wide and yet the result is not the unmasking of the hypocrite. One sees the dilemma of choice, sympathises with Anupam Roy's predicament, and realises that in real life the-option between right and wrong is hardly unequivocal.

Toward the end of the novel Anupam Roy faces a moral crisis, aggravated by an almost symbolic physical infirmity, the loss of his voice. After a period of nightmare and self-searching, he wakes up to find many of his problems recede because he can now come to terms with a different view of himself. The end comes dangerously close to sentimentality, specially in the affirmation of the values of his mother, a temptation no Bengali writer can resist (Is idealisation of the mother-figure an essentially Bengali trait or is it Indian?) yet the competent blend of circumstantial realism with evocative use of language finally steers the novel clear of mushiness.

Of the positive qualities of this rather remarkable novel I will single out only two. One: the authentic portrayal of a character in terms of his work and professional commitments. Very rarely do we see in Indian novels such a credible, convincing character seen largely in terms of his own career. Popular fiction and films have conditioned us into accepting career stereotypes too easily-the reference to a test-tube makes a scientist, khadi kurta a politician and absent-minded idealism a professor. But Anupam Roy is a three-dimensional individual, whose complex predicament is seen in terms of his changing political views, his rewriting of a particular piece for a newspaper, his guilt at the recognition of the gap between his academic stand and his personal behaviour.

The first test of his integrity comes when a high official of the intelligence branch invites him to his club for lunch and in between gin-and-tonic and sizzler steak, with the accompaniment of polite pseudo-cultural talk on Kurusawa, Joan Baez and Satyajit Ray, lets him know that the police is aware of a kit bag in his house left there by a young Naxalite; and if he values his own life, he should give it up to the police.

A period of conflict follows, but the decision is not difficult Roy surrenders the bag to the police which is found to contain, among other things, a note book with names and addresses.

So it is possible to bring many young men to the torture chamber for confession. One of the boys Anupam Roy knew well is found murdered soon after.

His guilt becomes difficult to live with. His facile and fearless-pen is unable to churn out the brilliant pieces he was so famous for. His own servant, the only witness to his act, accuses him silently-and a drunken artist in a bar publicly charges him of betrayal. At this point 'he becomes aware of a strange affliction he is losing his voice-possibly for ever.

Several issues converge after this. The necessary surgical operation for restoring his voice can only be done in Europe for which he urgently needs money. There is a growing guilt about the two women whom he rejected for his own convenience, and his hatred for his dead father becomes obsessive. He hates himself because he carries his father's genes. Having lost his voice and his ability to write, his self-confidence ebbs away, and his favourite metaphor of a proud charioteer holding the reins of his seven horses firmly in hand, no longer applies to his own life. A mute contrast develops between Anupam and his ordinary middle class brother Niru, who stayed with the mother while the elder brother was busy getting international recognition.

Niru had the courage to marry the girl he loved while Anupam spurned emotional entanglements; Niru loved animals, collected maimed creatures around him to feed them, while Anupam hated animals and the orised about the way they exercised tyranny of the weak. Finally when there was this desperate need of money for Anupam's surgery, Niru was ready with his meagre provident fund money and his wife's unit trust, while Anupam could not only think of accepting the editorship of a national daily which would advance him a large sum in return for his freedom of belief. "Niru does not earn much" his mother told Anupam, "but he is richer than you."

The second strength of the novel is the solidity of a specification which gives the moral and ethical issues a concreteness and credibility. Lower middle class life has been portrayed in Bengali fiction often very effectively, but is very rare to find an unbiased documentation of the life of successful people. The fact that the affluent level of society is seldom presented in Bengali novels without exaggeration or satire may have interesting sociological implications. But in this novel Nabaneeta Deb Sen portrays this life effortlessly with a very sure touch, although in very rare movements, it seems that because she can do this so easily, there is a slight tendency toward over-indulgence.

In the early chapters of the novel she establishes Anupam Roy's character by a simple device-describing a routine day in his life. The busy and varied life of this international-known man is indicated when he quickly goes through his morning mail consisting of a letter from Geneva in connection with a conference, a Sapru House circular about a seminar, the current issue of South Asian Bulletin, a request from an ex-student for a testimonial, a letter from a professor in Tokyo commenting on his recently published paper, a love letter from a woman (which he tosses away without reading) and a telegram about a selection committee meeting in Hyderabad.

As we follow him through the course of one day we learn a lot about him-his ability to handle difficult situations without losing his calm, his 'calculated control over himself and others including the woman with whom he spends one measured hour each day, and the charisma that he has acquired.

The collage of conversation at the tobacco executive's party, the coffee-house talk where the writers congregate, the four-lettered words of a drunken artist at the bar or the rhetoric of the lunatic at the Gariahat cross roads, all these have a ring of authenticity that vividly recreates contemporary urban reality in India. One wishes the novel could be translated into English or other Indian languages so that it becomes available to more readers, because the issues and conflicts dealt with here have relevance beyond the merely local.

Note how the reviewer subtly interweaves story-telling and apt comment, how analysis is blended with narration. The reviewer provides us with the full flavour of the work making the piece an adequate study of the times in which we live. This gives added relevance, while giving details of the book, to the mentioning of when it was published. The time frame of the novel would thereby be firmly established.

The Editorial: The editorial has been grandiloquently described as the mirror of the newspaper's opinion, its great and undying soul and its conscience. Like John Brown's body, the souls of many dead newspapers keep marching on. There is no doubt whatsoever about it.

Though a newspaper is hardly ever known as a *views* paper, it is remarkable how often a newspaper is known not for its news, but its *views*. Foreign correspondents especially are aware of how often they quote the major newspapers of the country they are assigned to. "*The Times* said today...", "The New York Times said today..." "In an editorial *Die Welt* said today..." are common enough beginnings to them. While news is sacred and opinion free and possibly profane, it is the opinion, evidently, that counts. News frequently is transient, but views have the aura of a certain permanency about them. Today's news may be tomorrow's garbage, but today's views can remain fresh for a long time to come.

Considering that not more than 15 per cent at any time read an editorial, it is still an impressive fact that editorial writers are held in such awe. The truth is that though only a few read editorials, the latter help form and nurture public opinion, especially opinion of the elite that alone frequently counts. A good editorial can incite action, inspire deeds, subvert legislation, stir revolution. Ideas, a public opinion expert once remarked, have legs and they can run.

There are editorials and editorials. Long ones and short ones, pompous ones and perceptive ones, thoughtful ones and titillating ones, editorials that are hard-hitting as well as caressing, inspiring as web as denigrating, editorials, in fact, that reflect as wide a range of human emotions as are known to man.

In the early days of journalism, news and views were published separately, the one in newsletters, the other in pamphlets. It is said that Daniel Defoe first united these two journalists streams in one publication in *The Review* which he published in London in 1704.

In the early days again, the newspapers had no separate editorial page. Opinion merely took the form of observations tacked on to the end of the news or more usually of letters to the editor signed by some pseudonym. To Noah Webster goes the credit for first placing his editorials under the masthead of his paper.

In those days editorials were written by one man-the editor and every reader was aware of the fact. Today newspapers have a battery of editorial writers-leader writers, as they are sometimes known-who write anonymously, but obviously under the guidance and direction of the editor to whom, of course, all opinion is attributed. This is only but natural and as it should be, for no single man these days can emulate Francis Bacon and "take all knowledge for his province."

The complexity of our world is such that too often no single person is competent even to write on a single topic-say, Foreign Affairs. So there are in some of the great newspapers of the world men who specialize in European, African, Soviet, American or Asian Affairs.

The men and women who write editorials have a heavy responsibility to bear. They have the obligation to read extensively to be well-informed. As Geoffrey Parsons, when chief editorial adviser' of the New York *Herald Tribune* said: "The richer the writer's background, the larger his ability to stimulate thought about anything. A good editorial writer addresses the largest classes ever 'reached by a teacher, philosopher or critic. He cannot know 100 much, if he is to hold their attention."

An artificial difference is sometimes made between an editorial and a "leader." The "leader" is defined as the principle article in a newspaper. But definitions have revealed a great deal of confused thinking. One writer insists that it is the first editorial; another derives its origin from the practice of "leading" out the article in order to draw greater attention to it; and yet a third would restrict it to editorials which give a lead to the readers. As S. Natarajan, a former editor of the *Free Press Journal* has noted, "neither position nor manner of display can lend importance to an article." The difference between an editorial and a leader, in the circumstances, can only be a matter of personal consideration.

That editorials writers both individually and collectively realize their responsibility as moulders of public opinion is evidenced by the tone of the Code of Ethics which the U.S. National Conference of Editorial Writers compiled and adopted. The preamble to this code points out that "the editorial writer, like the scientist, must pursue Truth no matter where it leads if he is to be faithful to his craft and to his society." The basic points of the code are the following:

(1) The editorial writer should present facts honestly and fully.
(2) He should draw objective conclusions from stated facts, basing them upon the weight of evidence and upon the considered concept of the greatest good.
(3) He should never be motivated by personal interest.
(4) He should realize that he is not infallible and should give voice to those who disagree with him in a public letters column and by other suitable devices.
(5) He should review his own conclusions and correct them should he find them based on previous misconceptions

(6) He should have the courage of well-found conviction and never write anything that goes against his conscience. Where editorial pages are more than the product of one mind, sound collective judgement can be achieved only through sound individual judgements. Therefore thoughtful individual opinions should be respected.

(7) He should support his colleagues in their adherence to the highest standards of professional integrity.

This editorial code though compiled in the United States could well serve as a model for editorial writers everywhere. They may even remember what ortegay Gasset once wrote:

> The present-day writer, when he takes his pen in his hand to treat a subject which he has studied deeply, has to bear in mind that the average reader, who has never concerned himself with this subject, if he reads does so with the view, not of learning something from the writer, but rather, of pronouncing judgement on him when he is not in agreement with the common places that the said reader carries in his head.

The ultimate purpose of the editorial, of course, is to express the editor's opinion. A distinguished editor, Arthur Brisbane, who had a vast following in his time, believed that the editorial writer's opportunity was four-fold: he could teach, attack, defend, and praise. He explained this further:

Teaching is the most important and the most difficult.

Attacking is the easiest and most unpleasant though sometimes necessary. The defending of good causes, of the weak against the strong, of the new idea against ridicule; is important and usually neglected by editorial writers.

Praise also is neglected, except in a partisan sense without meaning... First have something to say. Then say it so that people will see it, read it, understand it, and believe it.

The editorial writer must have first something worthwhile to say writing an editorial just for the sake of filling in space is both a waste of time and space. Some editors prefer not to write an editorial if there is no subject worthy of editorial attention. This should lend credibility to an editorial when it is subsequently written.

To have something to say, an editor must take as his theme an, event of significance. In other word, he must hang his editorial on a news peg. The editorial could then explain the event in its perspective, when it would be informative, comment favourably or unfavourably on it, when it would be reactional or subject it to objective and constructive scrutiny, when it would be deliberative.

Frequently the caption of the editorial will reveal the motivation of the writer. Mahatma Gandhi was a past-master in the art of chosing titles, as editorials in Young India will aptly testify.

An editorial writer should not only have encyclopaedic knowledge, at least in his own particular field, but should have an easy, graceful style that endears itself to the reader. He should remember that the enemy of style is pomposity and verboseness. At its best an editorial is creative writing. When it is imbued with passion and earnestness it rises to Garrison's credo that appeared in each issue of the now defunct *The Indian Social Reformer:* "I *will* be as harsh as truth and as uncompromising as justice. I am in earnest-I will not equivocate-I will not excuse-I will not re treat a single *inch-and I will be heard.*" It is this spirit that was immortalised in Lowell's poem on Garrison:

> In a small chamber, friendless and unseen,
>
> Toiled over his types one poor, unlearned young man;
>
> The place was dark, unfurnitured, and mean;
>
> Yet there the freedom of a race began.

Help came but slowly; surely no man yet
Put lever to the heavy world with less;
What need of help? He knew
How types were set,
He had a dauntless spirit, and a press.

Most newspapers in India carry three editorials and just as often only two. What is known as "The Third Editorial" is usually given to light treatment of subjects. There is no fixed style of editorial writing, though, obviously, an editorial has a clear beginning, a well-argued middle and a distinct ending that sums up the editor's views on a given subject. An editorial that hangs loose reflects, poorly on the writer.

But an editorial point can be made in many and diverse ways:

> The space meant for an editorial could even be left blank-as-some editors ordered, during the Emergency-to make a point. 'The space could be filled by an apt quotation as one Indian paper indeed did when it published Rabindranath Tagore's Prayer during that same period. Henry L. Mencken on 10 February 1938, filled six columns of editorial space of the Baltimore *Evening Sun* 'with black dots-some 10,00,725-to dramatize the number of Federal employees. The late Rollo Ogden, when editor of the New York *Evening Post,* commented on The odore Roosevelt's early procedure (in Panama by reprinting from Kings 1: 21, the 'story of King Ahab's seizure of Naboth's vineyard under the caption: "Panama, 899 B.C." During his great days as editor of the *Free Press Journal* of Bombay, S. Sadanand would recount stories from the *Mahabharata,* the *Ramayana* or even Aesop's Fables, drawing a parallel with contemporary events, to great effect. Originality kowtows to no fixed formula. Communication is all.

Not least of the editorial's function is to entertain. Many editors do this with the "Third Editorial," writing done with tongue, firmly in check, often in the manner of a "Middle."

Take this from an American paper, the Richmond Va., *Times Dispatch:*

PUT THOSE PREPOSITIONS WHERE THEY BELONG TO

Columnist Robert Ruark made some strong statements Monday concerning the rule against using a preposition to end a sentence with. He said there was no logical reason why you shouldn't put one of those "lousy, skimpy little words" at the tail end of a sentence if you wanted to.

There's really nothing for Columnist Ruark to get excited about. Prepositions always are supposed to govern other words, called their 'relatives', and only the laziest writer should find it difficult to arrange the sequence of his words so that the relative is last and the preposition is before.

Sometimes, with all the belittling of the old tried and standard rules, we wonder what modern literature is coming to Instead of polishing their sentences, as did the old masters of the language, many of today's writers sit down and simply dash something off. Prepositions are left dangling naked at the end of sentences, and you can't tell where they are going to or where they came from. These unclad words, tied on to nothing, appear about to take off.

In the speaking art, too, conformity with standard rules or grammar should be striven after. Here errors are easier to fall into. A person who wishes to leave a good impression with his listeners should use the very best grammar he is capable of. With anything less, he should refuse to put up.

It is a sad commentary on the literary world today that fundamental rules of grammar are laughed at. This is the age or skepticism where there's little left to cling to. Fortunately, however, there are a few purists in the writing and speaking arts who refuse to cut corners and whose work can be depended on.

Yes, Ruark, end your sentences with prepositions if you want to. But don't try to influence other writers, who to such a flagrant violation of rules of grammar will never give into.

Note how the editorial begins. It takes a statement by a columnist to hang its theme on and has a hilarious time putting the unfortunate writer in his grammatical place. The editorial is "timeless" since it can he enjoyed any time; in fact a third editorial deals often with timeless things.

As an example of how a "timeless" theme is handled, here are two editorials on the same subject, "The Resurrection" from *The' New York Times* and *The Washington Post* that appeared on the same day (14 April 1974).

Rebirth and Resurrection : Now comes the festival of spring, of rebirth, of resurrection. The whole earth celebrates. The religious holiday we call Easter is its spiritual symbol, but even the grass in the meadow and the trees in the woodland participate, even the beasts of the field and the birds of the air. This is the time when the winter of the earth, as we know it, as well as the winter of the soul, yields to the universal urgency of life and more exalted being.

Easter is everywhere. Winter has run its course. Spring returns. Out of dark desolation and chilling doubt comes the inevitability of new life, of enduring truth beyond the words or the management of man.

The Psalmist, knowing the wonder and the glory of life resurgent on the hills, in the valleys, in the woods and fields, sang, "The little hills rejoice on every side". They shout for joy.

They also sing. And again he said, "I will lift up mine eyes unto the hills, from whence cometh my help." His symbolism was broad as well as deep: for the world of faith and the human soul was also the rich, green world that his God had made. Man's arrogance was tempered by humility in the face of spring.

The hilts still stand. The grass still grows. The still waters and the green Pastures endure. Man may search the infinite and probe the infinitesimal, but the essence remains close at hand.

All around us is the evidence, the truth of life, rebirth and resurrection, which at least approaches understanding.

The New York Times

THE RESURRECTION

In the Jewish community of Jerusalem when Pilate was the local representative of Rome, the Day of Rest was Saturday. It was on this day, after dying on the cross on Friday, that the body of Jesus was laid to rest in the tomb. Early on the following morning-the first day of the Jewish week and what is now Sunday-a woman who had overcome her past reputation came to the rock—hewn tomb to minister to the body with ointments and spices, as was the burial custom.

But the stone before the walk-in tomb was moved from place. Mary Magdalen left. St. John in his gospel does not tell us if she fled in fear or confusion but, whatever the reason, she :sought the advice of her friend Peter. Alarmed, he and John came immediately, though we are told that Peter-evidently overweight and unused to morning sprints, no matter what the occasion-was not as fast as the other disciple. On examining the tomb, the two men saw evidence that indeed it had been vacated, because the burial linens were left behind. Weare not told in St. John's narrative what Peter said-doubtless the excitable Peter had plenty to say-but are given only the information that he went back home, perhaps because it was nearing breakfast time.

Mary stayed on. Full of natural emotion, she wept. After a time, a man-it was still dark and Mary took him for the gardener-came before her and asked why she was weeping, and who did she seek. "Sir, if you have removed him, tell me where you have laid him and I will take him away." To this the man answered one word: "Mary." She knew immediately it was the risen inaster (Rabboni) and she moved to embrace him.

Although each of the four gospels provides slightly different accounts of the details of the resurrection, the major dramatells us of Christendom's greatest moment: when a mystery of faith was joined by a triumph of life. In the masterful book "Easter" by Alan Watts, the author writes that "the story of Jesus lives on, not because he was an innocent man who died a cruel death with bravery, for others have done as much; not because he was a great teacher of spiritual principles; for there was nothing peculiarly original in his doctrine; not even because he returned from death, for that, too, has been recorded of others.

The Christ story lives because it has fascinated man's mind with the thought of a God who had shared the life of his creatures, a King who has become his own subject. It is the revelation that the Lord of the universe is not a cruel puppet master who watched his playthings writhe in the toils of tragedies which he has plotted. It is that he himself has entered the play, has become the victim of the tragedy, and has turned it into triumph."

Of the two great feats of Christianity-Christmas and Easter it is usually the former that receives more celebrational attention. Yet in both the liturgical and biblical expressions of these two events, the greater by far is Easter. The liturgy of the Resurrection includes 40 days of lenten preparation; while the advent season for the Nativity is much shorter, almost by half.

In the four gospels, only two writers, Matthew and Luke-tell of the birth of Jesus, whereas the details of the Lord's death and resurrection are reported by each of the four writers.

The original agony, death and resurrection of Chirst was singular also because the entire community was involved-from the crowd outside Pilate's praetorium who called for

Barabbas to Joseph of Arimathea who took away the body from the cross.

Deep human emotions stirred, as in no other places in the gospels, from the blunt doubts of Thomas who would not believe until he had seen for himself to the denials of Peter whose faith was troubled even though he did see. About the latter, though, the wavering was only temporary; in the poem *Saint Peter* Daniel Berrigan, the poet, writes:

> No Christ at a tombstone knocked me awake. A
> cock mounted the tall rock where his body bled.
> I choose that rock to stand: man and clean of hand
> and blessed, whose even second choice was Christ.

The alleluias of Easter not only commemorate an event to be celebrated but express a hope to be shared. Those who keep Easter know the rites of its liturgy are embedded in the renewal of the earth's life in another spring. All mysteries are reflected in reality, but where the mystery reveals a coming of life-a resurrection-it is hard not to share in the joy.

The Washington Post : The same theme, but two different voices that tell us that no matter how routine an event-and Easter comes every year-it is a dull and unimaginative writer who cannot see the beauty and mystery In Its recurrence.

Letters to the Editor : Few features are held in greater disdain than the Letters to the Editor column. In the first place it is presumed that, as with book reviews, *anybody* can write a letter to the 'editor. Anybody, of course, can, but as Shakespeare makes one of his characters say, you can summon the spirits from the deep, but will they come? And will editors accept such letters and publish them? The main characteristic of a letter should be that it should be timely and appropriate. Writing a letter to an editor about last year's tidal wave would be irrelevant unless the writer wants to suggest that another, and deadlier wave is due and could be more devastating. Letters, in the circumstances, could be in the nature of a warning against disaster, crime, riots or whatever. The sheer variety of letters that an editor receives on any given day reveals the nature of the needs of the community and the need to communicate between man and man. Most letters are commentative; they are natura, reactions to something that the editor has said or a newspaper has reported or a magazine has featured. They could raise new issues, seek to bury old ones, be laudatory in content or querulous or argumentative. Some letters may merely be informative-the London *Times* has carried letters from readers who claimed that they were the first to see a hedghog at a particular time and place.

The New York Times once ran a lively controversy as to whether white eggs were better than brown and distinguished men and women engaged in scholarly and hilarious debate.

In fact it is not uncommon for some newspapers to start off a controversy by "planting" a letter in the letters to the editor column that was written in the newspaper office itself. While this practice may be deplored by the purists, the fact remains that recourse is often taken to it to get the circulation going.

The letter to the editor reveals not only the nature of the paper's readership but also the nature of the problems confronting it. It-is an excellent feedback for the paper. An editor should be concerned if he does not get this feedback for then it would be clear that (a) either his readers do not care (b) or that they do not have an opinion. And if they do not have any opinion, what role can an editor possibly fulfil as an opinion-maker?

Letter-writing, like all other features is an art, but an art worth cultivating. The best letters are those that are contemporaneous, that come to the point and are courteous. The reader may be intensifiably angry with the editor but that is no reason why he should be abusive and vituperative. Politeness always pays, beside which a polite rebuttal always is sure to win the approbation of others. Anger is by and large counterproductive.

It is well to remember that newspapers belong not just to proprietors and editors but to readers as well. As one journal put it, because newspapers are bought every day, a habitual choice in time becomes an emotional allegiance. And that is further strengthened when the paper creates close links with its readership. Whatever the reader may think of *his* paper's policy, he should be certain that he will always have access to its letters to the editor column to air his own views. Apart from anything else, the letters to the editor column is a safety valve.

A good editor will never be afraid of publishing letters criticising him and his views. In fact he will quickly learn that the more he publishes such critical letters, the more his credibility is restored.. And he will also come to appreciate the further fact that in addition to getting unpaid material, he can use those very critical letters to increase his circulation.

Some useful hint to editors:

(1) See that every letter is recorded and acknowledged.

(2) The acknowledgement serves two purposes: first, it is an actor courtesy But even more importantly, if some malicious person has used a false name and address, the acknowledgement card will come back.

(3) Beware of bores (those who write regular letters or who sign under a pseudonym like *pro bono publico)*, sycophants and pressure groups, also of fakes and malicious writers who could land you in trouble.

(4) Beware of begging letters, for if you give space to one charity appeal, you may find it hard to deny others.

(5) *Never* print a letter from someone whose identity you do not know. Many newspapers check on letters that could be potentially damaging by trying to identify the writers. Some papers like the *London Times* provide the full address of the writer so that it is clear to the other readers that the writer is real and could be traced.

A letter to the editor column-especially if it is just one column in length-cannot take more than 1,000 words in all; short letters therefore would get preference. If they are overly long, then it is the editor's privilege to shorten them. It is courtesy, again, to seek the writer's permission for doing the editing. The shorter and snappier the letter the better are the chances of its getting published.

Anti-features: Editors are often flooded with articles that have no compelling merit other than that the writer thinks it has. Recapturing the heroism of old battles because the anniversary has come round may be patriotism but can be done once too often. It is no good writing about a foreign country just because the public relations department in the tourist office is pushing or the editor has been given a free, all-expenses-paid trip. That is no reason to saddle the reader with a general article on the country, unless the magazine happens specifically to cater to the tourist trade. And all copy submitted by Public Relations men should be put to the sternest of scrutiny, no matter how well it is sugar-coated and made to seem relevant.

4

Practical Angles

For success, a journalist must posses and uphold certain noble qualities in order to be professional. Integrity of character, commitment to the truth and reasoning power of mind are essential to any reporter. These qualities also contribute to the credibility of the reporting organization. Besides, a journalist has to be truly responsible. This responsibility extends to different groups of people at the same time. A journalist is responsible to the audience as much as to the news organization. Again, a journalist is always responsible to the source(s) who reveal information. Should the need arise, a reporter has to submit to a source who may request anonymity. A reporter must also have a healthy respect for news values. A journalist must inculcate other positive features besides clear perception. For instance, one must have specific skills to elicit information in a question-answer session.

The Profile : It is said that a reporter is both eyes and ears of a news organization. It is not possible to strictly prescribe qualifications which a good reporter must Posses. However, novice reporters must train themselves informally for the job so that they would be able to discharge their responsibilities with confidence, courage and competence. In order to quality the role of a reporter you must prepare yourself in many ways.

It helps to be well-read, and you can do full justice to your reporting beat. You must equip yourself adequately with all aspects of your beat. If you are covering the civic body proceedings, you must be fully knowledgeable about several laws and rules under which the proceedings are regulated. In addition, you must know its various functions, areas of operations and jurisdiction. You should cultivate wide contacts with all kinds of sources in your beat, some times even outside your area of activity. As a reporter, you should be able to find out information; you should have a bent of mind for research. You should be a perfect talker, you should possess inexhaustible patience and the ability to get along with any kind of people in difficult situations. To be a successful reporter and to accomplish your job competently, you must be able to perceive, calculate, predict and plan your action appropriately in anticipation of a news event.

The sole aim of good news reporting should be writing with a certain amount of responsibility to oneself, to an organisation, to society and to humanity at large. You must use your pen consciously, carefully and should bear full credit (or discredit) for what you say: "Just as an unclaimed torrent of water submerges the whole countryside and devastates crops, even so, an uncontrolled pen serves but to destroy." Besides, as you must write everyday, you should write to build your own image, as well as the image of your institution. You have a responsibility towards your city, state, region, country, even the world at large. Echoing this, the noted editor M.V. Kamath once said: "A newspaper's sense of purpose and integrity, rather than its circulation, would determine its influence." And it is the reporter who is a builder of a newspaper's sense of purpose and integrity.

It is essential for a news reporter to be alertminded and curious. In addition, one should be in excellent health and should have inexhaustible stamina to chase difficult assignments. Most of all, a reporter should be a sociable person. It is true that one must posses the right attitude toward the vocation. This would include intelligence, initiative, industry, general competence, objectivity and accuracy. There are several other features' of one's personality and character which can contribute befittingly to one's profession as a journalist. In this section, we shall elaborate the salient qualities.

The reporter is the most important functionary of a newspaper, as far as news operations are congruence. So one must know what constitutes news in order to be able to gather news. A reporter's job of discovering the news has been simplified in one way and rendered difficult in another sense, in this age of information. While there are the usual press notes on which news reports can be based, there are other sources of information on a variety of news event. The range of sources stretches from official spokespersons and press conferences to unidentified members of the public and the regular sources which one meets on the beat.

But quite often, most of the material before a news reporter may just be publicity matter or advertisements in disguise. Therefore, as a reporter, you must check the material and squeeze the news that would interest your reader. When you are overwhelmed by an ocean of facts, you can always rely on the readers' interest for guidance. Here is where Your ability to select the right information and present it to the reader comes to your help. Besides, most of the time you will cover routine matters such as press conferences and press notes that are hardly exciting. At least you may have to begin at quite a low level like covering local matter. Later you may be given the opportunity to cover major national issues. For the most part you may find yourself reporting the speeches, declarations and announcements by V.I.P.s, persons in authority, politicians and political parties. Occasionally, you may get an exciting newsbreak. But your routine reporting should not prevent you from looking for something unusual that may lurk under the ordinary occurrence. You have to be a keen observer so as to discover unusual and exciting material even in routine stuff. A sharp sense, of observation may also help exciting material even in routine stuff. A sharp sense of observation may also help you to gather amusing sidelights' of interest to your readers. Your alertness will help you to discover contradictions and problems while you are on your daily beat. This can be the basis for an exciting news story even where apparently there was none.

Professional journalists are never armchair writers. Introverts normally make poor reporters. Reporters have to move about meeting people, making their acquaintance and winning their confidence. This would help them to establish contacts, which in turn helps in writing well-investigated reports. This is the era of investigative reporting and readers are keenly interested to know what is going on behind the scenes. To get that kind of stories, you have no alternative but to be outgoing. You have to develop and affable temperament and an easy-going nature.

An outgoing nature is, the basic quality to establish contact and develop sources. During the course of your duty, you may meet several people who may help you in gathering information. You must have the ability to win the confidence and respect of those who may be potential sources of news. During the course of your regular duties, people may voluntarily offer you information. Alternately, this might not be the case when you are working on an investigative story. People may hesitate to talk on sensitive matters. They may like to reveal yet are afraid to in case it were to affect them adversely. Such people may be government officials whom you may meet while investigating matters ranging from inefficiency to corruption. They could be informers of the underworld, if you are doing an in depth crime investigation. What may be at stake for them could be their jobs or their lives. It may be quite difficult to win their trust. In such situations, you must be able to assure your sources that they will remain protected and their identities kept secret if they so desire. While you are establishing contact, there may be some among them who may want to plant information on you to sever their vested interests. Such information may consist of half-truths and even lies. So, you must have other independent contacts through whom you can verify the information.

Remember, even the most ordinary source at times can become very valuable, providing important leads and a wealth of information. A couple of years ago a newspaper carried a story about a footpath hawker who once was a wrestler of international repute, thus throwing light on the neglect of the sportsmen in the country. You must make it a point, therefore, to pay attention to your sources howsoever 'ordinary' they may seem by appearance. Remember, the classic case of the Watergate scandal. The scandal that shook the United States and the Nixon presidency was not exposed by any ace newsperson, but by ordinary local reporters acting on a tip from an ordinary source. What matters is the alertness and ability to pursue your sources to get the right lead. Take the case of the securities scam. The entire expose began with a source contacting Ms. Sucheta Dalal of the Times of India, Bombay, with an unconfirmed report about some activities in the State bank of India. Ms Dalal, Assistant Business Editor of the paper, followed the lead provided by the source and got the story confirmed from reliable contacts bringing to light the stock scam concerning stock broker Harshad Mehta and others involving a staggering Rs. 6,000 crores.

Reporting not Prejudiced

The reporter must be an unprejudiced observer of events, one who presents the facts to the reader in a balanced, objective manner. Now, objectivity is a much debated topic. It has been said that reporters mix comment with fact and so their reports are quite subjective. While reporters may have their own views on the subject of coverage, they should not allow personal opinions at any place in the copy. One must be able to throw light on unclear aspects if any, of the news event. At the same time, the news reporter must endeavour to write a report which is only a statement of facts. An observation or viewpoint, might occasionally creep in and one must be alert to such strips in straight news items. How do you maintain balance and objectivity in your coverage?

The first and foremost thing to do is to source your copy properly to assure the reader that what you are passing on as news, is not your opinion or some publicity matter in disguise. The sources must be quoted except when they want to remain anonymous. Even when you are not able to quote the sources, you must ensure that the story is balanced, by giving adequate coverage to all the sides of the subject. You should always ensure that the information you are presenting is true. You can do this by counter checking. Remember, what may appear fair to one group will amount to bias for another. So, always ensure that you give both sides of the picture.

But, remaining an unprejudiced observer does not mean adopting what is known in American journalistic parlance as "man from the mars" stance, i.e., seeing each event afresh, unconnected to any previous expectations or future possibilities and passing them on untouched by interpretation. In an increasingly complex world, this would not amount to objectivity or fairness. In many cases, it would simply mean an irresponsible attitude, a refusal to make the reader understand the event in its proper context and realise its significance.

In many cases, you not only report the events but interpret them for the reader. But, remember, interpretation does not mean back-door editorialising. It is not an excuse for colouring the story with your personal opinions.'

As a reporter, you may cover several complex and specialised subjects, such as science and technology, law and economics. Your command over the language must be such that you can explain even the most complicated issues in single terms to any general reader. In addition to specialised subjects such as science and technology, even government press notes are written in complicated language, burying the news point. You must be able to simplify it and bring out the news point. Except for routine coverages which can be handled by one person, many investigative stories have to be handled by a team. The Bofors Investigative stories in the Indian Express and other papers were based on reports from Geneva and Stockholm, besides New Delhi. The securities scam investigations by the Times of India involved, besides Sucheta Dalal, one more correspondent, R. Srinivasan, who posed as an investor and went to the State Bank officers in Bombay to get confirmation about the going on in the bank.

With investigative journalism seeking to bring out scandals and exposures, there is bound to be pressure on journalists to keep someone's wrong doings hidden from public view. This 'someone' is usually a person with considerable clout. The 'pressure' on journalists is exerted in the hope of preventing exposure. The concerned journalist may also be bribed with attractive favours in return for silence on the matter. As a newsperson you may provide helpful or harmful exposure to persons holding important positions in your beat. Since may of them need publicity to perform their functions, they seek you out to provide them with the required exposure. They are on the lookout for a minimum of harmful and the maximum of helpful publicity. If they consider it necessary, they may use their power and influence to pressurise you for this.

The pressure could be used to make you change the news or "kill" a story. This constitutes censorship. Pressure could also be applied with the hope of inducing journalists to volunteer the change or omission which is then equal to self-censorship. While groups like the government and the advertisers could indirectly pressurise you through your news organisation, direct pressure could also come from the government and political parties. In case you are doing stories on something which could lead to harmful exposure for someone, they could take recourse to a range of legal and illegal options, including legal action, threats and violence to pressurise you.

There are three ways of coping with pressure: fighting it, giving in, and anticipating the pressure and taking preventive measures. The first one is the most noble of the three options and history is full of shining example of this category. During the British rule in India, many papers decided to close down, rather than submit to censorship and government pressure. The father of the nation, Mahatma Gandhi, exemplified this spirit when he wrote during the Quit India Movement: "It is better not to issue newspaper than to issue them under a feeling of suppression." Even during the 1975-77 internal emergency, journals like Mainstream closed down rather than submit to government censorship. But the heroic option is not always feasible. Remember, running a newspaper is a business, apart from being a service. Thousands depend on it for a living. You are in it as a professional, seeking to earn your daily bread. So few expect you to be a hero or a missionary. If you give in to pressure which you cannot fight on your own and if your news organisation does not back you, the consequences could be disastrous for you as' a professional journalist. The reporters who generally brave powerful pressures are those who have the full support of their organisations or their professional colleagues backing them unitedly. But, still, you must have the strength of character to fight pressures that come in the form of inducements like lavish gifts, favours, etc. to influence your reporting.

Preventive measures to fight pressure could be legal steps, like seeking a court stay on any law or ordinance that could affect the freedom of the press. In case you feel threatened by some physical violence, you can always seek security from law and order authorities. The journalists of the "Punjab Kesari" group of newspapers, who have taken a courageous antiterrorist stand in Punjab, work under extremely tight security. The group has lost tow of its owners to terrorist bullets, but has not given in to pressures.

The reporting profession is unlike any other profession. At times, some slight carelessness is doing one's duty, can cause incalculable harmful repercussions, both for the news organisation and society. A slight laziness in checking or cross checking certain facts could endanger the credibility of the news organization, proving to be a major block in the way of advancement of the reporters career. A reporter has been likened to a solder on the field. Even as the quality of the soldiers on field determines to a large extent the quality of an army, so also your abilities and the way you discharge your duties as a reporter go a long way in determining the quality and reputation of your news organisation. As a reporter, you have to follow the character, style and policy of your newspaper or magazine or news agency. There are conservative papers which may prefer to stick to routine coverage, not bothering about investigation of scandals. In such papers, you have to stick to their policy even if it cramps your style. But in a news organization with a more dynamic approach to news, you must develop the skills of an investigator. Whatever you do as a reporter will affect the newspaper and its reputation. So, you must take pains to ensure accuracy and objectivity in your stories.

Remember, your sources are sacred. Your credibility in their eyes could be a major factor in your performance as a newsperson. There are sources with whom you will have to take great pains to establish your credibility to make them open up towards you. You will have to assure them that no harm will come to them, and if they so desire, you must keep their identity a secret. There have been instances in the United States of America and some other countries where reporters have defied court orders and gone to jail rather than reveal the sources. In 1960, an American magazine reporter alerted his editors that the ruler of a Middle East country was receiving large amounts of money from several governments for his personal use. But the reporter held back the story till 1977 as he felt that its publication would compromise his source. The matter became news only when the American Intelligence

Agency (CIA) files, made available to the press in 1977, contained the same information.

You may well ask whether the responsibility of protecting the sources is absolute. A situation could arise when the information given by a contact who wanted to remain unidentified could lead to a major inquiry of a court case. You may be ordered by the court to reveal who your contact is, for giving witness before the court. What would you do in such a case? Should you commit contempt of court or violate your commitment to the confidentiality of your source? If you reveal the source who wanted to remain anonymous, you could lose your credibility among your contacts who may hesitate to volunteer information in future. Such extreme cases have to be dealt with, on their individual merits. It is sufficient to say that under normal conditions, you have a commitment to protect your sources. As a news reporter, you have a duty to provide accurate, unbiased and objective information to the reader. Every effort must be made to ensure that the news is accurate, free from prejudices and that all sides of the news event are presented fairly.

To maintain your credibility with the reader you have a duty not to accept things or favours or pursue any activity that might compromise your integrity.

However, in these days, publicity seekers including those in private business, organise press conferences and conduct tours with attractive gifts and other incentives. While private firms depend mainly on advertising for publicity, they sometimes want their activities to be carried as news items since news carries greater credibility than advertisements. News reports are written by newspersons who are supposed to be independent and objective. While in these days of corporate and business journalism.

Business and corporate journalism is a field where you have to exercise a tremendous sense of responsibility. With the proliferation of big companies including multi nationals and their role in the liberalisation of the Indian economy, their activities form a major subject of public interest. But, it is a subject that must be handled with utmost care. On the one hand, you risk becoming a publicity agent for corporate houses and on the other, you may be risking people's investments and reputations. Remember, anything you write for a news organization could have its impact in terms of money and reputation.

Opinions about the newspaper industry have ranged from it being a mere business to an instrument of social change. Even if it is to be considered a mere business, it is deeply involved in matters of public interest. Every thing you write could have its repercussions in the society. Even under normal circumstances, you have to exercise great care about what you write.

You have to be particularly careful when reporting in a communally sensitive country like India. This is because there are a host of religious and social diversities and several linguistic groups. It would be unbecoming to be partisan to a particular faith, linguistic or social group. As a reporter you will have to wield your pen with due respect for everyone.

What may be considered correct by one group may be held wrong by another. Take the example of the Ramjanambhoomi, Babri Masjid dispute at Ayodhya. Two concerned communities have a conflicting stand about the disputed structure. If you have been following the controversy in the papers, you would have found that the disputed structure is referred to neither as Ramjanambhoomi nor as Babri Masjid. It is referred either as the "disputed site" or as the "controversial structure", of simply as the. "Ramjanambhoomi-Babri Masjid site".

Apart from the Ayodhya dispute, the communal tension in the country has been aggravated by the Punjab and Kashmir problems. News organisations are extremely careful about reporting events of a communal nature.

A similar procedure is followed when reporting communal riots. The step is taken to prevent any further tension from developing between the communities if they are to be identified in the news reports. For this reason, places of worship affected in riots are not referred to, by name.

Desk Work : The editor and the publisher of a newspaper are responsible for whatever is printed in it. It many Indian newspaper the editor and publisher is the same Person. In such papers editors is also proprietor and manager.

But where the editor and the publisher are different people, the editor looks after the editorial Content that is anything except advertising. An advertising manager looks after the advertising. The publisher, general manager or managing editor or executive director look after the management of the paper.

A number of assistant editors assist the editor in looking after editorial and feature pages. The news content of the paper is looked after by the news editor under whose guidance a number of sub-editors and reporters work.

In India the entry into the profession of journalism is normally as a trainee journalist who is later absorbed as a reporter or a sub-editor.

The job of a reporter is to gather news and write it for his organisation. Sub-editor makes it fit to print. Reporters go out in the field while sub-editors work at the news desk where all the news that comes, is selected, edited, each news story is given a suitable headline and its place in the newspaper is decided.

Reporters can become senior reporters, correspondents, senior correspondents, chief reporter, special correspondent and foreign correspondent. Sub-editors are promoted to the positions of senior sub-editor, chief sub-editor, deputy news editor and news editor but the basic job of a reporter remains news gathering and filing the report or "copy" to' the news desk. Similarly, the basic job of the sub-editor also remains the same; to "sub" copy to make it fit to print which includes collecting, selecting, arranging, reducing, farming, translating and adapting for publication according to the importance of the copy, Sub-editor is also called copy editor as what he edits is called copy. Whatever is field by reporters special correspondents etc., is copy for him whatever comes to the news desk from wire services is also copy.

But reporting and editing sides are not water-tight compartments. Reporters can exchange places with sub-editors. In many newspapers it is a routine. A sub-editor is sent on a reporting assignment many a time. He is also asked to write news items from the handouts that land up in the newspaper office when reporters away.

To be a good reporter or a good sub-editor what one needs is common sense and command over language. These two requirement in fact summarise the qualities newsmen should have as other qualities flow from these two and the basic human values.

It is customary to describe desired qualities of a reporter and sub-editor separately, but as both of them deal with the same commodity, news, and their basic job is to communicate effectively many of these qualities have to be common.

News Sense: it is the basic quality of newsmen. Every reporter has to have news sense or nose for news to distinguish news from non-news. He should be able to compare various news values and decide where to begin his story and should not miss important details. News sense is essential for a sub-editor also, he is the first reader of a reporter's copy, and if the reporter has made a mistake he has to correct it. A bad copy may have the most important element of the story buried in the fourth paragraph. It will be left to the sub-editors nose for news to bring that to the first paragraph.

Clarity: A reporter should have clarity of mind and expression. A person who is confused himself cannot tell a story to others. Only clarity of mind is not enough unless it is accompanied by clarity of expression. Without clarity of expression clarity of mind has no meaning.

Sub-editor is the judge of clarity of the copy. A good sub-editor will never allow a copy escape him unless the meaning is crystal clear. He has every right to make life miserable for a reporter who is not clear and does not write is simple language.

Objectivity: reporter and sub-editor should not allow their personal bias or ideas to creep into a story. They should not take sides but try to cover all the different viewpoints to achieve balance in the story.

Accuracy: A reporter should strive for accuracy, he should check and re-check his facts till he is satisfied that he has them accurate. In this respect he should not take any chance as accuracy is directly proportional to the credibility of a reporter and his newspaper.

The role of a sub-editor is to check for accuracy, it is particularly important when background is involved. In the case of dates and names the reporter may rely on his memory but the sub-editor must check them from reference material available in the newspaper office. When there is a doubt he should leave it out this is the golden rule of journalism. It is better not to say a thing than to say it wrong.

Alertness: A reporter should always be alert while dealing with his subjects. Many major news breaks in the past were possible because of alertness of reporters. Scoops don't walk into newspaper offices-alert reporters catch them in air and pursue. A sub-editor has to be alert while working on news-desk. Lack of alertness of a sub-editor can be seen by readers in the morning for he will be leaving or introducing mistakes for everybody to see.

Speed: In today's world speed matters everywhere. A person who cannot work fast cannot be good reporter. While maintaining all other desirable qualities a reporter should strive to work faster. He should think fast, decide fast and write or type fast for he has to meet deadlines or may have to go to another assignment.

A sub-editor also has to work with speed. He cannot sit with a copy for long. He has to do swiftly whatever is required of him for a lot more copy is waiting for him. A slow sub-editor is a curse at the news desk and is treated with contempt. Such people are misfits in the profession.

Calmness: Reporters and sub-editors often work in trying circumstances. They have to remain clam and composed in most exciting and tragic circumstances. In many situations they have to be calm-devoid of hysterical actions or utterances and apply appropriate mental and physical effort to write or edit the story.

They have emotions but they have to stifle them in the face of disturbing influences-they have to develop resistances to excitability. Being in the field reporters face many such occasions when they have to control their emotions. Sub-editors should develop a temperament to work under pressure of deadlines. They should not lose their cool if they are behind the clock for calm mind can work faster.

Curiosity: Reporters and sub-editors should have an unsatiable curiosity. For reporters it is useful in developing just for facts that may lead to better stories. This characteristic will keep on improving a sub-editor for with every passing day a curious sub-editor will have a better back ground to do his job the next day. Reporters and sub-editors should read as much as possible to constantly improve their awareness level.

Scepticism: It is another necessary quality which a reporter and a sub-editor should cultivate. They should not take anything for granted. They should have an unwavering posture of doubt until faced with undeniable proof. Reporters should be more vigilant for many forces constantly try to use them and through them their paper. Many people try to plant on reporters a wrong story for their own ends. Many a time reporters fall into such traps in good faith. They should have enough scepticism to avoid such plots.

Sub-editors should also be careful for some clever politicians, public relations men and product advertisers keep on trying to take them for a ride. They should not allow anything to go in news columns that should actually go as advertisement. They should not fail to check even reporters' copy for such foul play.

Punctually: It is a goods habit. For reporters it is a must for if they are not punctual they may miss something for which they may have to depend on secondary sources, it is always better to be punctual and then wait than reach late and ask others a rival may misinform, you or hide some important information.

At the desk too punctuality pays, if a sub-editor is punctual he will be treated with respect by his co-workers, if he is late he will irritate them and spoil the working atmosphere. Besides, he may have to face the problem of backlog of copy which he will have to clear under the pressure of deadline.

Patience: It is quality which helps a reporter in a big way for many a time almost daily he has to test his patience, the voluntary self-control or restraint that helps one to endure waiting, provocation, injustice, suffering or any of the unpleasant vicissitudes of time and life. Most of the time a reporter waits for someone or something and patience gives him the willingness to wait without becoming disgruntled or anxious. Many a time he has to tolerate other people's shortcomings and has to remain unperturbed by someone else's slowness or other quirks. Patience also helps sub-editors as they work long hours in trying conditions. They have to put up with many annoying situations everyday vis-a-vis reporters, proofreaders or printers.

Imagination: this basic mental faculty helps reporters in writing better stories that retain the reader's interest. For a sub-editor this creative faculty is very useful as he can add sparkle to somebody else's copy and make it lively, besides, imaginative headlines attract the reader and improve the quality of a newspaper farsightedness: An intelligent envisioning of the future helps newsmen in general. The quality helps them in identifying processes and people who will be important in future. Reporters can watch such processes and cultivate people who may become important news sources in the future.

It helps reporters and sub-editors in determining the importance of an event. A reporter with foresight can think ahead and prepare for eventualities. With a little forethought sub-editors can plan their work so as to avoid tension and it results in better functioning of the desk.

Self-discipline: One can achieve a degree of proficiency in sub-editing or reporting by systematic effort and self-control. In this sense self-discipline suggests dedication and firm commitment. It helps in Journalism as in any other field.

Integrity: It is a virtue in itself and implies undeviating honesty and strict adherence to a stern code of ethics. This human quality is important for journalists. It is more important for reporters for they are more exposed to temptations compared to sub-editors.

Fearlessness and Frankness: These qualities help reporters in asking unpleasant questions and taking risks to find out truth. Nobody gives a story on a platter. The reporter will have to probe, question, authenticate and exercise his power of deduction to get a good story.

Tactfulness: A reporter should be tactful, he should have the ability to handle sensitive people and situations gracefully without causing hurt or angry feelings. He should considerate of others and should be careful not to embarrass. Upset or offend them. A reporter should have flexible and sociable personality and should have a nature that relishes variety of experiences. He should have an understanding of human behavior and emotions. This will help him in developing contacts that are so essential for news gathering.

Initiative: A reporter works in the field should have an outgoing nature with initiative and drive. These qualities will help him get acquainted with news sources and get stories from them. A meek, retiring or shy person is not fit for reporting, he may be good at his desk. Reporter need a fair mount of assertiveness and aggressiveness to be successful in their career.

Mobility: A reporter should be mobile. He should enjoy moving ground and should not hesitate travelling distances to get stories when required, he should go to his news sources as often as possible for such constant contacts help him get news. A mobile reporter is seldom caught napping when a major story breaks.

Reporters and sub-editors should be diligent. There jobs require painstaking exertion of intense care and effort, alertness and dedication to the task and wary watchfulness. They have to make extremely fine distinctions while writing or editing copy. A sub-editor should insist on perfection and should love his job for he can make or mar the newspaper.

These qualities are basically qualities of good and efficient human beings. Good and efficient human beings make good and efficient sub-editors and reporters. All other things being equal reporters need additional qualities to deal effectively with all sorts of people they meet in the field. Sub-editors should have better command over language as they improve what reporters write.

A very authentic way of gathering facts, figures and opinions on various issues is to interview the persons concerned. In this unit, we shall discuss the importance of the interview in reporting, besides the skills required to master the art of conducting an interview. Having done this, we shall proceed to the next block where our main theme will be "specialised reporting".

There are carious way of gathering information and knowledge for the media. One can do so from books, magazines and journals, or incidents, and by meeting people who hold important positions. Meeting or interviewing them is one of the most significant and important ways of gathering information, facts and knowledge. The interview is a very useful input for all media-print and electronic. It depends on how one would like to use an interview. It may be used and a programme to make the audience/reader get information/ facts from the source directly. The interview can form the basis of an article, a feature or a commentary. Or, segments of an interview can be used to substantiate an argument or a point in an article or a radio/television feature.

One may like to presume that you have written something in your life; a letter, an application, an article or a poem. One can also assume that you might not have been satisfied with the first draft. Therefore, you may have re-written it changing sentences, paragraphs, words, etc. It is also possible-that after changing the draft twice, thrice or more times, you were satisfied with your written material. Let us call this the preparatory stage. To do and interview is also something like doing an original work in which you create something. Thus, to do a meaningful interview-both for yourself and for the person whom you plan to talk to-it is necessary that you do your home work right. It is only then, that an interview conducted after proper preparation, would make a certain impact.

It is said that to speak for five minutes over-radio, a person must prepare himself/herself at least for five hours. Therefore, preparation is very important. Interviews can be on the record or off the record. On the record interviews are those whose contents call be attributed to the person interviewed.

In this lease, unless there is a prior agreement to use the whole of the interview verbatim, portions of the interview, that have some use for the reporter can be utilised and the rest discarded or canned for future use.

Off the record interviews are those in which the information is given, but the source is not to be identified by the interviewer. In such cases, the source identified is "a source in the Defence Ministry" or "a General Commanding a division" etc. In such cases it is normal to cross-check the facts from another source, since the man giving the information is not willing to stand up and be counted. There can be interviews which are partly on the record and partly off the record. That is, some information given can be attributed to the person who gives it and some can be attributed to "a source" or "a Defence Ministry Official" or "a General", etc.

Knowledge of Subject

The most important part of the interview is to know your subject as completely as possible. It could be a VIP, an important member from the bureaucracy, the art world or the corporate sector or just an ordinary citizen. Accordingly; you should prepare yourself by reading about the person. It is imperative for you to not only fully research the information you want from your subject, but also the person behind it. You should also have all the essential background information of the interviewee, e.g. his/her family, hobbies, interests. This will help you to build an instant rapport with the interviewee. It will enable you to get on with the job most comfortably. A reluctant interviewee only acts as an obstacle and foils the very purpose of the interviewer. It is most important to research your subject matter. It could be a subject in which you neither have any interest nor adequate knowledge. But once you are fully armed with the basic and important information acquired through books, newspapers, journals or magazine, articles, you will be much more comfortable and should be successful in your venture.

For example, if you are required to interview a criminal lawyer, a policeman or an accused, you should have enough knowledge of criminal law-cognisable and non-cognisable offences, various Acts Sections which govern the offences, and other legal provisions. This will help you extract the required information. You must know your subject matter as well as the person whom you intend to talk to about the subject matter.

All journalists must remember two fundamental factors: First, all interviews are subject to editing. So there is no harm in culling more information than you can use. The information that you need to buttress an argument or to refute another or to make a point, can be used at the appropriate place. The rest can be stored for use in future.

Second, no statement made in the interview is allowed to be used out of context. If, for instance, a Government authority vehemently denies that any human rights violations were made during a particular clash in Kashmir, one cannot quote him to create the impression that no human rights violations are made by security forces during any clashes. If the authority interviewed does not generalise it, the reporter or sub-editor is debarred from generalising it.

It is important to establish contact with the interviewee much in advance of the interview. How do you do this? It could be a direct contact-physical or through telephone. More often than not, where important interviews are concerned, there is a channel yaw will have to go through. It could be the private secretary or the members of the family-referred to as the "protector of the interviewee." So, the first thing to do is to establish a rapport with the protector. To get to your subject matter or the person, you must be able to play to the gallery to defeat all the obstacles imposed by the "protectors". If the first thing is to establish contact and to build up a rapport, the most important part of the preparation is to decide what you want to get out of the interview. May be you want substantiation of a fact you have discussed; or the refutation of something; or may be you want the interviewer's views on some proposition you or someone else is making.

It is important and essential, to make a deep study of the individual you plan to interview. Let us say that he person is particularly fond of dogs. When you go to interview her/him, it will be fatal to talk about how you abhor dogs or how they are dangerous. As interviewer, you cannot afford to convey your general wariness about the capline species-not verbally, not even through body language.

The information you seek to extract from the person may have nothing whatsoever to do with dogs. Yet, the person may react by remaining uncommunicative through the rest of the interview if you start off on the wrong note. Paying attention to such minute, apparently insignificant matters really helps in conducting the interview smoothly. You must build a personal rapport to begin with, so you may start the interview comfortably.

In the electronic media, there are two ways of interviewing: with the Prime Minister or the President, the setting would be as designed by the Public Relation Officer or the Principal Information Officer. If it is a television interview, then you need the following:

(a) cameraman;

(b) sound recordist;

(c) lighting technician; and

(d) the sound technician.

The other way could be that the interview is to be held in a studio. In that case, you should adequately arrange the setting in the studio. For the radio studio interview, you would need a very good recording machine. You use a lip microphone which prevents extraneous sound from getting injected into the microphone. If the interview is only a part of what you are actually going to air, then it should be transcribed. Mark the important segments, and tailor the interview to the actual slot requirements with a suitable link to give necessary continuity. To do this, you would require an editor to do a proper cut and paste work of the tape.

Getting an interview can often be difficult because the

interviewer is generally viewed with suspicion. To overcome this handicap, the interviewer has to be imaginative. The interviewer labours between two competing factors. One, the public has the right to know and you are the tool employed to gather the information. Two, from the legal point of view nobody can be forced into talking and hence, the job can be tiresome and at times, very frustrating.

Be operational for the interview. This is-very important. It shows the importance of the interviewee and that he has not been taken for granted. In a nut shell, you must be ready right on time to start the interview. Arriving on time may be good in most cases, for one has to do things like setting up the camera, or recording devices before the interview. One should arrive 10-15 minutes before time in order to be operational on time. Outline your reasons for being there, unless you are working on something very sensitive. If you do not specify your reasons, it may create problems, start the interview with a broad question. This helps your to size up the person and also collect your thoughts. It also helps to receive information your may not have anticipated and to chart out your course of action-a correct direction that the interview should take. Do not interrupt until the interviewee has relaxed. Avoid making the interviewee uncomfortable at the outset. It would be of little value. An interviewee kept at complete ease can be most helpful. The interviewer must not only be conversant with the subject matter of the interview but must also be a good conversationalist. All the important features of interpersonal communication come into play in an interview. In a face to face meeting, the stress is on both the language used in speech and the no-verbal body language. But, in a telephonic interview, the stress would be on the tone and inflection given to the words. In this type of interview, it can be rather difficult to assess the intended meaning since the other person's actual expression is hidden from sight. We shall now discuss the salient points to be kept in mind when conducting an interview in person.

On occasion, an interview may not be planned or rehearsed before it actually takes place. But then there are a few thumb rules that are fundamental to any interview. Preparing oneself to interview a personality, a celebrity or eve the person-on-the-street is actually an on-going long-term process. This is because one must be well-rounded interviewer, skilled in the art of handling a variety of topics and areas as also a range of idiosyncrasies that are inherent in people in general. One must be prepared for any turn of events and still be able to take it all in one's stride, that is to say, with equanimity. One cannot acquire these skills overnight but must nurture them over a period of time. A great deal of deep study of persons and happenings is called for. The would-be interviewer must yearn to learn.

Some interviews are simply old wine in new bottles. Other seek to convey an innovation or idea that the interviewee has recently come up with. Yet other interviews are made out of the interviewer's idea(s): giving a new twist to an even, throwing new light on a discovery that had been accepted at face value, and such like. One must develop a keen sense of identifying material for use in an interview. One must also have the knack to rad more into matters that is at first apparent: something like reading between the lines. That way, a much-interviewed person may reveal a fresh side of the matter being discussed and perhaps also of his/her own personality hitherto hidden from public view.

Having a finely-turned news-sense helps to generate ideas for interviews. It enables one to capture a glimpse of the extra-ordinary in the most ordinary things and persons. It depends on the situation whether one come upon a fresh insight during the interview by asking hard-hitting questions or by putting queries in a gentle manner. These are tactics that ought to be learnt by assessing and recognising the opportune time and place when it come your way. Alternatively, you could create the right atmosphere to make your interviewee reveal material which would from the basis for a good interview. In effect, the interviewer gives shape and direction to the interview, always allowing enough leeway for the unexpected utterance. One could then build carefully on what is sometimes said in such an offhand manner. The interviewer must, therefore, remain alert and latch on to every word that is said during the conversation. One can become adept in this technique only with practice.

Advance preparation for the interview by way of well-thought out questions and a thorough consideration of approach is very helpful. One need not fear that the final outcome will sound stilted with not natural spontaneity. Usually the reverse is true. One will be able to pose the most appropriate questions when one is well-versed with the subject. But how should one conduct oneself when conducting an interview. At the outset, arrive on time for the interview. This will help keep the interviewee in good humour. Taking notes is an essential part of interviewing: the two cannot be separated. Some take down everything, even irrelevant and redundant remarks. Take down only what is important. However, that may not always be possible. People sometimes stop taking when you start writing. Your do not always know what is to have a flawless recall. A wrong quote can be most embarrassing professionally. It costs you your credibility. Now-a-days, there is the help of a recorder. Take permission of the interviewee before using it.

Crime Reporting : Crime stories, judging from the newspapers in the country, are more the staple, of evening papers than of morningers. And since evening papers are published mostly from the major cities it is hard not to draw the inference that crime is largely urban in nature and is only of interest to urbanites.

This, of course, is not true; there is probably as much, if not more, crime committed in rural India as in urban India but a murder in a distant village does not interest the urban dweller and small town papers have still to come into existence in numbers sufficient to draw journalism students to them.

Even in the cities it is the political story that largely makes the front page and very rarely the crime story though an occasional murder such as that of Prem Bhagwandas Ahuja (in what came to be known as the Nanavati Case) in Bombay can hit the headlines.

Though writing a crime story can be as complicated as writing a political story, it is mostly the novice reporter who is assigned to the police beat. Fortunately, the police beat is the best training ground for future diplomatic correspondents. As Richard Critchfield writes in *The Indian Reporter's Guide,* "while speech reporting rains the ear and sports reporting the eye, crime coverage gives the new reporter a broad range of events on which to exercise his talents, usually providing action stories with a narrative as well as human drama."

What constitutes crime? The dictionary meaning says crime is "a wrong act that is against the law" or "a violation of law" and it is also defined as an act or omission punishable by law.

An offence means any *act* or *omission* made punishable by *any law* for the time being in force. Offences can be *bailable* or *non bailable; bail* is security offered by the accused for his appearance before the officer or court granting him bail. Any person is eligible for bail if he is accused of a *bailable* offence and arrested or detained without warrant by an officer in charge of a police station.

Some of the more common crimes may be classified as follows:

(1) Abetment, that is, aiding and assisting, instigating or facilitating, a crime (usually the punishment is the same as for the offence).

(2) Criminal conspiracy is an agreement between two or more persons to commit an offence where some act besides the agreement is done in pursuance thereof by one or more panics to the agreement.

(3) Offences against the state. These include sedition, assaulting officers of the state and others.

(4) Offences relating to the army and navy, such as mutiny, desertion, harbouring a deserter, impersonating a member of the military and insubordination.

(5) Offences against the public tranquillity, such as rioting, being a member of an unlawful assembly, hiring persons to take part in an unlawful assembly, assaulting public servants, promoting enmity between classes or committing affray.

(6) Offences by or relating to public servants. These include illegal financial gratification, corruption, impersonating a public servant or offences by a public servant such as disobeying a law with intent to cause injury, framing an incorrect document, unlawfully buying property or unlawfully engaging in trade.

(7) Offences related to elections such as bribery, false statements, failure to keep election accounts.

(8) Contempt of the lawful authority of public servants such as-absconding to prevent service of a summons, giving false information, threatening or obstructing public servants.

(9) Raise evidence and offences against public justice as giving false evidence, destroying documents, harbouring capital off enders, escape or resistance to lawful apprehension, insult to public servant during judicial proceeding.

(10) Offences relating to coin and government stamps. These include counterfeiting, possession of counterfeit money if it is known to be so, fictitious stamps.

(11) Offences relating to weights and measures such as fraudulent use of false instruments for weighing or measuring or constructing such instruments for false use.

(12) Offences affecting the public health, safety, convenience,

decency and morals. These include deliberately spreading disease, adulterating food and drink, adulterating medicine, defiling public water supplies, driving or riding on a public way so negligently as to endanger human life, dealing with poisons, fire, explosives or machinery as to endanger human life, omitting to guard against probable danger by fall of any building over which a person has right to tear down or repair, committing a public nuisance, sale of obscene books, obscene songs or keeping a lottery office.

(13) Offences relating to religion such as defiling or damaging a place of worship, maliciously insulting the religious beliefs of any class, causing a disturbance to an assembly engaged in religious worship, trespassing in place of worship or disturbing a funeral with intention to insult, or uttering any word or making any gesture with intention to wound religious feeling.

(14) Offences relating to the human body:

(a) Offences affecting life:

(i) Murder.

(ii) Culpable-homicide: act done with knowledge that is likely to cause death, with or without intention of doing so.

(iii) Causing death by rash or negligent act.

(iv) Abetment of suicide committed by child, insane, idiot, delirious or intoxicated person.

(v) Abetting suicide.

(vi) Attempt to murder.

(vii) Attempt to commit suicide.

(viii) Being a thug.

(b) Causing miscarriages, injuring unborn children, exposure of infant with intent of abandoning it and concealment of birth by secret disposal of dead body.

(*c*) Voluntary causing hurt by dangerous weapons or drugs, to export properly, information, to deter a public servant from his duty or on grave and sudden provocation.

(*d*) Wrongful restraint or confinement.

(*e*) Criminal force and assault such as to deter a public servant from his duties, to commit theft, on a woman *to* outrage her modesty, to dishonour a person or to wrongfully confine.

(*f*) Kidnapping, abduction, slavery and forced labour:

(i) Kidnapping.

(ii) Abduction in order to murder.

(iii) Kidnapping a woman to compel her marriage or cause her defilement.

(iv) Procuration of a minor girl, or importation of girl from foreign country of buying and obtaining possession of a minor for purposes of prostitution.

(v) Kidnapping to subject a person to slavery, grievous hurt or abducting of child with intent to take its property.

(vi) Unlawful compulsory labour.

(*g*) Rape, by a man with his own wife under 12 years of age and in any other case and unnatural offences.

(15) Offences against property:

(*a*) Theft.

(*b*) Extortion: blackmail, obtaining illegal compensation.

(*c*) Robbery and dacoity such as simple robbery, or robbery on the highway between sunset and sunrise, or belonging to a gang of persons for the purpose of habitually committing theft (dacoity).

(*d*) Criminal misappropriation of property.

(*e*) Criminal breach of trust, as by a clerk or servant, banker, merchant or agent.

(*f*) Receiving stolen property, or assisting in its concealment or disposal.

(*g*) Cheating, by impersonation or by dishonestly inducing delivery of property or by altering or destroying a valuable security.

(*h*) Fraudulent removal or concealment of property or false deed execution.

(*i*) Mischief, causing damage to the amount of fifty rupees or upwards, or by rendering useless, killing or maiming any animal of value, or by obstructing ora public drainage, causing dimunition of agricultural water supply, damaging public road or bridge, removing landmarks, mischief by fire or explosives.

(*j*) Criminal trespass such as lurking, house trespass by night or dishonestly breaking open any closed receptacle containing property.

(16) Offences related to documents and to trade or property marks such as forgery, counterfeiting seals or plates with intent to commit a forgery, defacing or destroying a will, falsification of accounts, using false trademarks, counterfeiting of bank notes.

(17) Criminal breach of contracts of service.

(18) Marriage offences such as a man by deceit causing a woman not legally married to him to think she is and cohabit with him on that belief, or enticing with criminal intend a married woman, or adultery.

(19) Defamation or printing matter known to be defamatory or selling defamatory matter.

(20) Criminal intimidation, insult and annoyance such as starting a false rumour circulated with intent of offending the public peace, or intimidation by anonymous communication, or by inducing a person

> to believe that he will be rendered an object of divine displeasure, or uttering any word and making any gesture to insult the modesty of a woman, or appearing in a public place in a state of intoxication and causing annoyance to any person.

This is a pretty exhaustive list of criminal acts and a reporter covering crime must familiarize himself with it. It is equally important that he is familiar with the processes of dispensation of justice.

In India there are following classes of criminal courts. To begin from the lowest:

Magistrates of the Third Class: He may pass a sentence of imprisonment not exceeding one month and a fine not exceeding Rs 50.

Magistrates of the Second Class: He may pass a sentence of imprisonment not exceeding 6 months, including solitary confinement and a fine not exceeding Rs. 200.

Presidency Magistrates and Magistrates of the First Class: He may pass a sentence of imprisonment not exceeding two years, including solitary confinement and a fine not exceeding Rs. 1,000.

Courts of Session (Sessions Judge or Additional Sessions Judge):

> He may pass any sentence, but a sentence of death is subject to confirmation by the High Court.

High Courts: They may pass any sentence, authorized by law.

Above them all, of course, is the Supreme Court of India. When a person is arrested and charged with crime, he is first taken to the police station where he is held until he is produced before a magistrate. Arrests may be made with or without a warrant, depending on the crime. (As an example, if someone is accused of buying or selling of any person as a slave, IPC

370 lays down that he may not be arrested without a warrant but if the crime is habitually dealing in slavery, IPC 371 permits arrest without a warrant).

A *warrant* is a written out authorization from a magistrate to the police giving them the right to carry out an arrest.

An offence can be either *cognisable* or *non-cognisable*. In the case of the former no warrant is necessary. In the latter case, a warrant will be necessary.

There is a further classification of cases into *warrant cases* (for offences punishable with death or imprisonment for a term exceeding a year) and *summons cases* (for offences punishable with imprisonment for a term not exceeding one year and fine.)

Arrest: If a person complains against another demanding the latter's arrest he must affirm under oath that he has reasonable grounds for belief in the guilt of the accused. A *search warrant* permits the search of a premise where there is reason to believe evidence of a crime may be found. But in certain specific circumstances, the police have the power to search without a warrant.

A person has a constitutional right to be brought into court promptly to be confronted with the charges against him. He cannot be held in custody for longer than 24 hours without a special order from a Magistrate (who can authorise the detention of the accused for not more than 15 days at a time).

Information relating to commission of a cognisable offence if made by a witness or informant is reduced in writing, read over to the informant, signed by him and entered into a book. This is called *first information*. Anyone acquainted with the circumstances of a case and whose statements are recorded by the police are called *witness for the prosecution*. (Remember the famous Agatha Christie play by that name?)

An *investigation* is carried out by the police starting with their first knowledge of an offence committed; this can go on until the police officer is satisfied that he has all the information necessary to form an opinion as to whether the offence has been committed or not.

An *inquiry* is begun after the police officer has sent up the case to a Magistrate. If no *prima facie* (on the face of it) case is made out the Magistrate dismisses the complaint and discharges the accused. If on the contrary, the Magistrate is satisfied that a *prima facie* case has been made out, he frames a *charge.* He may then *try* the case himself or *commit it for trial* to the Court 01 Session.

In his *charge sheet* or *completion report* that a police officer submits to the Magistrate he must state (a) the names of the parties (b) the nature of the crime (c) the names of persons who are acquainted with the criminal case and (d) whether the accused has been forwarded in custody or released on his bond with or without sureties. This is the final report of the police officer after completion of his investigation.

A police officer making an investigation has the following duties to perform on a day-to-day basis:

(1) He must set forth the time when the information reached him.

(2) He must put down the time when he began and closed his investigation.

(3) He must name the places he has visited and

(4) He must record the circumstances ascertained.

Trial of Summons Cases: In regard to a summons case, the accused appears before a Magistrate. He is told the particulars of the offence charged against him. He is asked to *show cause* why :he should not be convicted. But no charge is framed. If the accused *admits the offence,* his admission is recorded in his own words; he may be convicted, if he fails to show sufficient cause.

If the Magistrate does not convict the accused or the

accused, *does not admit* the offence, the Magistrate *shall hear* thee complaint (if any) except where the complaint has been brought by the Court itself. The Magistrate will then *take evidence* produced by the parties or *examine* the accused and if he finds the accused not guilty, he shall *acquit* him. If he finds the accused guilty, he shall pass sentence on him providing he does not ask a higher court for an enhanced sentence, or release the prisoner on probation with an admonition. The Magistrate's finding *is not limited* by the offence specified in the complaint or summons.

If the complainant *fails to appear,* the Magistrate shall acquit the accused unless he adjourns the hearing of the case to another day. However, the complainant may, before the final order is passed, *withdraw* the complaint with the *permission* of the Magistrate in which case the Magistrate then acquits the accused.

In a case not instituted upon a complaint, any Magistrate with the sanction of a District Magistrate may *stop proceedings* at any stage without pronouncing a judgement and *release* the accused.

Trials of Warrant Cases: In these cases the Magistrate hears the accused and any evidence produced for the prosecution. If the Magistrate finds *no case* has been made out against the accused, he *discharges* him. If he decides there is ground for presuming the accused has committed an offence, he will frame in writing a charge against the accused. This shall be read to the accused who is asked to plead guilty or not guilty and whether he has any defence to make.

If the accused pleads guilty, he may be convicted by the Magistrate. If he refuses to plead or does not plead or *claims to he tried,* he is asked to state whether he wishes to cross-examine any of the witnesses for the prosecution already examined. Thus the accused is called upon to *enter on his defence* and produce evidence. If the accused is found not guilty, he is acquitted. If found guilty, the Magistrate passes a sentence on him if he does not submit the case for enhanced sentence or release the prisoner on probation with admonition.

Trials before High Court and Court of Sessions: In the High Court all trials are by jury, though in the Court of Sessions the jury may be substituted by assessors. The accused is brought before the court, the charge is read and explained to him and he is asked whether he pleads guilty or claims to be tried.

If he pleads guilty, the plea is recorded and the accused can be convicted. If he refuses to plead or does not plead guilty or-claims to be tried, the Court shall *choose jurors.* These are chosen by lot and their number is nine. They then appoint one of their number as *foreman* and are *sworn.* A juror may be objected to by either the prosecutor or the accused, though the Judge's decision is final. In the High Court the judge is bound by the unanimous verdict of the jury. In the Court of Sessions, the Judge, if he disagrees with the unanimous verdict, can submit matter to High Court, giving the grounds of his disagreement.

It may be remembered that in the Nanavati Case, in which the Jury acquitted the accused 8 to 1, the Judge, Mr. R.B. Mehta,-declared that the decision was "perverse" and announced that he would refer the issue to the High Court. The Jury's verdict was reversed by the High Court and subsequently the Supreme Court confirmed the sentence of life imprisonment for Commander K.M. Nanavati, for the murder of Prem Bhagwandas Ahuja.

How does one report crime cases? Here below is a partial list of questions to be asked by a reporter:

Casualties: Was anyone killed? If so, how? Similarly, was any one injured? How? What were the weapons used? What happened to the dead? Was any of the killed well-known?

Property Loss: What was the value of the property lost or damaged? What exactly was stolen, defaced or destroyed?

Method of Crime: How was the crime committed? What weapons, if any, were used?

How were the victims treated by the criminals? Was this a repetition of any similar crime? (Remember the similarity of crimes committed by the murderer Raman Raghavan in Bombay and its suburbs).

Motive: What moved the criminal to commit the crime? What did the victims report? What did the police or other witnesses have to say?

Arrest: State the names of the arrested people, along with their age and occupation. What formal charge was preferred? How did the police apprehend the criminals? Where were they taken to?

Clues: Did the criminal leave behind him any clues? What clues did the witnesses provide? What clues are the police investigating? Is there a description of the criminals available?

In the following leads, note how these different elements are emphasised:

Sample News : The city police have arrested two persons for allegedly defrauding the Jammu and Kashmir Bank Ltd., to the tune of Rs. 10,41,120. K.K. Dhar, Bombay Manager of the bank and Roopa, alias Roopmala Sain Khosla, a small-time film actress, were nabbed Thursday as they alighted from a cab at Pali Hill Bandra.

Two other accused in the case, Sudhir Sain Khosla, husband of Roopmala and S.R. Sheth, are absconding.

Sunday Standard, 1 July 1979

Casualties : Patna, June 25: At least 21 persons were killed and nearly a hundred injured in a pitched battle between Army and Central Industrial Security Force (CISF) personnel at Bokaro in the early hours of this morning. The condition of 17 of the injured is stated to be serious.

Indian Express, 26 June 1979

Clues : The city police are on the hunt for a foreigner who has reportedly cheated several people on the pretext of providing them jobs as chauffeurs in a chain of hotels in Canada which, he said, belonged to his father.

Operating under the name of Capt. Sheisya, he extracted from each a sum of Rs. 4,000, the police said. The wanted man appears to be of Malayasian or Korean origin, is tall and slim and has an accomplice in Bombay whom the police are tracking.

Indian Express, 26 June 1979

A ticket stub to the Liberty Cinema for the 6.30, Aug 8 evening performance of "Hercules" may hold the solution of the mystery of who killed Hislop College professor Chandralal Rao and why.

The Hitavada, 29 Aug 1961

Property Loss : A hunt is on to trace a con-man who is alleged to have conned the father of Davis Cup per Sashi Menon into parting with an electronic wrist-watch presented to the tennis star. The watch had the inscription "Seiko Super Tennis" and was one of the prized possessions of Menon.

The police said the con-man goes by the name of A.B. Murthy and claims to be the Sales Executive of HMT (Watch Division), Bangalore. His *modus operandi* is that he gains the confidence of people by his glib talk and friendly ways and lures them into parting with their valuables under some pretext or other.

He was described by his victims as of medium height, wheat complexioned, long-haired and adept at speaking and writing English, his age was stated to be around 30.

Indian Express, 28 June 1979

Judgment : Found guilty of culpable homicide not amounting to murder and of causing hurt, Shamsuddin Rahim

Babaji, a 32-year old fisherman residing in a hut at Ghas Bunder, Sewree, was sentenced to rigourous imprisonment for 7 years by Judge B.P. Talathi, at the Sessions Court for Greater Bombay.

The prosecution said that on November 8, 1977, at 9.15 p.m. Farida Abdul Rashid and her mother Khatija Kassam were sitting near their hut at Ghas Bunder when they heard a commotion near Kadar's garage. When they rushed to see what had happened, they saw the accused, who was in a drunken state, assaulting Ayeta, sister of Farida, with a kitchen knife. They intervened and they were also assaulted by the accused. As the accused was running toward the seaside, he was chased and caught, but he managed to throw the knife into the sea. The injured women were removed to the J.J. Hospital where Khatija died on November 10, 1977. The knife was subsequently recovered from the seashore. The accused denied the charges. Mr. G.M. Coehlo appeared for the prosecution. Mr. P.K. Nair defended the accused.

Indian Express, 27 June 1979

Suicide : The compound of the Air Force station at Madh Island was the scene of a tragedy in which a 21-year old aircraft maintenance man was found with a bullet in his head in the early hours yesterday, According to the Malavani Sub Police Station which received the information of the death from the Station Security Officer, they rushed to the spot to find Nilkantha Bhikari Raut, lying on the ground with injuries near his right ear and the left side of his head. Inquiries revealed that the tragedy could have occurred any time between 11.30 p.m. on Wednesday and 3 a.m. on Thursday. An empty shell was found in the rifle chamber and the weapon itself was entangled in his legs. The body was taken charge of by Inspector Gaikwad under a *panch name.*

A poignant note was struck when, on a search of his personal effects, the police turned up six letters written by the deceased and all addressed to relatives. On the envelope of one of them was the plea: "Please post this as soon as possible".

Raut had no relatives in Bombay and was a resident of Orissa. His relatives are being informed.

No information was forthcoming as so the possible motive of the apparent suicide. Neither is any foul play suspected.

Mid-Day, 29 June 1979

It is the duty; of the reporter to check in every day with police sources, whether at Police Headquarters or closest police station depending on where the reporter is situated, for information some information is given orally; on other occasion the reporter is given a written report, which is factual, but has to be extensively rewritten to make sense to a newspaper reader. In his book *The Indian Reporter's Guide,* Richard Critchfield quotes this sample actually issued by the Nagpur Police Press Liaison Inspector:

1. PLOT TO DUPE MERCHANTS FOILED BY NAGPUR POLICE
2. THE COMPLAINANT IN A ROBBERY CASE BECOMES.

   AN ACCUSED IN A CHEATING CASE

On 11-8-61 one Nathulal Shrawan, a Grain dealer in Dana Bazar, Itwara Nagpur had lodged a complaint with Lakadganj Police that the same afternoon while he was preparing himself in his shop situated in the upper story to go to the bank to deposit a huge amount of Rs. 23,500, some two persons (with a dagger had appeared in the shop all of a sudden and had decamped with the entire amount after causing him injuries at two places. On this a case of robbery was registered by the Police and immediate steps were taken up to deal with the matter. It was a problem for the Police especially when the incident was reported from thickly populated area of the City where lot of sensation was obvious among the business class. The Police adopted: the best methods of elimination off acts and on the basis of certain clues and traces, it had come to a reasonable conclusion suspecting the bonafides of Nathulal himself regarding the reality of this crime. They had a definite data that the incident was false and this Nathulal was out with such an alarming report with, all obvious cause to maintain his credit in the market, which in fact was at stake.

The Police had no other alternative except the legal means and as such they had to register case *u/s* 420 IPC against this Nathulal who had very obviously planned the show to dupe the payments of other merchants to whom he owed. He was arrested and thus had an awkward position, when confronted with a data of contradictory facts ascertained through Police investigation. When firmly and cautiously interrogated by Police Inspectors Mushtaque Ahmad and Khandagale, under the direct supervision of Shri N.S. Khedkar, S.D.P.O. Kotwali Dn., he had to' divulge his secrets and ill designs and had to recover the huge amount which he had reported to be looted from his own Possession only in the dead of night.

The Police Sources have given to understand very interesting details regarding this crime, especially when the complaint of a robbery case himself is traced to be the accused of a cheating case.

A Police report is not expected to be like a news report. It purports to give all the facts sequentially, but it is left to the reporter to make a coherent story. This is how it appeared in one daily:

> An Itwara grain dealer was arrested and charged with cheating today when police discovered he had falsely reported a Rs. 23,500 robbery in his shop on August 11 to maintain his credit in the market.

Contempt of Court: It is extremely difficult to define the term "contempt of court." It is an aspect of reporting that the crime and-court reporter has to be constantly aware of and guard against. By and large contempt of court can be defined as any conduct or action that tends to' bring the authority and administration of the law into disrespect or disregard or will interfere with or prejudice the parties litigating or their witnesses during litigation contempt is of two kinds: (1) contempt committed in the face of the court and (2) Indirect contempt or contempt out of court.

Some instances of contempt are obvious: A reporter surreptitiously returning to' the court room after having once been excluded from it violates the order of the court. A reporter who photographs an accused person in spite of the order of the court not to do so is again in violation of the court and can be cited for contempt. Similarly publication of proceedings of a case being heard *in camera* is a disobedience of the court's orders.

The out of court contempt may be divided generally into (a) false and grossly inaccurate report of court proceedings (b) such publications that may have a reasonable tendency to interfere with the orderly administration of justice and (c) publication that scandalize the court, judges, counsel, parties or witnesses.

Pending Cases: The courts win resent any comments or mis-reporting in pending cases where such comments or mis-reporting could, in the least, be taken to have the effect of prejudicing the fair trial of an accused person. In the circumstances a wise reporter and his editor will make no comment on a case that is *subjudice*. The reporter is well advised not to assume the role of investigator, counselor tribunal and in any event no extra-judicial opinion regarding a pending trial should be made. The point is not whether the publication in fact interferes as much as whether it *tends* to interfere with the due course of justice. If a paper reports prosecution evidence it should also report defence evidence. The paper must not appear to take sides. And reports must not be partial or garbled.

In the case of a criticism of a judge, the criticism must take the form of reasonable argument or expostulation. It must be made in good faith and must be free from the imputation of improper motive. Criticism of a judicial officer which takes the form of representation to the Government, expressed in terms which do not overstep the limits, is not contempt. It is contempt to criticise a judicial act so as to interfere with the administration of justice but it is not contempt to criticise adversely the purely ministerial act of the court.

Newspapers must be particularly careful in attributing to judge the corruption, incompetency and dishonesty, irrespective of the facts whether the offending remarks are made in a case before trial, in a pending case or a case that has been decided. Contempt may have been committed again and this is why it has been said that contempt of court is hard to define-a person may be guilty of contempt even though there was no intention of the publication of contempt. The question is not what was the intention of the publication but what was the effect of the publication. The intention is to be inferred from the consideration of the natural meaning of the words used and the impression which they convey to an ordinary reader. All that may be in favour of the publication is that want of intention may be considered as an extenuating circumstance.

When reporting proceedings of a court, a reporter must remember that there are four stages of proceedings:

(a) before trial

(b) pending trial

(c) after the decision and

(d) when appeal is pending.

Once a trial is over, newspapers enjoy the privilege of fair comment, fairness implying that criticism is based on actual fact. Newspapers may review the facts of the law and express their opinion even if their opinion may be contrary to the decisions of the court. But personal attacks on the judges attributing incompetency, and partiality, judicial dishonesty, political bias and improper motives or "other consideration" are in contempt of court.

The Contempt of Court Act XXXII of 1952 says: "Save as

otherwise expressly provided by any law for the time being in force the contempt of court may be punished with simple imprisonment for a term which may extend to six months or with fine which may extend to Rs. 2000 or with both."

Provided that the accused may be discharged or the punishment awarded may be remitted on apology being made to the satisfaction of the court.

A full and qualified apology takes out the sting of the contempt. Courts shall take a very strict view where the apology is not tendered and refusal to apologise is considered an aggravation of the offence carrying deterrent punishment.

Editors, news editors, chief sub editors and reporters therefore have to be extra careful about what is written and when it is written. The majesty of the court shall not be trifled with in any way or form.

Contempt of Parliament and State Legislatures: The Parliament expects "a newspaper writer should be more cautious than a private citizen as his criticisms are widely published." Such comments in respect of Parliamentary proceedings or the performance of any member on the floor of the House, if they contain any personal attacks on individual members or if the language of the comments is vulgar or abusive, are not protected and cannot be deemed to come within the bounds of fair comment or justifiable criticism.

Such writing constitute a breach of privilege and contempt of the House on the principle that such acts tend to destroy the House and its members in the performance of their functions and duties by diminishing the respect due to them and by bringing them into odium, contempt or ridicule. (See *Searchlight* case, AIR 1959 S. C 395 and *Blitz* case-Lok Sabha debates on 20 April 1961 and 18 August 1961).

It is one thing to criticise the performance of a member of Parliament and quite another to report Parliamentary proceedings. The Parliamentary Proceedings (Protection of

Publications) Act of 1956, popularly known as Feroz Gandhi Act, provides that no person should be liable to any proceedings-civil or criminal in respect of a publication in a newspaper of a substantially true report of any proceedings of either House of Parliament. This Act was repealed during the Emergency but has now been re-enacted.

The Act permits the press to report defamatory statements in parliament without committing a breach of privilege of Parliament and by implication no legal action for the publication of any such statement referring to any outsider would lie. This Act, how ever, applies only to the proceedings of Parliament and not of State Legislatures which are left free to enact their own legislation in that respect.

The Official Secrets Act, 1923: This Act consolidates the law relating to official secrets and deals with two kinds of offences: (a) Spying and (b) Wrongful communication etc. of secret information.

Under Section 3 of the Act, it is an offence if any person for any purpose prejudicial to the safety or interests of the State :

(a) approaches, inspects, passes over or is in the vicinity of, or enters any prohibited place; or

(b) makes any sketch, plan, model, or note which is calculated to be or might be or is intended to be directly-or indirectly, useful to an enemy; or

(c) obtains, collects, records or publishes or communicates to any other person any sketch, plan, model, article or note or other document or information which is calculated to be or might be or is intended to be directly or indirectly useful to an enemy. Under this Act it would be hard for any Indian reporter to publish the Indian equivalent of The Pentagon Papers.

Fashion Reporting : Fashion in the modern age has become a craze everywhere. There was a time in the past, when it was thought that only the females have a monopoly over the fashion.

It was then a popular belief that since women are concerned for their appearances and looks, therefore, they spend a lot of time on their make-up and dressing. But now-a-days it is not so, because both the boys and the girls are crazy after fashion. There are special magazines which are wholly devoted to different styles of fashion. Fashion is an expression of some permanent attractions of humanity, viz., sex, snobbery, beauty and money.

High fashion is very expensive and it attracts those who have enough and want to show it off. It also attracts those who do not have money but would like to adapt fashion if they ever had. Fashion now-a-days has become a big business in which huge investment is made. With the change of fashion a lot of money is lost and earned. The mini skirt, midi, and hot pants all have made news in their own times. It is a fashion to print photographs of pretty girls to make the magazines saleable.

Paris, London, Rome, Hollywood etc. are the centres of fashion in the world. Fashion shows are organized in big cities all over the world to popularise the new dresses and other fashionable wears. The moment a fashion makes appearance in these big centres, it is publicised by the fashion magazines which are eagerly awaited by the fashion conscious people all over the world. It is generally said that fashion in Paris—the home of fashion—changes very fast. At times, it changes even before it had been introduced in other centres of the world.

Fashion can be used for anything, for dress, hair style, shoes, manners, etiquettes, in all spheres of life. Some persons may be crazy to wear fashionable clothes, others to keep fashionable hair style, or to keep an expensive library, while still others may adopt fashion in their speech and manner. In fashion nothing is stable and eternal. Here everything changes fast like the law of Heraclitus, in which everything is in a flux.

Fashion moves in a circle and goes on changing like the round globe. Sometimes, past fashions are also repeated again after a long time with minor or no changes. Sometimes, the lengthy dresses are invoked and at other times mini dresses become fashionable. Sometimes, gaudy and colourful dresses enter the world of fashion, while at other times, simple and sober dresses are considered to be fashionable. Still at other times, wearing uncouth hippie dresses are invoked and sometimes wearing an indifferent dress becomes the craze.

A few years back, keeping closely cut hair and wearing tight dresses like drain pipe trousers was the fashion, whereas the latest fashion is to keep long flowing hair and wear bellbottom type loose trousers with high heel shoes. Of course, now again tight pants are making appearance.

Sometimes, what the famous actors and actresses wear becomes the fashion. Pop music, pop art and hippie-cut clothes have also been fashions for a long time. Now-a-days, youngmen and women especially students have become highly fashion conscious. All this has increased the importance of the fashion writer.

A fashion reporter should be always on the look out for spontaneous fashion. Such fashions are self-generating and spread like wild fire. A fashion writer, of course, should be in touch with the fashion designers. He should visit the fashionable shops and attend the fashion shows. He should also visit the college and university campuses, coffee houses and restaurants for collecting new ideas about the prevalent and future fashions. Now-a-days, the masses, especially the young boys and girls, create their own fashion. It is the job of the fashion writer to observe them and write about their ideas of fashion.

Certain stores also use the media for advertising their fashionable wears. In this way, sometimes, fashion advertising and fashion articles are linked up for the promotion of certain fashions. Of course, a fashion reporter is not to be influenced by businessmen in his comments, but he has to keep contact with the stores selling the latest fashionable dresses and other goods.

Writing for Women : Many newspapers and magazines devote one page to the women's problems and their likings. This page is called women's page. It may be published once or twice a week. This page generally gives information to the women regarding the home and other domestic things. It might include features on decoration of the house, cleaning of the house, recipes for the preparation of festival foods etc. It may include articles on women's diseases and health. It might also tell the women how to reduce weight and remain slim.

In some women's pages, questions by women are also answered. Women readers may ask questions on diverse matters like health problems, domestic problems, recipes for dishes, fashion etc. In this page, features can be written about the latest fashion, dresses, decoration styles, tips on shopping etc. In this page the women can also be informed about the latest cooking gadgets available in the market. Sometimes, articles regarding women's lib and other problems faced by them can also be discussed.

Some of these women's pages give very useful information to the women regarding women's diseases as well as child care. Some magazines invite the medical problems of the women and also give solutions to cure the same. In this manner, these women's pages are becoming very popular and the reporter who writes these pages also gains much popularity and importance.

Sports Reporting : The importance of sports reporting has increased greatly all over the world. The sports fans eagerly await the news and comments concerning their favourite sport or game and the performance of their favourite players. For this reason every newspaper and magazine gives a lot of importance to its sports page or columns. Some newspapers and magazines employ the reputed sports commentators to write their sports comments. In fact, there are many magazines which are wholly devoted to the field of sports.

Sports reporting should capture the complete atmosphere

of a particular game while giving the facts concerning the game or the match. There is no doubt that first of all a sports lover wants to know the facts of the match of his favourite game. Sports reporting should be done in such a way that even those readers who have no knowledge or little interest in the sports should be tempted to read it. Like other international events, sports reporting is also done now-a-days on an international scale. People all over the world are interested to know the results of the famous World Cup matches of football, lawn tennis, hockey etc.

Sports reporting has become an art. The reporter must learn properly the rules of the game about which he is asked to give his comments. He should try to know the famous players and their past performances. He should equip himself with as many facts as possible before the game starts. In sports reporting the time factor is very vital, because the report regarding today's play must reach the newspaper's office in time, so that it can be published in the next day's newspaper. It is better if you can identify the players at the very start of the game, so that you can report back the achievements of the individual player accurately.

A reporter working for an evening newspaper may have to write his report as the game progresses in the afternoon, so that his report is published in the evening newspaper. A reporter working for a morning newspaper or weekly magazine, has a bit easier time, since he may not be required to send his report by telephone in separate 'takes'.

You should try to remember the following points as far as sports reporting is concerned:

(i) You should try to know the name of the Manager and other officials of the team.

(ii) By knowing the Referee and the Manager well, you can sometimes get a good sports story from them.

(iii) Try to know something about the personal lives of sportsmen, because now-a-days readers are quite interested to know about their earnings, expenses and even the eccentricities and their love affairs.

(iv) There is a difference between a sports writer and a general reporter. The general reporter simply makes a report regarding what happens, whereas the sports writer is at the same time a reporter and a critic.

(v) The sports reporter judges the quality and the skill of the players at the same time, when he is writing his reports. But his opinion must be authoritative and effective.

(vi) The sports reporter must know the correct names of the goal scorers with their proper spellings, so that he should not misquote them at any time.

(vii) In your report you must give the essentials of the game like the names of the teams, the ground at which the game takes place and the correct score of the team.

(viii) Never try to unnecessarily exaggerate the quality and importance of a particular sporting team or a match.

(ix) You should watch out for any news-worthy event at the match site which may prove to be more important than the game itself, just like a fight among the supporters of different teams or breakdown of a spectator stand etc.

(x) Generally, every sport has its own jargon and technical terms. When you use these technical terms, you must explain them properly for the benefit of those who are not very much familiar with the game.

(xi) The successful sports reporter also justifiably accentuates the dramatic event in the game, so that those who could not see the game should feel the dramatic effect.

Reporting Abroad : Some big newspapers can afford to have their own special correspondents stationed in the big cities of the world. These foreign reporters regularly send reports to their newspapers. Sometimes, special correspondents are also sent to cover special events like a royal coronation, general election in a foreign country, death of the head of a state or some international trade fair or exhibition. Due to the faster air travel now-a-days many newspapers instead of keeping resident correspondents, send their reporters from time to time to cover important events.

Certain newspapers also keep local 'stringers' who can be relied upon to give the news whenever any event takes place. Such local stringers sometimes give information to various newspapers and news agencies. The foreign reporter is faced with the problem of the time factor. Generally, there is a time difference between his home country and the country where he is stationed. When it may be dawn in his home country, it may still be midnight in the country where he is stationed. There is a Standard Time system throughout the world dividing it into time zones. Since 1833, this has been based on the meantime of the Greenwich meridian which runs approximately through London. The International Date Line, across which the date changes, is approximately down the 180th meridian.

A foreign reporter must try to know the time difference between his country and the country where he is stationed. For example, the Indian time is 5-1/2 hours ahead of the London time. It is better if a foreign correspondent keeps two clocks, one set to the local time of the country where he is stationed and the other to his home country's time. Sometimes, a foreign correspondent has a big problem, how to send back his story, especially when he covers an important crisis in a small town of a foreign country, because he may have the problem of long delays in contacting his country by telephone or sending a cable.

A foreign correspondent should be a good observer of things, especially when he is covering some crisis, war or insurgency. Sometimes, press reporters who do not have any rivalry, join hands together to exchange whatever information they can get. A foreign correspondent should also be a good judge of things and men. People might tell him very dramatic stories, but he should assess all the information with his common sense, so that he is neither taken in by the official propaganda nor by the exaggerated unofficial reports.

Knowledge of foreign languages will be very helpful for a foreign correspondent. Of course, it may not be possible for him to learn all the languages of the world. On the other hand, if he acquires the basic knowledge of three or four major languages like English, French, German, Russian etc. it will be possible for him to travel in most of the countries of the world.

A foreign correspondent, should also remember the following points :

(i) He must have a valid passport with him.

(ii) Some countries require a visitor to obtain a visa before entry.

(iii) He must get himself properly vaccinated before leaving his country.

(iv) Generally, countries require a valid vaccination certificate for typhoid and small pox. For tropical countries yellow fever and cholera vaccinations are also necessary.

(v) You should carry your money in traveller's cheques which is always quite safe. You must also know the rules governing the export of currencies.

(vi) Before going abroad, you should also take out a personal insurance policy against sickness or death.

(vii) If you know driving, then you should try to get an international driving licence from the transport authority in your country.

(viii) You must be careful about the customs, regulations governing the import and export of goods from one country to another, so that you do not get into unnecessary problems.

(ix) If you carry a camera and a watch, then you must have

their receipts with you, so that while coming back you are not charged any customs duty.

(x) You should be careful while using your camera in a foreign country. You should not photograph military installations and aerodromes, because in many countries photography of these places is strictly prohibited.

(xi) For a foreign correspondent it is a good principle to travel light. He should carry only a few clothes and a light weight portable typewriter, so as to keep the weight of his luggage quite low.

(xii) You should carry with you some woollen clothes also, if you are going to a very cold country, but on the whole there is no need of carrying unnecessary luggage.

(xiii) If you are going abroad for a short stay, then it will be beneficial to pack all your goods in a small suitcase, so that you do not have to carry a heavy hand bag.

(xiv) Do not forget to carry your shaving box, your first-aid kit, towel etc.

(xv) Also do not forget to carry a few writing pens and ball points in your hand bag.

(xvi) You must keep in touch with your home office by whatever method it is possible, like telephone, cable etc.

(xvii) You should not use the long distance telephone too often. Whenever you are going to contact your home office by telephone, it will be a good thing if you can have your reports written out before making the call, so that you can pass on the exact message properly.

(xviii) It is a good thing if you call on your national embassy in the country of your visit, because who knows you might need their help in case of any difficulty or if you are thrown into the jail.

(xix) In certain countries you enjoy a facility that telephone calls to your home office may be paid by your office, by reversing the charges. If you like you can avail of this facility.

(xx) Generally, the foreign correspondents make use of the cable to communicate with their office. For this, foreign correspondents carry a cable card which entitles them to send cables at press rates.

The main value of a foreign correspondent to his paper is the prestige that he is in a foreign country, whereas some of his paper's rivals may not be able to send their correspondents abroad. There is no doubt that a foreign correspondent can give only a single man's view, as he has only one pair of eyes and one pair of ears. There does exist a very good professional friendship among the foreign journalists stationed abroad, but in reporting the stories every foreign correspondent has to rely upon his own judgement. He must always be cautious and careful; because all that glitters is not gold, and he should try to go behind the facade of the news. Things are not always the same as they seem to be.

There is no doubt that the life of a foreign reporter is full of problems and difficulties. But it is also fall of adventure, excitement and has its own rewards. Foreign travel is a great experience in itself. It has a great educational and enlightening value.

Group Responsibility

The Setup

Chief Reporter : The chief reporter has a team of reporters working with him. He holds discussions with the news editor regarding the coverage of news. He plans the special coverage of the expected news. On the basis of his planning he allocates duties to the reporters. Many of the reporters are specialists of different fields like politics, sports, business, crime etc. It is the duty of the chief reporter to see that all the activities are covered properly and nothing important is missed by the reporters.

The chief reporter decides regarding the relative importance of the happenings in the city which should be covered and reported. He receives many invitations for press conferences, public meetings, demonstrations, agitations, strikes etc. He deputes his reporters to cover these events after assessing their relative importance. Many social and voluntary organisations also invite him to cover their annual functions and other activities.

The chief reporter also receives a lot of Government handouts, press releases and other publicity material for publication. He selects the important items for printing after assessing their news-worthiness. Sometimes, he also goes out to cover some very important news or function especially when there is a heavy rush of work. Sometimes he also looks after the administration side of the reporter's holidays and other routine matters.

He has also to keep contacts with the various sources of news. He tries to cultivate new contacts of likely information. He keeps in touch with all the important happenings. He tries to be fully aware of the activities of the rival newspapers. He also plans new investigative and interpretative reports by deputing his men.

The Correspondents : There are different kinds of correspondents who work for a newspaper. Some of these are discussed below :

The Liner : The liner is not a full time journalist. He may be living in a small town. From time to time he may send news stories to the newspaper. He is paid on the basis of the lines of the news stories published in the newspaper. He is only a part time journalist whereas he regularly pursues some other profession.

The Stringer : The stringer is also not a full time journalist. His whole time profession is quite different which he is doing in addition to writing for some papers. But he is in a little better position than the liner. Because he is attached to a newspaper through a string on payment of a small amount to cover his expenses. He is generally paid some fixed amount to retain him for the newspaper.

The Correspondent : There are various categories of correspondents. The most important of them are special correspondents. They generally cover some specified fields in the capital of a country. Some of these attend the Parliament sessions. They keep in touch with the government agencies and other news sources. Sometimes, they are also assigned to cover other special areas. Then there are the foreign correspondents. Some people consider the foreign assignment as the most glamorous part of the job. They are stationed in the capitals of important countries of the world.

A newspaper may also have its correspondents at important district headquarters. Generally, they are full-fledged journalists. The correspondents of a newspaper at the stale capitals are called 'staffers'. They do full time reporting work and are the regular employees of a newspaper or an agency. The correspondents in the different state capitals are in direct contact with the newspaper office. Generally, messages and reports from them are received on the teleprinter. Similarly, instructions are also sent to them on the teleprinter.

Newspaper's News Service : Sometimes, important national newspapers also have their own special news service. This news service is run by a chief of news service in consultation with the editor. The chief of the news service keeps in touch which its correspondents stationed in the country and in other parts of the world. These correspondents, spread all over the world, send their reports to the chief and the sub-editors working under him to shape them into news stories. Sometimes they also revise or even rewrite them. These sub-editors are experts in rewriting the reports sent by the correspondents. The chief of the news service keeps himself in touch with all the important happenings in the world through his correspondents. As a head of his department he also looks after the administration side of the staff under his control.

From Grossroots : The staff of a big newspaper consists of many persons, those who work on the front desks, like the employees in the advertising and circulation departments, and those who work behind the scenes, like the editor, leader writer, sub-editor, manager etc. But the most interesting and the most familiar person for the public is the reporter. For the public the reporter is the press itself. At all important meetings, demonstrations, national or international gatherings, and trouble spots the presence of the reporter represents the mysterious and invisible power of the press.

There is no doubt that no other single member of the staff has a greater influence upon the life of the newspaper than the reporter. The reporter is in touch with life every day under all sorts of conditions. It is his duty to go out to see, find, hear, and know about the latest events and happenings and then write about the same in his newspaper. The newspaper today is a reflex of the day to day life and this reflex is made possible through the stories of the reporter.

Prime Duty : It should be the duty of every reporter to make his copy pulsate with life and full of interest for the readers. His stories should be bright and sparkling, something that should make people think and talk and look forward to the next issue. To do this a reporter has to put his heart and soul into his work. Of course, the reporter of today has to work at a greater speed and under more stressful conditions than his predecessors in the past. But he also gets more remuneration today as compared with the past. It goes without saying that a reporter has also to sacrifice many of the pleasures of home life to answer the call of duty, at all odd hours.

A reporter must appreciate the importance of having a good reputation for absolute reliability. For this purpose he must be systematic in his habits and punctual in keeping his appointments. He should be quite careful while making inquiries to know the facts and should be fair in his comments. The most important thing is that he should be efficient and prompt in turning out his copies. By observing these principles, every reporter can make his path smooth and trouble free.

A reporter should have the ability to write good English or the language of his paper. He should possess the quality to write in a condensed manner according to the availability of space. This goes without saying that whenever a reporter writes his copy in his own hand, it must be readable. In fact, he should write his reports in such a way which obviates any possible chance of mistake and subsequent query regarding spellings of words and meanings.

The reporter should type or write his reports clearly only on one side of the paper in double space so as to allow enough space for sub-editorial corrections. Every good reporter should develop the habit of turning out a neat and clean copy. Sometimes a reporter may give headlines to the report, but generally the headlines are given by the sub-editor. Now-a-days the reporters usually type out their stories but whenever a hand written copy is to be filed, it must be written in ink.

Unique Position : The reporter of a local newspaper occupies a unique position and he becomes quite popular with the people of his town. He reports the local events, functions, fairs, socials etc. and comes closer to the social life of the town. A reporter should follow some professional ethics in his work. Sometimes, while engaged in his profession, he may come closer to some persons and develop confidential relations with them. Some persons may also tell him their personal, private and business affairs. But a reporter should never betray their confidence under any circumstances by divulging their secrets which they have told him in good faith. This quality of trustworthiness increases the popularity of the reporter and he is welcomed wherever he goes. This will also enhance his reputation in all sections of the society.

Sometimes, a reporter may be asked to write short length paragraphs regarding the local intelligence or about the city news. For this he should keep his eyes and ears open and develop a nose for local news. He should develop a system to ensure that none of the interesting news is missed by him. He should try to know the secretaries of social, religious, political, musical, dramatic, legal, official and other organisations and should call upon them regularly to get some interesting stories. He should make inquiries from the police regarding news of accidents and crime. He should also contact the fire station for the particulars of local fires. Similarly, he can contact hospitals for collecting information regarding accidents and deaths. In the same fashion, he can get a lot of good news from the sports clubs and other organizations.

Systemised Working : Every reporter should keep an engagement diary. In this way he can systematise his working and attend to all his appointments properly and punctually. By keeping an engagement diary he can know about the important engagements and other events in the future and cover them without fail. Now-a-days, it is very necessary for a reporter to possess a good knowledge of shorthand and typing. This helps a reporter greatly in writing down verbatim reports of political meetings and speeches made at some political functions.

Generally, the reporter types the copy in the office or telephones it to a copy taker. Whenever the reporter types the copy in his office, he should prepare it in such a way that it should not need much sub-editing. It should be so neat and clean that it could be photographed and put in the paper as it is.

The reporter should not forget to give a catchline to this copy. Every copy which goes to the printer to be set is given a catchline. The catchline is a key-word, because during the production it identifies all the sheets of the copy. The catchline is given on each sheet so that the printer can collate the whole story. The catchline should be chosen very carefully. It is better to choose an uncommon word, which may not resemble with another catchline. If you choose a very common word as a catchline like 'accident', it might be confused because there may have been half a dozen accident stories in that edition of the paper.

The word chosen as a catchline may not have a very close identification with the story. But there should be some mental link with it. You should put the catchline and the page number at the top. Before starting the story you should leave half page of the first sheet. At least two inches margin should be left on the left side of every page. The space which you have left at the top of the first sheet can be used by the sub-editor for writing the headlines or any other instructions for the printer. On the left side margin, the editor might write corrections if any. As already mentioned you should always type the copy in double space to leave some space in between the lines for corrections which might be made by the sub-editor.

Good Rules : It is a good rule to end the page at the end of a paragraph. Similarly, you should not continue a sentence on to the next page. At the end of each sheet you should type the word 'more', or the letters 'm.f.' or "more follows". Whenever you finish your story you should write at the end of the last page the word 'end'. All these things are very necessary, otherwise, sometimes a page or a paragraph of your copy might be lost on the printer's desk. You should also try to follow the house style adopted by your newspaper thoroughly. Every newspaper has its own style, which must be adhered to.

Besides the above a reporter should also remember the following points :

(i) As already discussed above, a reporter should never repeat a story which has been told to him confidentially or in good faith, unless he takes the prior permission of the person concerned to make it public.

(ii) While collecting the local news, a reporter should keep in mind the great value of giving the names of persons in his stories. However, the names should be spelled correctly.

(iii) Every reporter should try to develop the qualities of a descriptive writer.

(iv) A reporter must remember that practice makes a man perfect. Therfore, he should always try to improve his method of reporting and his style.

(v) Every reporter should use plain English. He should avoid difficult words. He should enable his reader to visualise the scene described by him as clearly as if he had seen it with his own eyes.

(vi) A good reporter should avoid the use of stereotyped phraseology.

(vii) A reporter should try to be accurate in his reporting. Whenever his accuracy is called in question, he should be able to produce his original note-book.

(viii) One main cause of the complaint against misrepresentation in newspapers is that certain persons in the heat of excitement say things, which they do not mean. And when reported accurately in the press, they deny having said such things.

(ix) Whenever a reporter has to report on the court proceedings, he should be very careful in his report. For example, use of a wrong name or adverse comment might land him into legal problems.

(x) While reporting ordinary public meetings, a reporter has to produce only a summary, which he should try to write up as the meeting progresses.

(xi) The reporter must master the art of condensing while reporting the speeches made in the public meetings. This will greatly help him in writing his summaries.

(xii) A reporter must know what is news-worthy and what is not. Recognition of news values implies the need of "news nose". Without it a reporter cannot hope to achieve success in his career.

Special Correspondents : There was a time when Indian newspapers had two kinds of correspondents at New Delhi:

the Special Representative and the Special Correspondent. The former species seems, for a variety of reasons, to be dying. But the Special Correspondent remains, the aristocrat of the profession, often better known to readers than the editor himself since it is the former's by-line that often features on the lead story on the front page.

Special Representatives : The Special Representative, however, ruled the roost for a long time, in fact from around the turn of the century when leading newspapers used to keep high-powered; influential special representatives at Simla whenever the government shifted its headquarters there from Calcutta (the then capital) during the summer. The era of the Special Representative, then, may be said to have started in 1899 during the Vice regality of Lord Curzon. The reason for sending a special representative to Simla grew out of the fact that there was no powerful daily in the Delhi area at that time, the nearest one being the *Civil and Military Gazette* at Lahore. Leading newspapers wanted one of their men to be where power was, not only to get news, which an ordinary reporter may have obtained without great difficulty, but to negotiate favours and facilities with the high and the mighty. Since those in power were Britishers, with their own sense of racial superiority, it was inevitable that those appointed to hobnob with them were also Britishers, naturally of some eminence, so that they could easily socialize with their fellow compatriots and wrangle favours from them.

Such a one was Howard Hansman of the *Pioneer* of Allahabad who quickly earned the reputation for getting exclusive interviews. The *Pioneer*, it may be remembered, was very much a British-owned paper; so was *The Statesman* which had its own Special Representative in Everard Coates. *The Englishman*, another paper, had Sir Edward J. Buck and the *Indian Daily News* a man called Dallas. Viceroys, Governors, Commanders-in-chief and their minions patronized these men, who wore the right sort of ties and came from the right sort of schools. It was the world of the whiteman into which the brown man had no entry. It was many years later that K.C. Roy and Ushanath Sen joined that strange band of lobbyists and preened themselves as a special breed of newspaperman, with more interest in newsprint than in news.

All Powerful : Today, however, it is the Special Correspondent who is accredited to New Delhi and his fare is special news. He is expected to rub shoulders as did his professional forebears again with the high and the mighty, and while 'it is no more necessary to know how to tie your knot or to wear formal dinner dress, it certainly helps to have the right kind of contacts in ministerial circles. Indian ministers these days have no use for formal dinner wear and at least one minister decided he could even dispense with a tie when he was appointed Minister-in-waiting to President Carter when the latter visited India in 1977.

Nevertheless the glitter is there. As Sir Philip Gibbs, no mean. Special Correspondent himself, once said: "The noblest and most amusing career in journalism is that of the special correspondent, because the special correspondent sees a great deal of life at other people's expense and it is very much worthwhile."

That is looking at it somewhat cynically and while it is true that a special correspondent enjoys a great number of privileges, dines and wines (when that is permitted) with the powerful in the land travels abroad at some one else's (usually his government's or newspaper's) expense and comes to see a great deal more than other ordinary mortals, it is not roses, roses all the way.

Often, it is necessary to remember, the special correspondent does not reach his eminence overnight. He has probably come up the hard way, via reporting the police courts and the municipal corporations of his home town, though it is not unusual for some leading newspapers to pick up a bright young man with a foreign degree to do the job, probably on the theory that if the young man had an opportunity to study abroad, he comes from a sufficiently high social stratum that ensures self-confidence in dealing with the world of officialdom.

For certainly the Special Correspondent has not only to meet the dhoti-clad minister who would probably be only too glad to talk to him, but he will also have to deal with the Chief Secretary to a Department and some of his minions who may think they are a cut above the elected representatives. In this, as in other spheres, self-confidence and the air of a man who knows he represents a major paper and can afford to swank about, helps. If word goes round that his salary, not to speak expense account, is measurably higher than that of his less fortunate brethren, he would find that he has entry into normally reticent circles.

In Delhi, a Special Correspondent, once he is accredited, gets certain facilities that go with the job: reserved seats at public functions, entry into the Secretariat, housing facilities and of course, the right to ask questions from the Prime Minister and other ministers and get answers. This puts him in the category of a man who has access to news at the highest level. If he is familiar with ministers he would call them at their homes or be invited as their guest. All too often, if he represents a national daily, he may find that instead of his calling up ministers, the ministers, or their men may be wanting his ear. If the Special Correspondent wants news, the minister, on occasions, may be only too willing to provide it. One feeds on the other.

This, of course, puts a terrific burden on the Special Correspondent. He has to be familiar to-and not necessarily with-the minister, but he must know how to keep aloof from his source as well. He has to be especially aware of the planted story, the deliberate leak intended to damage some one else's reputation or power base. News is not always what a minister tells the Special Correspondent. It is the latter's job to find why a minister is confiding him and what axe the latter has to grind. In the circumstances, a Special Correspondent is the sifter and the interpreter, the guide and the diplomat. James Gordon Bennett once described a Special Correspondent as "half diplomat and half detective" which is a pretty good description of the job.

News Interpretation

It is his dexterity to interpret news, as much as to get it, that marks the Special Correspondent from the run-of-the-mill reporter. A good Special Correspondent will not only get news-that, after all, is his major responsibility-but will make it meaningful to his reader. Facts, admittedly, stand by themselves and are self-explanatory. But only partly. What do the facts mean in terms of a possibly emerging pattern? What does it mean to say that the rate of industrial growth was three per cent in a given year? Is it low or reasonably high against a background of economic stagnation? What was the rate of growth a year ago? How does it compare with the rate of growth in the neighbouring countries? It is the Special Correspondent's special responsibility to inform the reader of the *meaning* of facts. This is where his talents are most called for. He has to express an opinion. But the opinion must be so interwoven with information that together they provide the reader with the full story. Facts without opinion are barren; opinion without facts is arrogance. What the Special Correspondent has always to beware of is the tendency to offer opinion without supporting data. It is difficult enough to give an opinion with available data; it is unjournalistic, if not unethical to spout opinion with no hard information to base it upon. A columnist may get away with it but a Special Correspondent cannot.

Sometimes what passes for special correspondence is a caricature of what it should be. A Special Correspondent may be called upon to provide an "intro" to long parliamentary proceedings or to. "open" stories such as are meat to the news agencies, but that is not really what a Special Correspondent is paid for. It is poor journalism to stay put in one's own office or home and then, when the evening is over, pore over the news agency reports and condescend to write an "intra." It will be more professional if the Special Correspondent attends parliament and sits through the often tedious proceedings to make his own assessment at first hand. Then his effort at providing an "intra" becomes relevant and sound.

A good news editor will ask the Special Correspondent not only to provide an "intro" but to give a running story as well, telling the reader what the parliament was discussing, with adequate background as to the importance and significance of the debate. If the newspaper has plenty of space to allot to parliamentary proceedings, it may be left to the agencies to report who said what. In any event, that is the function of the agency. But it is the Special Correspondent's particular responsibility to place debates in their proper perspective. This calls for in depth study not just of past parliamentary proceedings, but of political science, history, economics and allied subjects. Special Correspondence does not come easy. It is earned by dint of hard work and home studies. To believe, as some do, that all that a Special Correspondent does is to attend cocktail parties and drop names, is not to appreciate his avocation.

Home study includes poring over voluminous government reports and publications of all sorts relevant to a Correspondent's job. One never can tell where one can get a good lead. The Correspondent may pick one in the day's newspaper by sheer chance because he notes that a report reveals a missing link that is worth chasing. Or he may get it in a report that is hard to read but should, perhaps for that very reason, be read with greater attention. Even usual government handouts under trained eyes could yield profitable leads to be developed by further research and interviews.

So a Special Correspondent will perforce have to do a large amount of reading, not only of reports and documents available in India, but similar ones from abroad. His reading has to be very catholic and embrace a wide range of interests such as foreign affairs, defence, agriculture, industry and commerce, trade, imports and exports, taxation policy. Well might he say with Terence: *Homo sum; humani nil a me alienum puto.* (I am a man, I count nothing human indifferent to me).

Friends and Foes : A high powered Special Correspondent attracts equally high powered friends and not a few enemies. He has to learn to live with them. Friends may-and often will provide him with valuable information. He should know how to use such information. Some of it may be spurious; it will have to be checked for accuracy. Some will be confidential and then the Special Correspondent will have to use his judgment. A confidence betrayed is a friend lost for ever. But sometimes an important source will deliberately provide information in the hope that it will be used, even though he may swear you to secrecy. To assess such situations requires experience and confidence. The best thing in such circumstances is to refuse to be party to confidential secrets and information dubbed "off the record." This calls for courage. It is some what flattering to be taken into confidence by ministers or high officials. But ministers may want to take you into confidence precisely because they do not want the Special Correspondent to delve deeper into certain kinds of news.

Besides, the Special Correspondent may be aware already of what the high official seems eager to tell on an "off the record" basis. Even if he is not, the chances are that he would soon learn of it from other, independent sources and so why tie oneself to observing secrecy? It is certainly not prudent for a Special Correspondent to receive conditional information when for all he knows, his rivals may be getting it from other sources unconditionally, thereby scoring a scoop. A Special Correspondent's loyalty is not to his ministerial or official friends but to his newspaper and to his readers.

A Special Correspondent cannot afford to live in an ivory tower, nor can he disdain social life. It is at putties that he makes important contacts under relaxed conditions. But it is a woeful mistake to believe that he can get information while swapping drinks.

Some notable Special Correspondents do not touch a drop of liquor. One does not have to be a drunk to get news. Senior officials-who, after all, are the real source of meaningful news-do not pass information to Special Correspondents over a gin-and-tonic. And not even two Patiala pegs may loosen their tongues. If that happens they may find that they are transferred. A cocktail party is not a place to gather news; it is a place to make friends in congenial surroundings. It will not hurt to have a drink or two; but it will certainly be no handicap to be a teetotaller. Drinking does not make a journalist, though a journalist may drink. If that was all to journalism, pubs in every city would provide the best correspondents.

Writing in the mid-fifties, Krishnalal Shridharani, himself a distinguished journalist summed up the qualities that a Special Correspondent should possess. These are :

(1) Vast and varied contacts with official sources, with opposition sources, with embassy sources, with fellow reporters, with private secretaries and with one or two high and mighty.

(2) Ability to keep a confidence.

(3) Courage, occasionally to refuse confidences with strings attached. Ability to avoid hearing things that bind one to secrecy.

(4) A bent for research based upon previous training in social sciences and the humanities. A craving for facts.

(5) A bit of brass (especially in foreign countries and in a war zone), the knack of bluffing one's way through forbidden areas.

(6) The art of conversation which primarily consists of encouraging others to talk, without yourself being a wet blanket.

(7) The ability to get along with people and in difficult situations. A friendly smile. This will invoke "human interest" confidings.

(8) Physical stamina and moral courage. The ability to do with out sleep on occasions.

(9) Ability to be freshly impressed by action, colour, life.

(10) Imagination, and a simple, sparkling style.

Shridharani then went on to outline the pitfalls in the path of a Special Correspondent which he said are more numerous than in the case of the routine reporter. And what were the pitfalls?

They are deeper, too and their openings more obscure. He may begin to take himself too seriously because of the stir he creates and that is the beginning of the end. Then again, he might begin to accept the wishful thinkings of his 'important sources', and thus lose the power to judge and predict. And exclusively top-level contacts might make his stories hollow: they supply leads, but meat is to be found with men who work out the details. Exclusively top-level connections may turn him into a party-going butterfly, progressively more and more incapable or applying the seat of his pants to his working chair. Just when things become easy, he stands in the need of doing things the hard way. Much of what is said about Special Correspondents holds good' for Foreign Correspondents as well. A Foreign Correspondent comes to his job with a good deal of experience behind him. He would probably have spent some years in New Delhi as a Special Correspondent, learning the nuances of being a diplomatic correspondent at home. That ought to stand him in good stead when he leaves for foreign capitals.

Indian correspondents abroad at one time were mostly concentrated in London which used to the most important capital for India in pre-independence days. After all there was a need to know the pulse of the British public and what Parliament did or said about India and its nationalist movement. Indian newspapers regularly sent correspondents to cover the Round Table Conferences come of them like Dr. Shelvankar stayed on. London increasingly became the home of Indian Foreign Correspondents.

But as the centre of political gravity shifted to the United States, so did to some extent the interest of Indian newspapers which first began to send correspondents to the United Nations and then, as the United Nations' glamour and relevance began to' fade, to Washington. Indian correspondents sent to Washington were simultaneously accredited to the United Nations as a matter of course.

Accreditation rules to Washington are simple enough. The news paper informs the State Department through a letter from the editor of its intention to appoint the correspondent-named, for guidance-to his post in the capital. The letter is processed and the correspondent thereafter is duly informed that his appointment is accepted. He is then given a press card that permits him to enter the State Department and to attend news briefings and other press conferences. He could then join the State Department Correspondents' Association which also issues him a card acknowledging his membership of the Association. He will meanwhile have to be processed by the security offices and be fingerprinted after which he will get a White House press card that will enable him to attend White House press briefings and also presidential press conferences. Armed with these he could apply for membership of the Senate and Congressional Press Association; membership would qualify him to observe Congressional sessions from the press gallery, and also to attend hearings. He will also be entitled to receive the *Congressional Record* gratis.

Foreign Correspondents : Time was when a Foreign Correspondent would have had to take his copy to the nearest telegraph office where he would have been asked-unless, by then, he was sufficiently well-known-for his press card, his telegraphic or cable authority and identity card. But time marches on and so does technology. These days it is easy to apply for and quickly get international telex machines that link one with one's own office and the world at large. The correspondent therefore does not have to go to the cable office to hand over his copy. He can have a telex machine installed in his own office or home and send his message directly to his office and have the satisfaction of knowing that it has been received without any distortions. The telex is a major boon to Foreign Correspondents. The author had the mortification to find out, while covering the non-aligned conference that met in Algiers that his copy did not land in Bombay for four days. By then naturally, the story was dead.

As long as the Foreign Correspondent remains in his chosen capital, his problems are easily handled. It is when he is sent to another capital or country that he has to be familiar with a number of items of professional interest, such as the place where the international conference is held, the facilities available for cabling, the availability of hotel accommodation, costs, distances to be covered in commuting from hotel to conference site or to cable office, the nature and cost of transportation, the kind of medical and dental service available at short notice etc. Sometimes the government of the host country will provide the information; at other times it will be necessary to call on the local residence of the Indian Ambassador or at the Chancery to register one's presence. Certainly it is a wise Foreign Correspondent who will stay in touch with the Embassy of India, not only as a source of information but for safety reasons also.

It is presumed, of course, that a Foreign Correspondent will know the language of the country to which he is assigned, Russian if he is in the Soviet Union, German if in Bonn, French in Paris and Spanish in many Latin American countries.

The Foreign Correspondent will be under pressure to say kind things about the host country. He should have the courage to resist such pressures. It is also unwise to run down the host country, no matter how much its society and administration differs from one's own. It is not the task of a Foreign Correspondent to sit in judgements on alien governments and institutions but rather to explain them in the context in which they chanced to be set up. Different countries have different historical backgrounds and they are what they are because of their special and unique pasts. Wisdom lies in understanding the process of history and to interpret each nation in the context of its own history and immutable past. Wisdom also lies in knowing that several international conflicts and controversies have no simple, immediate solution, that the conflict generally is between right and right and not between right and wrong and that one's patriotic bias, although justified, is not always just. And that takes some time to learn, especially at the United Nations where the urge to take sides, to pontificate and to prejudge can be very pressing indeed.

The Foreign Correspondent, under all circumstances, will keep to the law of the host country and never break it wittingly or even unwittingly. The Foreign Correspondent is an Ambassador of the press of his own country and has to be on the best of his behaviour. A Foreign Correspondent who cheats, who indulges in questionable practices where foreign exchange is concerned and who gets a notoriety for being unscrupulous not only brings disgrace on himself, which is his private business and should be of no concern to anyone but his own office, but will make it difficult for fellow correspondents from his country to follow him. Foreign Correspondents are usually under constant and quiet observation, a fact that they must be aware of, especially in communist or authoritarian countries. Getting into trouble of any kind just would not do.

In this regard the Foreign Correspondent cannot do better than take guidance from his Embassy which could give him some simple obvious do's and dont's. Embassies are generally helpful to correspondents if only because they themselves do not want adverse publicity. Also, they would like to be briefed on what the Foreign Correspondents have learnt in the course of their work. In most instances, there is a fair exchange of information between Foreign Correspondents and their Embassies but the correspondent must remember and realize that he works for his newspaper and not his country's government and should, at all times, learn to keep his distance from officials, if for nothing else, to respect his professional ethics of independence. Over dependence on Embassies will result in Foreign Correspondents relying on what for all practical purposes become government or embassy handouts. A Foreign Correspondent is sent abroad to give his personal assessment of the situation prevailing in the host country or countries, not to peddle Embassy views on the same. To retain one's independence in foreign lands is not always easy and embassies sometimes come under pressure from host governments to keep the writings of the correspondents in check, but this is part of the game and must be faced with courage, good humour and firmness.

Of all types of correspondents, the War Correspondent is in a very special class by himself. Think of the names: Winston Churchill, William Howard Russell, Edwin Lawrence Godkin, Richard Harding Davis, James Creelman, Luigi Barzini, Irvin S. Cobb, John Reed, Ernest Hemingway, Evelyn Waugh, Herbert Matthews, Wilfred Burchett, David Halberstam.

There are very few Indian war correspondents and such wars as India was compelled, after independence, to participate in have happily been of short duration. Frank Moraes, D.R. Mankekar and D.F. Karaka, among others covered the second world war. But they are in a different class form Emie Pyle or Edward R. Murrow.

Actually, the war correspondent is comparatively new to history. In years gone by Generals preferred to report their own victories and resented a civilian snooping around the battlefield as William

Howard Russell of *The Times* of London quickly discovered in the Crimea. During 1914-1918 the war correspondent was very much part of the military machine and kept quiet about the extent of the slaughter till the war was over. Not until Vietnam did the war correspondent begin to emerge as a partisan for truth and compassion. The British press failed miserably during the Russian Revolution. Looking back on its own coverage of the Revolution 35 years later, *The Times* in fact, admitted its shortcomings: "The idea of a *campaign ad maiorem proletariatis gloriam* was so foreign to Wilton (the correspondent) that he never understood it. More unfortunately still, the idea was equally foreign to Steed (the Foreign Editor), Dawson (the Editor), Northcliffe (the proprietor), to Lloyd George (Prime Minister) and to Milner (soon to be Minister of War). No one had heard of the forces of the Left except in terms that indicated them to be madmen.

Not all War Correspondents were so dumb, though some were more Jingoistic than stupid. James Creelman, along with J.A Mac Gahan' and the Italian Luigi Barzini, was one of the few correspondents to protest the conduct of war and write with truth and-compassion. His report of the Japanese massacre at Port Arthur in 1894 caused the Japanese to offer him a bribe to tone down his report, but he refused. American opinion was changed overnight. Barzini was a misfit among war correspondents of his time for he saw no glory or heroics but only senseless slaughter in war. Yet newsdealers had only to shout "Article by Barzini!" for his paper, *Corriere della Sera* to sell out. American journalist and poet John Reed, author of *Ten Days' That Shook the World* and correspondent for the radical publication *The Masses* achieved journalistic greatness with his unparalleled description of the November 1917 events in Petrograd. Ernest Hemingway, reporting from Spain for the North American Newspaper Alliance (NANA) became the most influential figurehead in the fight against fascism.

The Spanish Civil War remains a watershed in the annals of journalism. No other war has left such a profound and lasting impression on those who reported it. "Today wherever in this world I meet a man or woman who fought for Spanish liberty, I meet a kindred soul" wrote Herbert Mathews.' "In those years we lived our best and what has come after and what there is to come can never carry us to their heights again."

The second World War had its crop of outstanding war correspondents like Emie Pyle, Drew Middleton and Edward

R. Murrow. It must have taken Murrow some courage to depart from the propaganda line that the fall of Dunkirk was Britain's "finest hour" and to assert, if somewhat, mildly, that "there will be disagreement an that point" Emie Pyle won renown by speaking up far the infantry soldier. "I lave the infantry because they are the underlags. They are the mud-rain-frost-and-wind bays. They have no comforts and they even learn to live without the necessities. And in the end they are the guys that wars can't be won washout" was his credo.

The wars since 1914-18 have made many war correspondents heroes in their awn right. Same have 'been killed. This is the price that wars exert even an journalists. A revolution, Mao Tse-tung once said, is not a tea party. Nor is war. Those who have reported one do not glamourize it, Vietnam was probably the most dangerous affairs for corespondents. Forty five of them have been killed there and eighteen listed as missing.

Fortunately wars are not as regular as international conferences; true, they provide all the drama far a correspondent to work an. "If you have not seen a battle" Herbert Matthews once wrote, "your education has been same what neglected-far after all, war has never been one of the primary functions of mankind, and unless you see men fight you miss something fundamental" Other journalists may fervently pray they may be spared such fundamental education but the fact remains, as another War Correspondent, Charles Mohr said, wars, "in an add way provide good stories." The hell they do.

The trouble is that many corespondents fight shy of telling the truth about war far a variety of reasons: ignorance of what really is going an, a false sense of patriotism, fear of being sent back far reporting reality. In his fascinating book *The First Casualty,* Phillip Knightley, himself a special correspondent, recalls instance after instance of War Corespondents failing to tell it all, of Ernest Hemingway suppressing the unpalatable facts about Republican Spain, Evelyn Waugh making a mess of covering the Abyssinian-War but gathering material far his navel *Scoop* and the Russians crushing Quentin Reynolds because they believed that Western corespondents were spies. Perhaps they were. War is a distressing affair in many ways and the first casualty turns aut to be truth.

The Vietnam war was better reported than any other war since the Crimean was a casualty to truth. As journalist Murray Kemptan has remarked, with a million-dollar corps of correspondents in Vietnam, the war in Cambodia was kept hidden for a year.

That takes something. The best comment on war coverage is perhaps given by Gavin Young, a British newspaperman who covered Vietnam. "Correspondents" he wrote, "are bound to be haunted by the feeling that there is probably only one way to work the various elusive aspects of the war into one wholly satisfactory picture. Apart from the aid programmes, the military operations, the political ups and downs, how can one depict the human facets of such a complete tragedy? What of the thoughts and feeling of the Vietnamese? How has the war affected their lives and art, their outlook on foreigners, and different cultures? How if at all, have the Americans been changed by contact with the Vietnamese?.. The Vietnamese war awaits its novelist."

Knightley asserted that on the whole, writers-be did *not* call them War Correspondents-for non-daily publications like *Tom* Buckley in the *New York Times Magazine,* Jonathan Schell of *The New Yorker* and Sol Sanders of *U. S. News & World Report* came out better than most of their news colleagues because, he said, they were "free from the tyranny of pressing deadlines" and could look at the war in greater depth. Are regular war correspondents, then, a useless tribe?

One suspects that even at the risk of not being able to tell the whole story every day, the War Correspondent will be necessary though wars may not. Only, the War Correspondent must know his limitations and be honest enough to admit to them' It is the most important service he could do to his reader who otherwise depends upon him to tell the truth as he sees it.

The Accreditation : Every capital has its own rules of accreditation. Given below are rules for accreditation of news media representatives to New Delhi.

(1) These rules apply to the accreditation at the headquarters of the Government of India of news media representatives.

(2) An application on the prescribed form should be submitted by the editor in the news media organization concerned to the Principal Information Officer, Government of India, New Delhi. Full details about the professional experience of the representative seeking accreditation should be furnished with the application. The Principal Information Officer will refer the application to the Central Press Accreditation Committee for their advice and approval.

(3) The applicant should fulfil the following conditions for accreditation:

   (a) His residence should be the headquarters of the Government of India during the period of accreditation.

   (b) He should be working journalist as defined by the Working Journalists (Conditions of Service and Miscellaneous Provisions) Act, 1955 and should be whole time engaged as a correspondent or cameraman or correspondent-cameraman or a cartoonist.

   (c) At the time of application he should have spent five years in the profession of journalism.

(4) The professional norms applicable to Indian newsmen will also govern the grant of accreditation to applicants on behalf of foreign media.

(5) Editors of news media may in exceptional case be granted accreditation if CPAC is satisfied that the applicant is genuinely engaged in covering current affairs and needs accreditation for this purpose. Such applications will only be considered by the CPAC. No temporary accreditation will be granted by the PIO in such cases.

(6) The Central Press Accreditation Committee may grant accreditation, as an exceptional measure, to journalists of long and distinguished service of at least 25 years who may be contributing special articles to a number of newspaper regularly but not attached to any newspaper which qualifies for accreditation.

(7) Accreditation will be granted only on behalf of a news media-organization having a minimum circulation or coverage as prescribed by the Central Press Accreditation Committee. The Central Press Accreditation Committee will lay down, from time to time, the number of accreditations for various classes of news media organizations, taking into account the coverage required by the organizations and the service limitations of the Press Information Bureau.

(8) In the case of news, features, photo and TV news and feature agencies, following factors will be taken into consideration for determining the entitlement for and the number of accreditations:

(a) The news, features, photo or TV news and features should be based on the news emanating from the capital.

(b) The agency should provide regular service to media network on commercial basis. For the purpose of classification of the agency, only the revenue, as certified by a Chartered Accountant by way of subscriptions from news media for supply of news material will betaken into consideration.

(c) An agency whose service operations extend to at least half of the State of the Indian Union or to electronic media network shall be deemed to be an all-India agency.

(d) In case of agencies of all classes and types, accreditation will be given to the whole-time employees only.

(9) In case of daily newspapers and weeklies, the following factors will be taken into consideration for determining the entitlement for and the number of accreditations.

(a) The paper concerned should be published regularly.

(b) Its circulation should not be less then 5,000 copies as certified by the RNI.

(c) The contents of the concerned weekly should be mainly related to current affairs.

(d) For newspapers and weeklies with circulation above 50,000 copies, only full-time employees of such organization will be granted accreditions.

(e) In the case of smaller newspapers combined circulation may be taken into consideration if they ask for accreditation for a common representative or a journalist himself seeks accreditation jointly on their behalf.

(10) Periodicals of longer than a week's periodicity will not be granted accreditation. However, fortnightlies and monthlies published abroad for the benefit of Indian communities or for dissemination of Indian news would be granted accreditation on the merits of each case.

(11) A press card will be issued to each accredited representative. Admission to special functions including press conferences however, will be governed by invitation.

(12) Accreditation is personal and not transferable.

(13) Accreditation does not confer any official or special status on the news media representative. It merely

recognizes and identifies him as a representative of the media organization which employ him. It must be used only for journalistic purposes. The words "Accredited to the Government of India" should not be used on visiting cards, letter-heads or any other literature.

(14) When the representative ceases to represent the media organization for which he is accredited, the fact should be brought to the notice of the principal Information Officer in writing within 15 days by both the representative and his editor. Failure to comply with this may result in withdrawal of facilities.

(15) The list of accredited news media representatives will be subject to review every year by the Principal Information Officer in consultation with the Central Press Accreditation Committee.

For the purpose of review, the PIO may call for (a) information about the revenue of the Indian agencies (b) dipping of published dispatches or photographs of dope sheets from the concerned news media organization or representative. To ensure that only genuine news media representatives remain accredited on behalf of foreign media organizations, the PIO may, from time to time, go through their published dispatches or enquire through the Indian missions abroad about the representative's work.

(16) The Principal Information Officer may:

(a) accord accreditation by issuing a temporary card in case both the applicant representative and the media organization qualify

(b) accept substitution of an accredited representative for a temporary period

(c) grant temporary accreditation to visiting pressmen

(17) A representative will be liable to dis-accreditation if:

(a) He engaged himself in work other than journalistic, such as soliciting business or advertisement.

(b) He uses for non-journalistic purposes information and facilities provided to him as an accredited representative.

(c) He publishes official secret the inviolability of which is accepted by general understanding and the Central Press Accreditation Committee concurs with this view after giving opportunity of a personal hearing to the concerned representative.

(d) In the course of his duties, he behaves in an undignified or unprofessional manner.

(e) He ignores or violates the conditions on which information and facilities are provided by government.

(f) News media organizations will also be liable to dis-accreditation if they are responsible for wilful publication of mala fide reports or abuse confidence.

(18) In all cases relating to dis-accreditation, the Principal Information Officer will take action warranted by the circumstances in each case in consultation with a locally-based sub-committee of the Central Press Accreditation Committee. All such cases will be referred to the Central Press Accreditation Committee within a period of not more than three months.

(19) These rules come into effect from 17 February 1978 and supercede the earlier rules.

5

Ideal Profession

All copy reaching a newspaper office from different sources is processed at the news desk. The desk is manned by sub-editors and usually a chief sub-editor leads the team and works as copy tester and also as revise editor or slotman. He sits in the very useful slot of the horseshoe-shaped copy desk facing other sub-editors on the rim. After distributing copy to other subs he also checks their work for any mistakes and passes it on to the composing room.

Prime Listed Job

The sub-editor does some or all of these to every story:

— Reads the story for clarity of language and meaning and rewrites where necessary.

— Shortens the story while retaining the essentials and maintaining coherence.

— Combines one story with another or perhaps combines running reports from several news agencies, correspondents and reporters to produce a single intelligible report from different and sometimes contradictory messages.

— Saves space when verbosity creeps in.
— Corrects the grammar and checks for house (or office) style.
— Checks for apparent errors of fact.
— Checks for legal errors (libel, contempt of court, etc.)
— Checks for taste.
— Adds important background facts and provides answers for any implied questions.
— Writes headlines which attract the attention of the reader and also writes sub-headings if necessary.

The chief-sub or revise editor checks the work of sub-editors ensuring accuracy of details. He also becomes the first reader of the story and sees whether the headline and copy make sense.

Another senior sub-editor or chief sub-editor looks after the work at 'the stone'. He is called 'stone editor' also. Though with change in technology the stone has vanished but the term persists. The job of the stone editor is to ensure that all plans mature on time in the composing room where the pages are made up with metal types and picture blocks or with strips of film or bromide. The stone sub can also be called production editor, or make up editor. He deals with minor disharmonies. If the text is too long, he cuts it. If the page plan does not work, he changes it. If there is late news, he makes room for it. He checks the galley proofs and page proofs and finally sends them to the press.

Thus, a sub-editor has to know all about news writing and how a reporter should write news copy. He is supposed to improve upon the work of the reporter. He should not change something for the sake of change but he must make sure that every correction or change he makes improves the copy.

News Agency Copy : The bulk of copy which comes to the news desk is from wire agencies. The teleprinter keeps on creeding information almost all the time during peak news hours of the afternoon and evening. This copy comes in takes—the unit of news agency transmission or unit of newswriting. Let us look at the following news agency take from PTI.

ZCZC

URG GEN

New Delhi 26

Sobhraj-Style

Playboy Of Prisons Once More Outwitted

New Delhi Apr 7 (Pti) A Playboy of Prisons

Who Charmed His Way To Freedom Time And Again Has Once More Been Outwitted.

The Living Protagonist of Two International Best sellers—charles Sobhraj—who Had Literally Walked Out Of The Tihar Jail On A Sleepy Tropical Sunday Three Weeks Ago Was Not To Be Inhibited In His Style By The Massive Hunt For Him.

Along With The 41-year-old Frenchvietnamese National Was His Old British Friend David Hall, A Dairy Chemist Known For His Dexterity With Soporific Concoctions. Wanted For Crimes In Thailand, Nepal, Greece And Turkey, The High School Drop-out, Fluent In A Couple Of Languages And Proficient In Law, Will Soon Be Back In Tihar, His Home For Years At The End Of His Third Escape From Indian Jails. More Pti

RR RT BDS

Here ZCZC is selector code.

URG is the priority assigned to the item. The priority markings used by PTI in descending order of importance are Flash, Snap, Urg (for urgent), Pri (for priority) and Rush. Flash is reserved for a matter of supreme importance. It gains precedence over all other items. It is just two or three words and is followed by the story at the earliest. 'Snap' usually consists of no more than a sentence carrying the very important news point. 'Urg' items take precedence over all others barring 'Flash' and 'Snap' items.

GEN is the classification. PTI has a system of three way classification of news which enables the agency to tailor its news to the needs of subscribers. The *general* classification (abbreviated Gen in marking) is the basic service provided to all subscribers and includes, in compact form, the important news of the day. The *special* (marked SPL) and *extra special* (marked ESPL) classifications provide details about the news already given in the general service as well as additional news.

New Delhi is the place of origin of the story.

Del 26 is the number of the item. It is issued serially with the abbreviated name of the originating centre preceding it.

The first metropolitan centre handling the item changes this to another serial number preceded by its own abbreviated name. Thus items will be serialised under Del, DNI (for items from north Indian centres other than Delhi), Bom, Cal and Mds. Parliament copies are issued Par numbers.

On events spread over several days, where the daily wordage is very large, special serials are started.

For example, Oly (Olympics), AICC (All India Congress Committee), etc.

Foreign news items have their own serial numbers, FG (Foreign General), FS (Foreign Special), FES (Foreign Extra Special) PTF, PAS, and POOL. Whereas FG, FS and FES files carry news items received from Reuter, AFP and UPI and are credited to those agencies, the PTF file is made up of reports received from PTI's own correspondents and stringers abroad. Items taken from the services of agencies like TASS, Xinhua, Antra Bernama, Tanjug and other agencies with which PTI has exchange arrangements go under the PAS series. The POOL file is devoted to agencies participating with PTI in the Press Agencies Pool of Non-aligned countries.

Sobhraj-Style is the *slug*— an identification tag. Every story, even a story consisting of only one take must carry at the top a suitable slug. Generally the slug is one word which is often the key word in the story. Thus a story about rain would be slugged "rain" and one about the police firing, "firing". Slugs are nouns and not adjectives or various forms of verbs. When copies on the same subject pour in from various points, a *master slug* should be used with *sub-slugs* for individual story. In the above example *Sobhraj* is master slug while *style* is sub slug.

Playboy of prisons once more outwitted is the headline. This is a new development. Agencies normally are not supposed to give headlines but now to lighten the burden of newspaper sub-editors they have also started putting headlines. If the sub-editor at the newspaper desk likes it he can indicate the type size for the headline.

New Delhi Apr 7 is dateline and PTI is credit line. It appears just after dateline in the first take of the story and again at the end of each take. All the takes of the story except the last end with More-PTI as in the above example. The last take of the story is closed with PTI. For Spl or Espl services, or sometimes for all stories, the story can be reopened. In re-opening an item, reference is given to the previous take by its number for instance, "Sobhraj five—New Delhi-re-open del 33".

RR RT BDS are initials of the reporter, deskman processing it and the teleprinter operator punching it on the tape. Each take also carries at the end the time at which it is transmitted in the services.

The Lead : In news agency lead is used in the case of developing stories for updating the top, as necessary, in the light of fresh facts as they become available. Examples of such stories could be a train or air mishap, a conference or meeting, an election, a state visit by a VIP. Such stories may require one or more leads as the story advances with the day. A lead can also be used to tie up loose ends of a dispersed story, or to provide combined top for two or three different items about a single subject or related development.

There can be one or more leads to a story. For example, the leads on an air crash story slugged "Crash" could be "Lead Crash", "Second Lead Crash", and so on. The final wrap-up story would be "Lead all Crash".

Pick Up : A lead often overhauls a substantial part of a story or even the entire story. Such a lead is also called a "round up". Close to deadlines of newspapers roundups are not useful and therefore the lead is in the form of a brief one or two para top, that is, just the new intro. This intro introduces the new element that has emerged in the situation. In such cases, an appropriate pick-up line is given, linking with the part of the earlier story specifying the item by number, slug and dateline and giving the location of the point of pick-up.

Kill Note : If an agency wants to withdraw or kill a story which has come on the ticker, it puts out a kill note. The kill note has priority marking 'Kill' and is without a dateline. It gives the number, slug, dateline and subject of the story which it kills and also indicates whether a substitute follows.

Similarly, corrections are also issued, specifying the take line and words of the earlier story and then the whole take is re-issued with corrections.

Service Messages : Sometimes service messages which are meant for internal use also reach newspapers. Such messages have the word "service" at the top. Ordinarily a service is addressed to the Ed (editorial department) at a particular place. These messages should not be confused with messages and stories sent for use in newspapers.

In order to prevent mistakes the words *not, now* and *nor* are repeated in news agency copy. While editing the copy a sub-editor should delete one of these words.

Choice Making

News agencies keep on creeding takes of different stories one after the other, while reporters and correspondents also continue filling copy so that subjects covered by news agencies are also covered by the members of newspaper staff.

If the same story is covered by a member of newspaper staff his copy should get priority over the news agency copy. Additional information given by the news agencies can be added to his copy giving credit to the agency.

News copy coming from different sources is sorted out at the desk and all copy relating to a particular story is kept separate. This helps the sub-editor doing that story to read the whole copy, analyse it and do justice with it. This sorting helps also in knowing whether the news agency has completed the story or some more takes are likely to follow.

Judging the importance of the story the chief-sub decides the space to be given to it. This has to be in relation to total news fall. The relative importance of the story also determines the page where the story would go. Except developing or running stories, all other stories are edited as soon as it is decided that they are to be used. For running stories the deskmen wait for more information. When they come close to the deadline of the edition they proceed with what they have. When additional information comes, the story is changed again for the next edition.

A word about copy. Good copy, also called clean copy, has the name of the reporter and the date on the top of the first page. At least a third of this page is left blank to allow room for instructions to sub-editor and the printer. Sufficient margin should be left on both sides of the copy—say one and a half inch on the left hand side and one inch on the right hand side of all pages of the copy. At least a two inch space should be left at the top and the bottom of each page. News copy should be typed double space.

Every page of the copy should start and end with a paragraph. If there is a mistake in typing a word, it should be typed again. Corrections should be made above the line.

A reporter should leave underscoring paragraph, indents and all other typographical markings to the sub-editor. Wrong underscoring and paragraph marks make a mess of copy. At the end of each page before the last 'more follows' or MF is essential and the end of the last page should be marked 'End'.

On the copy the sub-editor crosses out certain things and circles others. Neither will be set in type but the distinction is that what nobody needs to see any more is crossed out, but essential service messages are circled. The page and edition where the story will go are written on the top of the story and encircled. For example, P 1/2 would mean page one of the second edition. Sub-editor's name or initials are also written and encircled, if there is a printer's or proof reader's query it can be referred to the sub-editor who has edited the copy. Type size and columns are also indicated and encircled. For example, 8 x 1 would mean that the copy is to be set in 8 point type of the newspaper text print across one column. There is no need to specify the face or to say that it is in roman. The Rule in newspaper setting is to specify the unusual and otherwise to keep the copy clean. The fewer the marks the better it is.

Catch line or slug is also essential on edited text takes and headline folio, the operator setting the text sets the catch line and it can be married, with the other folios of the same story. Thus a story may have 'Rajiv' as slug or catchline. Its headline folio will carry 'Rajiv 1' and its first text take would have 'Rajiv 2', and so on.

News Headline : Every headline is written on a separate folio. The headline should be written clearly—in capitals if necessary. The letters which need capitalisation should be double ticked. Edition and page mark go on the top left hand corner and the catchline on top right hand corner. It also carries instructions regarding type and the columns over which the headline will be spread and the headline style. For example, '14 CBLC × 1 set left' would mean that the headline has to be set left over single column in 14 point century bold type in lower case. If the normal headline style is set left in that case it need not be specified in the instructions. However, it is essential that the style breaking headlines should be marked with words and symbols.

Simplicity, informality and impact are the essential characteristics of a modern headline. It should give a clear signal about the content of the story and should be economical in editorial production and reading time and in news space. It should be read quickly. It should be proportionate to the news and flexible. Many of these requirements can conflict with each other. The sub-editor has to match the headline with the story and maintain a balance to give required importance to the story.

Headline Pattern : Headline can be multi-deck or multiline in a single deck. They may be set in capitals, lower case, italics. Headlines may be spread over one or many-columns. Arrangement of words could be centered or indented lines.

One should not confuse deck and line. A deck is a distinct headline on its own and as such it may consist of one or more lines. A headline of five lines is a single deck if the lines are in the same type and read from one to the other. If there are two such units, say of two lines each, the headline will be double-deck.

The old trend which survives in some papers is of multi-deck headlines. The more the decks, the more important is the story. The purpose perhaps was to give all the important news points in different decks of the headline.

The modern school of thought is against the multi-deck. The argument is that the multi-deck headlines consume more editorial time on writing, production time in setting, and the newsprint space. These wastes are further increased by the practice of separating each of the decks by a fancy rule or a dash. All this to little purpose. People normally do not bother to read beyond the main heading.

Single deck campaigners argue that the modern reader scans the headlines and expects to be able to take in their message almost at a glance. From the headline he wants a signpost and not a gazetteer. Single deck headline provides this. For single-column items, two or three lines are needed to write an effective headline. When the story goes beyond three columns often a single line is enough. There is really no need for multi-deck headlines anywhere. Single deck can meet any situation. Its weight and style can be varied enormously. However, in most newspapers one to two top stories on a page are multi-deck. One should not go beyond three decks even in such stories.

A deck should not be confused with a strapline—the subordinate line above the headline, usually one line in smaller type. It is also called an eyebrow or kicker. It is more useful than the traditional deck. The common use is as a departmental label business news, etc. It can be set left on a set left or centred head or it can be centred on a centred head. It can also be used to give a point or detail from the main story, or it can set the scene.

In terms of modern headline pattern one must remember that strapline should not be written full out. It should not compete with the main heading in any way, typographically or verbally.

Letter Form : Capitals of the body type were used in the early headlines. Then there were capitals produced by display founts. Today the range of distinctive headline faces gives us freedom to put headlines in lower-case. This is done for several reasons. Lower case letters are easy to read and therefore the readability of a headline improves when set in lower-case. We read by recognising the shapes of words and groups of words rather than individual letters and there is greater variety of word silhouette in lower case. Words in capitals have distinctive lengths but not shapes. Lower case words are distinguished by their ascenders and descenders.

Another factor involved in the better readability of lower-case is the fact that we have grown used to reading lower-case because it is the commonest style in all reading material. Headlines in roman capitals are difficult to read than headlines in roman lower case. But roman caps are easier when compared with italic caps. All headings in caps need extra spacing between the lines and consume more newsprint space. Lower case headings are more economical in space since the ascenders and descenders create their own white space within the face of the type. Caps are static and formal while ascenders and descenders in lower-case give the impression of life and movement, and therefore are better for conveying news. Moreover, one can say more in a given space with lower case headlines than headlines in caps.

Lower case headline means that all letters are lower case except the initial letter of the first words and any proper names. Many papers capitalise the first letter of each word and still others capitalise prepositions if they begin a line but not otherwise. But the lower case style is superior to all caps and to initial cappings on the ground of legibility and economy. More and more newspapers are switching to lower case headlines. However, newspapers can have an effective mixture of capitals and lower case heading while the staple headline remains in lower case. Thus, the deck can be in caps and the subsidiary deck in lower case.

Spread and Arrangement : The first headlines were single column. Now they can be spread over all the columns in the newspaper. Newspapers today use the opportunities for display by mixing single column and multi-column headlines depending on the importance of the news.

Banner headline (covering all the columns) should not be in lower case because lower case letters across such a wide measure look straggly. Moreover, headlines should be crisp and lower case headlines will be unduly wordy.

There is a wide range of possibilities regarding

arrangements of headline. A newspaper may standardise on one form, such as the centred head, or it can mix them between headlines. But much depends on the skill of the page planners and the ideas they try to communicate.

The basic typographic arrangements are flush left, centred, stepped, flush right and hanging indention.

Flush Left : Many newspapers have switched to this style. The flush left heading has one or more lines which are set flush to the left. This should not touch the column rule. The flush left headlines look better when each line is indented on the column rule leaving 6 points or half an em space on an II em column.

Centred : In this type of arrangement each line of headline type is centred on the white of the column. The well-constructed, centred heading, whether of a multi-line or a multi-deck has its own symmetry and it is neatly framed in white.

The patterns created by this need slightly more attention than the patterns the flush left heading creates, but neither needs as much attention as some other patterns.

If one is writing multi-deck headlines they should be centred where they look best. The common double column headline is a single deck of two lines with centred headings. The second line should always be shorter than the first at least by two units. One should never try to write headlines in tight caps. They need more white around themselves for legibility.

Stepped : In this arrangement the first line is set flush left and the last flush right and the middle lines centred. Each line has to be about the same length, and they look like steps. To achieve a smooth step requires great care in headline writing. This style is discouraged by modern experts of readability. However, the greatest difficulty is that the stepped style depends too much on a precise count and any failure can lead to ugly results.

Flush Right : Each line is pushed against the right-hand margin to create a stepped effect on the left. It has even more limited application than the stepped headline. It may be occasional variant in a paper but it cannot be recommended as a regular style. It is slow to set and difficult to read.

Hanging Indention : The first line is set full out and the others indented, usually to the left. It cannot be a regular style but can be used as an occasional variant.

Quotes : The old school considered that quotes and dashes were full letters. The new school thinks it is an ugly habit. No headline should need double quotes. Only single quotes should do. With flush left headings the flush line should be the initial letter of each line—not the quote. The quote should be left to hang in the white.

Writing Headlines : Writing headlines involves half the skill of a good deskman. The difficulty in writing headlines is in conveying in a few attractive words the essence of a complicated set of facts. In half a dozen words the headline has to inform the reader what the story contains.

The headline gives emphasis on a few words in bold types. Hence every word should be weighed. Accuracy, intelligibility and vigour are the requirements and any newspaper which is careless with its headlines is careless about its own purpose and vitality. Wordy and vague headlines leave a newspaper reader confused and irritate him. Where every headline goes to the print with precision or wit, the whole newspaper comes alive.

Headline writing is art and craft at the same time. The art is in imagination and vocabulary and the craft lies in accuracy of content, attractiveness of appearance and practicality.

Counting the Units : A headline must fit in the space available to it. A headline with too many letters to be accommodated in the width and type required is called a "bouncer". It bounces back to the desk from the printer's room and wastes time at various levels. The deskman should always write a headline which should fit. But if there is a superb headline which will not fit in the headline scheme, the scheme can be changed to fit it. A chief-sub may consider this if the merit of the headline so demands.

A sub-editor counts the units in the words he writes for a headline. These units must not exceed the number of units allowed by the size of the type, its style and the number of columns the headline is being allowed to run.

The unit count system begins by giving a unit value to every letter and figure in the alphabet. It is based on a count of one for most letters with adjustments for thinner or fatter letters, and for capitals when they are mixed with lower-case letters. While m and w are counted as ½ units; *i*, *l*, *f* and *t* are counted ½ unit. Other letters are counted as one unit. Where capitals and numerals occur in a headline which is otherwise in lower case, allowance must be made for the extra space the capital letter or numerals will take compared with the lower-case letter. In a headline set u/lc (upper and lower case), count any ordinary capital letter or numeral as an extra ½ unit, that is, ½ units. Exceptions are: *M* and W which should be counted as two units when in caps and *I* and *J* and numeral 1 should be counted as one unit.

If the headline is in all caps the letters M and W should be counted as ½ unit while *I* and numeral 1 should be counted as ½ unit. Other letters and numerals will be one unit. The space between the words is counted by some experienced sub-editors as ½ unit, while others insist that the space should be counted as full unit. It is better to count it as full unit as if it is in excess it is on the right side and it also simplifies the count.

How does one know the number of units available? In newspapers there is always a list of headline types composed and pasted somewhere for ready reference. It may be available in the style sheet or style book.

If it is not available then the sub-editor should prepare a unit count card which gives the various counts at a glance. Unit count card can be prepared from the type schedule or by counting headlines as published in the newspaper for each style, size and spread. Count a dozen representatives of each headline and average the unit count obtained. Working in this way from published examples the deskman can write headings that fit without the need to count them. Experienced sub-editors resort to a unit count only in case of doubt.

Language : But the real art in headline writing is in using the language to sum up the news item and attract the attention of the reader. Before writing the headline the sub-editor must read the copy carefully and decide on the basic news point. The sub-editor must think hard about the single element in the story which makes it worth its space in the paper. When he finds one or more such points he should write them on a piece of paper.

Some sub-editors prepare to write a headline first and sub the copy later. Their argument is that it concentrates the mind on the subject of the copy and becomes the test for intro. If the basic news point is not in the intro it has to be re-written. So, while the sub-editor tries to look for basic news point for headline he is also evaluating the work of the reporter. However, in many cases headline has to be given later, after a first few takes are composed. But even in such a situation the sub-editor must write down the basic news sentence. Often when edited this basic news sentence yields a good headline.

However, the headline writer should always be cautious about the meaning of the words when they are written in different lines of the same headline. There are a few rules. Never split a hyphenated word, look for another way of saying the same thing without using a hyphen at all; never split compound verbs or compound nouns between lines.

A sub-editor must pretest the headline on himself. He must read it to himself and at the end of each line think if it means what he wants to say. If there is any doubt or awkwardness he must re-write the headline.

When multi-deck headlines are used, there is no point in repeating the same information in several decks. Only the first deck should be completely self-contained. Once the first deck has declared the subject area, other decks can take it for granted and use the space to supplement and elaborate. The first deck should have the most important news point. The second deck may elaborate this with a significant detail without repeating any word or it may add a further newspoint. Repetition of a word should be avoided but in no case should it be replaced by a difficult or confusing word. In that case the general Rule is to repeat rather than to confuse. Overline, if it is there, should elaborate or supplement the main deck.

Accuracy and impartiality are the basic requirements of a good headline. A news headline expresses the news and not the views of the sub-editor who is writing it. Care should be taken to write headlines of political stories. They should not look as if the paper is supporting some political party's viewpoint while in fact it is just reporting the viewpoint. To avoid such a situation one may use quotes or name the person or party in the main deck. The headline writer must put his personal views aside. He must remember that his job is to reflect as accurately as possible the content of the story.

Quotes are one of the devices for dealing with strong opinions in headlining speeches or political party resolutions. One may put the name of the speaker or party in the headline. Headlines entirely in quotes are usually weak and should always be avoided. It is better to use single quotes for the part of the headline which really needs them. When a headline is in decks often the attribution is given in the second deck. It is a bad practice. A headline with opinion and without quotes cannot be made acceptable by putting an attribution in the second deck. Attributions must be contained in the same deck as assertions, otherwise the statement in the first deck seems to have the authority of the newspaper for it.

But there should be no quotes when the opinion is obviously of the paper or the critic or columnist. It is unnecessary and may mean that the critic or columnist has relayed gossip. Another word of caution is that the people in the news, particularly in crime stories should not be identified by race; colour, religion or nationality unless such identifications are pertinent in the news context. It is wrong to indulge in puns when the subject is death, injury or religion. Funny headlines should not be given for serious events. The sub-editor should always check whether the meaning of the headline is the same as the content of the story. Normally it is the duty of the chief-sub to check the work of subs as far as copy editing and headlining is concerned. He must also keep all these considerations in the mind, for he is again a person on whom the headline and the copy is pretested for clarity of language and meaning.

Strong Verbs : There should always be a verb in the headline. News is activity and verbs bring activity and life to a headline. In a normal headline there should be no room for adjectives. Its colour and spice must come from a rich verb. One should avoid using parts of weak verb 'to be' or 'to have' as the main verb in a headline. The verbs 'to be' or 'to have' are not needed even as auxiliaries. For example "Sobhraj arrested" is better than "Sobhraj is arrested". There are occasions when the verb 'to be' should be omitted even though this seems to leave the headline without a verb. This verb is better when implied. Its physical presence in the headline makes it weak. Passive voice has been a major culprit in headline writing. A verb should be used in active voice as far as possible. At least before using the passive voice the sub-editor should himself try the active voice and should explain to himself the reason for not using the active voice. Passive voice normally breeds extra words and burdens a headline. Usually, rejecting a passive voice construction can lead to a more vivid headline. However, care should be taken to see that the main news point is as close to the beginning of headline as possible.

The headlines have been using the present tense to describe events that have already happened. The arguments in support of this phenomenon is that the present tense is active, it puts the reader in the middle of the action and gives him a feeling of participation. The event described in present tense in the headline may be past, but it is the recent past and the reader is learning about it now. He also understands the convention and will imply that in the present tense his morning newspaper's headline is giving the news of yesterday. 'Yesterday' is almost never justified in a morning newspaper headline because in that case almost all items could have yesterday in the headline. The reader takes for granted that it was yesterday unless it is otherwise specified.

There is an added advantage in using the present tense. It is invariably shorter. It gives the feel of recency to the news below the headline.

Subject is an essential part of a sentence like the verb and headline is really a truncated, but still meaningful, sentence that the reader understands. It should be in the headline either as such or as understood. It may be possible to write a headline without a subject in many circumstances but one should remember a headline with a subject tells more about the story than one without it. The rule regarding the use of subject in a headline is to give the name if it is well known or the title if he is not well known. One must headline a name in case of obituary even if a person is not so well known.

The weakest form of subject in headline is 'he' or 'she'. It is not an identification. But it will be at times good to use 'he' or 'she' headline on a human interest story with a picture of the subject.

'Man' or 'woman' are weak identifications of subject but at times they are inevitable. 'Wife, husband, father, mother' are better because they narrow the field. But they should not be taken as another name for man or woman. 'Husband banned at club' will suggest that he cannot go while wife is allowed.

Thus it is better to be more specific about the subject but it should be ensured that there is no distortion. Don't say "child" in head, line if the child is not yet two. Better use 'baby' or say boy or girl and give the age.

Headlines should be as specific as possible not only in identification of the subject but also in other matters as well. One should be specific about the main newspoint and a headline should tell as much as possible. It does not however mean that 'where' of the story should always be included. One should, test by examining the headline whether the addition of a place name adds significance. It is sufficient to say 'Barnala condemns terrorism in a headline and it need not be 'Barnala condemned terrorism at a Chandigarh press conference'. Further place name comes as the first thing after the headline, as a part of dateline. But in stories where place is important it must be there in the headline. For example, 'Earthquake rocks Simla'. The language of a headline should be positive. Some stories must be negative but the headline writer should avoid using 'no' or 'not' and try to express the same thing in different words. Short and simple words should be used for longer ones. For example, talks can be used for 'negotiations' and 'goods' for 'commodities'.

A headline should express a single thought to ensure clarity. It is difficult to communicate a single idea in limited space; if more than one idea is involved it becomes almost impossible. Therefore the most important idea or thought or event should be identified to be put in the headline. The deskman has to decide what the news really is and then he should express it with verbs and nouns using positive, simple and short words. This is the rule. If the circumstances need the rule can be broken but the sub-editor should know that he is breaking a rule and should be careful about clarity and content of the headline.

Typography : The history of typography has shown that the type which is easy to read is better than any fancy type and the Italian humanist lettering now called Roman ousted

Caxton's Germanic Gothic in England and everywhere else because people found it easier to read.

Types bear many eighteenth century names of pioneers who cut type. William Caxton of London cut his famous type in 1720. John Baskerville of Birmingham and Giambattista Bodoni made his fame from 1786 in the printing office of the Duke of Parma. But these types were originally designed as small-sized types for books. When the type manufacturers had to meet the demand for display faces for posters, shops, advertisement and newspapers, they produced strengthened versions of the book faces and later wholly new designs of their own.

Though there is today a vast range of display type, a newspaper must select from a limited range. Speed of production requires that headline type in general use in the newspaper shall come as metal from key boarded machines of linotype and intertype or the semi-mechanized Ludlow system, or as film set characters from these and other manufacturers. An attractive hand set type from a founder can only be used for larger sizes at wide measure when hand-setting will be as fast as machine because the type setter will be setting just a few characters.

In hot-metal process the Ludlow system of slug casting from hand-set matrices is most popular for headlines as the key board machines do not set above 36 pt in upper and lower case.

There is no need to leave extra-white between letters and words. It normally spoils the visual impact of the headline. Spacing in the headline should always be judged visually. If it looks wrong it is wrong without any doubt.

Use of underscoring, bucket, hood or curtain and box should be avoided in headline particularly when it is spread over single or double column. It indicates failure to choose right type size and only therefore one needs column rules to separate this headline from the rest.

While using reverse block (a white letter on a black background) one should always choose an open bold face without fine serifs. Open sans or a slab serif is ideal.

Punctuations : Full point is not used in headlines. The last word is the end of a thought and therefore no need to put a full stop. When two thoughts are joined together in a deck (though one should avoid this) they should be separated by a colon. The use of semi-colon should be avoided for simplicity and typographic neatness for easy reading. Exclamation and question marks should be rarely used. Comma should be used to separate clauses and sometimes used to indicate the omission of 'and'. While using comma, care should be taken to ensure the right meaning. Quotation marks are used to indicate external authority for the statement and also to indicate doubt about an assertion.

New Technology of Type Setting : For many years the only kind of type setting was that done by hand and therefore the production of newspapers was necessarily slow. The invention and adoption of line-casting type-setting machines 'linotypes' enabled publishers to greatly speed up the production of newspapers. The Linotype continued to be the most widely used technique of setting type until about 1966 when a number of typesetting inventions began to be accepted and adopted by many newspapers throughout the world. The type is now set photographically and with the aid of computers and some related inventions revolutionised the speed of newspaper production. The video display terminal (VDT) allows the reporter to not only type his original story and have the words show up on video display screen, but he can also correct and edit that story without touching a piece of paper and operate the photo typesetter on a push of button.

The optical character reader (OCR) enables the reporter to type his story on a special electric type-writer, edit it on the same machine and then feed his written story to the OCR to 'read' the words on the paper and operate the photo typesetter subsequently. Hand-set and machine-set type were best adopted to letter press printing which consists of printing from raised letters, directly on paper. Photo typesetting is better with offset printing method in which after a, printing plate is coated with ink and water it first prints on a rubber sheet (called a blanket) and then from the blanket onto paper.

Photoprints, when used with offset, are pasted directly on a page format along with screened pictures. Then the entire page is photographed as a single entity, converted into a negative and finally into a printing plate. The basic photo type setting technique consists of placing a film negative of each letter in a sentence in front of a light source and then shining light through the negative onto light-sensitive photographic paper. The result is a picture of letters assembled into lines. Once enough lines have been set photographically they can be pasted on to a page form, photographed and converted into a printing plate.

The first generation of photo typesetters were really a modification of hot typesetting machines where each letter of the alphabet was first made in the form of a mould (called a mat). Hot lead was poured into the moulds thereby producing a line of metal type. These mats were modified by replacing the moulds with a film negative of each letter. After the first line was set, the photographic paper would be advanced ready to receive a new line of letters. Thus, the first generation photo typesetters were really photo-mechanical in nature and therefore relatively slow. The fastest could set twenty lines a minute depending upon the versatility of the operator.

The second generation of photo typesetters could set type faster and the method of photographing the letters was different. At least four different modes of negatives were developed by various competitors. All the letters of the alphabet, numbers and punctuation marks were prepared on a single film negative surface such as a disc, a drum, a film strip or a rectangular grid. It was possible to move these letters more quickly than older machines. This generation increased the speed of setting to about 150 lines a minute.

The third generation photo typesetting machines are almost totally electronic. They use a cathode ray tube (CRT) as a scanning device and throw light through a lens and then through each of the letters in a sentence on the negative surface. A photoelectric cell behind the negative picks up the light and delivers it to another cathode ray tube which eventually prints the letters originally scanned on photographic paper. This third generation typesetter can set upto 500 lines a minute.

The fourth generation typesetter has also emerged. The distinguished feature of this typesetter is that it uses laser beam in the setting process and has no photographic negative to shine light through. Instead a laser beam generates letters from a memory control, electronically through a series of strokes and builds letters somewhat like that of CRT machine but without a master negative. Fonts of type are stored in the memory unit of this machine and can be called forth by pressing a button. This machine can set 1000 lines per minute. It is also possible to generate line art and halftones in the laser typesetters. This will enable the user to make up all of the elements of a page on a video display tube. When the page is made up, it may be printed on photographic paper ready for conversion to an offset printing plate.

Most photo typesetters installed in newspaper plants are operated in conjunction with either a VDT or an OCR in addition to a computer. Assembly of these various operating machines wired to each other is called a "system".

In this system the reporter types copy on VDT keyboard. He then corrects and edits it. When he is satisfied he sends the story to computer for storage. Other stories are also in storage. Sub-editor or chief sub can retrieve it from the storage for checking and can do editing using the VDT. He can also write headlines, specifying the kind of type, size and width and return the story to computer for storage. If he feels he should edit it fully or rewrite it he can have it printed on paper at 360 lines a minute speed. Then he can edit it on paper and later on VDT and return it to computer for storage.

When the news editor is reading the dummy page, he can ask the computer to print all sluglines on VDT and decide what stories he wants. After this decision he calls up each story on VDT, determines its length and begins to dummy the page. After this he presses a button and sends body copy and headlines to be set on a photo typesetter which delivers a photoprint. Story now goes to the printer for paste up.

Photo-editing : Good pictures speak for themselves. While making selection of news pictures, the prime consideration should be the context in which the picture is being used. The picture should have information related to the story with which it is to be used.

A good news photograph should reflect the feelings and responses of the people photographed. Even routine events yield good photographs if the people are caught by the camera in action and their feelings and emotions are expressed on the faces. Animation is one of the prime quality of a good news photograph. A photograph should reflect the mood of the moment. Even when selecting from file pictures care should be taken to select a photograph which depicts the right mood. When a person is sacked a picture depicting him in a happy mood will be a misfit. Like words, pictures also have meaning. There are occasions when symbolism could be effective to impart meaning. Sometimes comparison provides meaning to pictures.

Looking at certain photographs one is surprised what little the eye can see when the event is taking place. Action photographs particularly come in this category. In sports events and cultural events, action photographs depicting the climax of a movement if captured by camera becomes an exciting picture.

A photographer must reach a scheduled event a few minutes before the time and look for a key moment while shooting. A camera is very much similar to the notebook of a trained reporter. It should catch the key moments of the event that are most relevant to the news event. A news photographer should have news sense and it should be sharpened by selection of his most newsy pictures by the photo-editor.

Only a photographer with a keen news sense will be able to catch decisive moments of history with his camera. In every event there is sequence of action of which only a few moments are at the climax and only one of them is really decisive. The nearer the photograph is to that moment, the better news photograph it is. The photograph, once selected, has to be edited for size, shape and story content. The basic determining factor is the story content because it determines the size and shape of the photograph or whether the photograph should be used at all.

It is debated whether a photograph should be cropped. Many photographers of international repute argue that a good photograph should never undergo cropping. But it may be true of only excellent news photographs capturing decisive moments. Most of the photographs can be improved by cropping. While cropping, the emphasis should be on the story and what is in the picture. One may remove irrelevant portion of a picture and emphasis could be added to the relevant portion of the picture. The shape of the picture is also decided by the story content.

While determining the size of a picture, emphasis should be on legibility and impact. It is pointless to give a photograph if it is printed so small that the relevant detail is lost. Legibility determines the minimum size of the picture and maximum has to be determined by the availability of space, competition from other news pictures or stories. It should also be seen whether giving a bigger size justifies the expense of space by increase in the impact. Space should be used with discrimination to ensure that the photograph which really needs it should get it.

Cropping is a creative job. Looking at the above factors

one has to identify the key image in the photograph and enlarge it to give maximum information or impact. The words with the picture should match. The reader must be told what, where, when and why of the photograph. If explanation improves the understanding of the key factor it should be given.

Design and Layout : It is essential to realise that newspaper design is part of journalism. It is not decoration but communication. Newspaper communicates news and ideas and design is an integral part of the process. A sub-editor begins with a blank sheet of newsprint and wants to communicate several ideas and the day's news. It is the function of newspaper design to present that mosaic in an organised and comprehensive way by using text type, display type, photograph, line work, white space and a sequence of pages in the most fitting combination.

Newspaper design has to care for the audience too. Researchers find out the readership habits and give it due consideration. For example, the broadsheet format of a serious newspaper will not suit a metropolitan evening daily which is produced for commuters on crowded trains or buses. Ideal format for such a newspaper will be tabloid for ease in handling. Front and back page of such a newspaper should have the widest possible range of appeal. There are other considerations of utility. A family newspaper should not publish women's column on sports page or on the other side of the sports page. Magazine sections are separate from news sections of the newspaper. Such elementary considerations form the framework of newspaper design.

There is an important role in newspapers for artists and designers but they must be closely involved with journalists and journalism. They must share the idea of communication and the audience. A designer should not think that a day's news can fit in his preconceived patterns. The design cannot be left to the artist alone. If he produces something which is more useful in communication of an idea it should be used.

Any refinement which interferes with function should not be allowed. There should be a balance between form and function where function is the priority. There is need for continuous dialogue between journalist, designer and the researcher to achieve a better balance between the form and function of newspaper design.

Organising the Content : Editorial content can be divided into two groups : (i) *Unpredictable-Spot* news in words and pictures which can be divided into local, national, foreign, and so on. (ii) *Predictable:* Stock-market prices, weather forecast, TV and radio programmes, film, art criticism, letters to editor, editorial, crossword puzzles, bridge column etc.

Predictable content should be in predictable positions. Television and radio programmes, share prices, weather, etc., should be anchored in the same place day after day.

When the unpredictable news is organised in departments (foreign, sport, business etc.) these should appear in approximately the same position in the newspaper every day. The space will vary according to the news and the size of the paper but the page should not be changed from day to day. Page sequence should be logical and consideration of reader habits should determine it. For example, right and side pages particularly at the beginning of the newspaper get more reader attention so they should have material in which maximum readership is interested.

The Front Page : It is the most important page of a newspaper. It induces the reader to pick up the paper and read it. It establishes the identity and character of the paper and also introduces freshness by its display and content. According to function visualised for the front page it could be ......

Signal and Text Front Page : It is a typical modern front page where a selection of the most important news items is signalled by headlining and positioning on a clear scale of priorities and supported with text. Less important items go to inside pages. Most broadsheet newspapers follow this style with exceptions like *Punjab Kesari, Jagbani, Akali Patrika.* Efforts should be made to give the full text of an item on the front page. If the text does turn to another page it may be because of more items that deserve the signal treatment on front page.

Poster Front Page : It contains all the important news items on front page just one or two paragraphs of each indicating the page on which details appear. Even as late as 1965 designers recommended this type for *The Times,* London. However, it was not accepted. Many newspapers use variations and combinations of the two styles. Part of front page of signal and text front page can be used everyday to encapsulate the main news (and features) presented inside. *The Times of India* uses this combination type front page.

Feature Front Page : *Punjab Kesari, Jagbani* and *Akali Patrika* give features on front page. Front page has normally nothing to do with news in these newspapers. This kind of front page is established in Punjab and it was regarded that change in this style may lead to fall in circulation. However, *Ajit* has changed from feature front page to signal-and-text front page and the circulation actually did not go down but has increased.

Page Layout : Make-up or layout of the page is determined by the format of the page-the number of columns in which the page is divided.

Eight columns of 11 or 11½ picas each is the standard for broadsheets partly dictated by advertising standards of 11 picas. Layouts can vary in this format and number of display positions are available if the nature of the newspaper is serious.

However, there are nine or ten column papers. This format provides excess of display portion. It is difficult to manage typography and make such a page attractive. Readability of such papers is poor.

There is a 7½ column format also. The standard 11 picas measure is retained for six columns and the seventh column is equal to 1½ and the remaining half column is distributed as white space in the gutters. Many papers use this format which is attractive and convenient and also provides variety.

Six-column is regarded 'optimum format' because it takes optimum text line for easy reading (about 15 picas). However, the display positions are less than the eight-column pages. In this format long stories can be handled with extra ease.

Five column format is also used by some papers. Some papers use this 14. 6 picas grid for editorials or long analytical articles requiring long text.

For tabloids five and four column layouts are convenient and widely used. However, this format may vary from page to page and even on the same page. The varying format is most justified when it signals a distinct change of content. For example, editorial comment from general news content. The column grid is part of the basic format of the paper and is more or less a fixed element of newspaper design. Layout or make up occurs in this format.

Layout means arrangement of headlines, text, artwork and white space on a page or pages. Layout could be *static* or *dynamic*. If one can predict the layout of tomorrow's page today because it has been similar, with minor variations day after day, the layout is called static. In such a layout one can predict that the first lead story will be on say the left hand side. There will be pictures and then there will be the second lead. There will be a third major story below the picture. *The Times of India* and *Statesman* provide good examples of such layout.

But layout is dynamic when no body can predict what it will be the lead may be on left or right and if there is a striking picture, headlines will be submerged to make room for it. Here the designer is attempting to respond dynamically to the news. *The Telegraph* and *Jansatta* are good examples.

Layout, whether static or dynamic, could be modular or irregular. Modular layout breaks the page into a series of rectangles-headline and related text form a four sided rectangular unit.

Irregular layout breaks the page into a series of interlocking shapes. Most or all headlines themselves are irregular in shape and most or all headline-text units on a page form irregular shapes.

Vertical vs Horizontal : Vertical layout gives the simplest page organisation. Headlines are set in the width of basic single-column grid and the text runs single column. This oldest layout style has limited range of news value expression. Though it is visually depressing, maximum number of stories can be given above the fold.

When headlines side by side are the same size and style the result is called 'tombstoning'. This is a major problem of vertical layout. It can be overcome with alteration of colour along the horizontal line. Colour here means blacks, greys and white and with modern display type, adjacent heads can be varied to express different news values or tone. The headings can be set left in the white to avoid clash of headlines.

Another way is to vary the width of the headline grid. For example, a two column head is used to express more important news. The width of text setting can also vary to avoid monotony of tombstoning.

Horizontal Layout : This is another, simple layout but with more capacity for emphasis. It is modular with text squared up under multi-columns heads to create a horizontal unit. Page is then made up of a series of these units lying flat on each other. In this layout a long story seems shorter. Complete stories can be read with page folded at the natural midpage fold and without the reader having to shuffle the paper up and down, headlines are separated from each other by text and thus each headline retains its emphasis. In horizontal layout full use of the width of the page is possible for display. However, there are only a few stories above the midfold which can be seen at retail outlets.

Quadrant Layout : It envisages the page as four separate sections divided by a line at the fold and a line down the middle of the page. Each unit has a strong display item consisting of either multi-column headlines and picture or panel. This formula reminds one that there is more to a page than its top half. But this formula, if followed with geometric rigidity, may lead to display of news item disproportionate to news value.

Diagonal Layout : Here the designer places headlines along two imaginary diagonal lines, which divide the page and cross each other. It reminds that headlines can be distributed anywhere on the paper. But it is difficult to coordinate display with the news values.

Frame Layout : The columns one and eight on an eight column paper should be solid text so that beneath the paper's title and eight-column banner heads the frame, the content of the page. It is more a gimmick than a formula for layout. After all, newspaper page is not a picture to be framed and put on the wall.

Brace Layout : In brace layout headlines are arranged in steps so that the one higher in the page is supported by another running parallel. In such a layout the headlines compete for attention with each other and lose emphasis. It also forces text away from the headline. Headlines can actually stand on their own. They do not need each other's support as is provided in this type of layout.

Circus Layout : In circus layout, emphasis is on variety contrast and movement, but not on order or news value. There are many points of attraction, not necessarily related to news values. The reader is to be distracted and entertained. The mast head of the paper may appear in any position above the fold.

Symmetrical Layout : This layout attempts to produce an equal balance of weight around an axis, classically the optical centre of the page. Each side of the optical centre should be a mirror image of the other. Optical centre, the pivotal point, is a point one-third of the distance from the top where the horizontal forces are in equilibrium with the vertical forces and is the point of perfect balance.

Symmetrical layout need not be static. The essence of axial symmetry is balance at the centre and this can be achieved in dynamic layout.

Symmetrical layout has a powerful appeal for serious papers as it appears to organise the heterogeneous content rationally and satisfies the human mind's natural demand for balance. It is of little use to the newspapers that thrive on excitement. Even in serious newspapers, the symmetrical balance threatens display in relation to news values. It is also difficult to produce a perfectly symmetrical page, particularly a news page. Further, perfect balance may be boring also.

Asymmetrical Layout : This layout is dynamic and excludes any axial symmetry, any predetermined point of balance. Here 'artistic balance' or 'informal balance' is achieved by a balance of unequal forces at unequal distances from the centre.

Asymmetrical layouts have a balance which is subtle. It enables the page to satisfy our natural desire for order, organisation and balance while providing emphasis and movement. Balance is there but it is not a mechanical balance and it does not force the news to conform to set pattern. This assists functional relationship of content and display.

The newspaper design and layout must be functional. There should be organisation and rational coordination of heterogeneous material but the news values should get priority in deciding the display. It should give emphasis to the most important news to attract the reader. There should be order, but the prime importance should be given to news value.

6

Different Levels of Job

A unified system for bibliographical references is described. The suggestions, which are in the main compatible with ISO DIS 690, allow the name/date (Harvard), the numeric-alphabetic or the sequential numeric system to be used for references in scientific books and serials; an optional dual-access system is also outlined. The 'master typescript' system described allows numbers to be substituted for names/ dates in the text when a paper is submitted to a publication that uses a numeric system. In reference lists, depending on what the author's target publication requires, references must be arranged either alphabetically or sequentially, in the order of their citation in the text. In all lists, whether alphabetic or sequential, references should contain the same elements, arranged in the same order, as follows:

> Able BC, Cain A D, Adam E, Eve A 1976 Bark thickness in apple trees. Tree J 12:90-99

Extra punctuation marks can be added if required. Authors may leave further capitalization and italicization to be marked by editors/ copy-editors. Titles of articles should be included; they can be easily deleted if the publication does not require them. Journal titles should be given either in full or abbreviated in accordance with the standards blamed in this document.

The suggestions made here form a two-part system dealing with the citation and arrangement of bibliographic references in scientific serials and monographs. The proposals are addressed to authors, typists, editors and copy-editors, and will also interest publishers and printers. The 'master typescript' method explained here can be easily adapted for publications using either the name/date or one of two main numeric systems for references (sequential-numeric and numeric-alphabetic). The standard layout suggested for references in reference lists can be used for all three systems. If there are differences between the suggestions in this document and an editor's 'Instructions to authors', the latter must lake precedence in the final manuscript submitted.

The purpose of citations (in the text) and references (in the list) is the identification and retrieve of documents (usually an article or a monograph). The connection between citation and reference is made either by repetition of the author's name and the year of the publication cited, or by repetition of a reference of the author's name and the year of the publication cited, or by repetition of a reference number. The two most common systems that use numbers assign them either in the sequence in which the references appear in the text or by numbering references in an alphabetic list.

These suggestions are similar to the recommendations made in the draft International Standard (ISO DIS 690) on bibliographic references, except that in the system described here initials are used instead of fore names, punctuation marks are kept to a minimum, ISSNs and ISBN are not mentioned, and (for monographs) the publisher's name precedes the place of publication. The theme of these suggestions is uniformity. They are put forward as a compromise between the best of the innumerable systems that at present take up so much time when manuscripts are being prepared for publication.

The master typescript method is based on two premises: first that it is much easier to convert the text from the name/date to one of the numeric systems than vice versa, and secondly that many authors use the name/date system in preparing the early drafts of their papers.

(***Note:*** Authors who are sure that their papers will be accepted by a publication using a numeric system do not need to use the master typescript method but they should follow the suggestions made here in sections 3 and 4).

The principal features of these suggestions are:

(1) a master typescript method is described that allows easy conversion of name/date citations to numeric citations;

(2) reference lists should be arranged according to the system (numeric or alphabetic) required by the author's first target journal;

(3) references should always be made up of the same elements, arranged in the same order;

(4) references should be styled with a maximum of informational and should conform as closely as possible with the conventions of spelling and punctuation of ordinary text in the language concerned. However, for easier transformation between reference systems, punctuation is here kept to a minimum.

(5) other than as shown in the examples, capitalization and italicization of elements in references need not be indicated by authors but may be left for editors or copy-editors to specify according to each publication's typographical style;

(6) an optional dual-access system is described that not only provides readers with a bibliography but also allows them to refer back from the reference list to find where the reference is cited in the text, using the reference list as an author index.

If a master typescript is prepared according to these recommendations, the author can-with a minimum of effort-alter copies of the master so that they conform to the requirements of individual serials or books, as follows:

(a) if the information contained in certain elements (e.g. titles of articles) that are listed here as standard parts of a reference is not wanted in a particular publication, the unwanted elements are deleted before the final typescript is submitted. If punctuation additional to that recommended in this document is required by the publication, punctuation marks are added as necessary.

(b) If the numeric-alphabetic system is required in the target publication, the list is numbered and numbers are substituted for the citations originally typed in parentheses in the text.

(c) If the sequential-numeric system is required in the target publication, the list is rearranged/retyped in order of citation (in practice if the first journal to which an author submits a paper uses sequential numbering, the references in the list should be typed in the order of their appearance in the text). Name and date citations in the text are then changed to the relevant numbers.

Principles and Rules

Citations in the Text : In the master typescript, citations should be in the name/date forms.

Jack & Smith (1977) report...

or

... as was recently reported (Jack & Smith 1977, Braun et all 1978)

If the target publication uses a numeric system, several spaces should be left after each citation in the text.

After conversion to a numeric system (1.5), names of cited authors will appear in the text only if they were originally cited outside parentheses:

Jack & Smith (1977) report that...

Becomes

Jack & Smith (22) report that ...

But

as was recently reported (Jack & Smith 1977)

becomes as was recently reported (22).

- For citations in the text that refer to three or more authors, the form Brown et al. should be used every time such citations are made, including the first.
- If citations refer to specific pages in books or in lengthy journal articles, those page numbers belong with the citations in the text, not in the reference list, and may be placed after the date. Reading is facilitated if the year or reference number is separated from the page number by adequate punctuation:

  (Smith 1977 p 302), or (Smith 1977: p 302).

  In a numeric system this would become:

  (22:p 302) or (ref. 22:p 302)

  Alternatively (and perhaps preferable where superior numbers are used), a new number may be assigned each time a different page of the same book or article is cited in the text; each such reference in the list then gives the specific page number as well as the other elements of the reference.
- Citations referring to communications which cannot be retrieved by readers do not belong in the reference list. If included at all, such communications should be described in the text as 'unpublished work' (not as 'in preparation') or as a 'personal communication' (not as a 'private communication') and the source should be included:

  ... as was found recently (J Smith, 1977, personal communication). or (for a meeting without published proceedings):

This project has produced significant results (M. Brown, unpublished paper 3rd Congr Psycho Eng, 25 November 1977).

- If a numeric system is required in the publication, appropriate numbers are substituted for the name/ date citations in the text of the master typescript.
- Where names/dates are used in the text, and if it is desirable for readers to be able to refer back from the reference list to the text, a dual-access system (About 1974) may be used. In this system, numbers are placed between names and dates in the text, with the numbers running consecutively through the text (as in the sequential-numeric system, but with each citations being assigned a new number, however many times a reference may be cited in the text):

  Jack & Smith' (1977) report...

  or

  ... as already described (Jack & Smith 1977)

  These numbers are then placed in parentheses at the end of each reference in the reference list in the way.

Reference Lists : Alphabetic lists. For Publications requiring alphabetic reference lists, entries should be arranged in strict alphabetic order, unless there are several citations of articles/ monographs by three or more different authors with the same first author References of this latter kind, where 'Brown et al' (for example) is followed by several dates in the text, should be arranged chronologically in the list, regardless of the number (above two) of authors and regardless of the alphabetical order of the names of authors other than the first (since the names of the other authors are not known when the text is being read). References arranged in this alphabetic-chronological way should be placed after papers by Brown or by Brown & X, as shown.

- Arrangement of entries referring to the same -first author (IUB-CEBJ 1973):

Citation in the Reference list

Brown & Green (1977)	Brown A 1977
Brown & Green (1976)	Brown, A, Green B 1976...
Brown & White (1975)	Brown A, White C 1975...
Brown et al (1974)	Brown A, White C, Green B 1974
Brown et al (1975)	Brown A, Black D, White C, Green B 75
Brown et al (1976)	Brown A, Black D, Green B 1976
Brown et al (1977a)	Brown A, White C, Green B 1977a Why wheels turn. Gen Eng 7:59-65
Brown et al (1977b)	Brown A, Green B, White C 1977b How wheels turn. Gen Eng. 8:10-15

- Authors' surnames should be given and alphabetized exactly as spelt, with prefixes, Mc and M' should not be alphabetized as Mac. Names beginning with prepositions such as de, De, van von, 0', etc. should be alphabetized under the first letter of the prefix. The term Fr or roman numerals may be added after initials. The important principle is conformity between the citation in the text and the entry in the reference list.
- Terms such as 'ibid.', 'idem', 'op.cit.' and 'loc.it.' should never be substituted for complete references in reference fists. In the text, if used at all, they should be used sparingly and with great caution. Later changes in the text can make such references misleading.
- If the numeric-alphabetic system is required, the alphabetically arranged references are first numbered: Adam E 1976... Adamson J 1975... The numbers are then substituted for the name/date citations in the text.
- If the dual-access system described in 1.6 is used, the numbers from the text are inserted in parentheses at the end of each reference in the reference list:

  Jack V F, Smith J 1977 Structure of seeds of Stellaria media

  (L.) Vill.J Bot 35:290-295 (1,5,149)

- Sequential-numeric lists
- If the sequential-numeric system is required, the name/date text citations are numbered sequentially in the order of citation in the text; the references in the list are numbered accordingly and the list is arranged so that the entries are in numerical -order, regardless of which letter of the alphabet the (first) author's name starts with. When a reference is cited more than once in the sequential system, either (a) the reference may retain the same number, thus breaking with the strict sequential principle, or (b) it may appear as many times in the list as it is cited in the text, each time numbered according to the sequence of citation. Before conversion or preparation of the typescript the author must consult the instructions to authors of the target publication to see how it handles multiple citation of a single reference.

References to Articles in Serials : References to articles in serials should take the following forms:

Jack V F 1977 The seeds of Stellaria media (L.) Vill. J Bot 35: 257-261

Abel B C, Cain A D, Adam E, Eve A 1976 bark thickness in apple trees Tree J 12:90-99

- This system uses the minimum punctuation necessary to present the information clearly. It also takes into consideration that punctuation marks can be added easily if the journal's style so requires, and that words and characters can be deleted more easily than they can be added. The references include the following features:

  Surnames and initials of all authors are inverted.

  The initials are paced to permit punctuation if required. A comma appears between the initials of one author and the surname of the next author.

  No ampersand or 'and' is needed between authors'

names but space should be left for its subsequent insertion, if required.

A stop is placed only at the end of titles of articles.

No elements are underlined.

- The date of publication is placed immediately after the authors' names. These two pieces of information are the most valuable in identifying of appraising a reference and are the key elements in locating a reference in a reference list when name/date citations are used.
- Titles of articles in serials should be given, as many readers consider this to be essential information. However, if the first target publication will not print them, the articles titles can easily be deleted or omitted.
- Serial titles should either be given in full, or be abbreviated in accordance with ISO 833, ANSI Z39.5), 1969), and BS4148 (1970, 1975) (these standards are compatible with each other) or with list (such as Index Medicus, BIOSIS List of Serials, etc.) based on the principles set out in those standards. One-word titles are never abbreviated.
- First and last pages of articles in serials and chapters in monographs should be given. This information tells readers the length of the article, i.e. whether it is a short note or letter or a full-length paper, and indicates how much photocopy is likely to cost.
- The issue number of a serial is redundant information unless each issue is paged separately; if issues are paged separately, the issue numbers should be inserted (in parentheses) immediately after the volume number:

  12. Jack V F 1967 Trees. Sci Am 17(3):38-47

  For newspapers or popular weeklies the full date of the issue may be given instead of the volume number

  Smith A 1974 Creating wealth. Times (Lond) 25 November 3

***References to Monographs* :** References to monograph should take the following basic forms:

- Monographs by one or more authors, without an editor:

  Jack V F 1977 Monograph of Stellaris media (L.) Vill. Pergamon, Oxford

  Zorba A, Quinn A 1976 Bone structure of early Cretans' 3rd edn. Elsevier/Excerpta Medica/North-Holland, Amsterdam

- Chapters or sections of edited monographs:

  Jack V F 1977 Seeds of Stellaria media (L.) Vill. In: Smith J (ed) Anatomy of Caryophyllaceae. Springer, Berlin, p 250-280

  or (preferred if there are references to several contributors to the same book):

  Jack V F 1977 Seeds of Stellaria media (L.) Vill. In: Smith (1977) p. 250-280

  Smith J (ed) 1977 Anatomy of Caryophyllaceae, Springer, Berlin

- Chapters in edited monographs forming apart of a series:

  Bull F, Friend A 1975 Jumping over the moon In: Jones M, Lloyd P (eds) Space travel. Galaxy Press, Houston (Soc Space Sci Symp 21) vol. 3:1-24

- The references is given in this chapter include the following features:

  Name(s) and initials of editor(s) are given as shown above. 'Editor'. 'editors', and 'edition', may be abbreviated as 'ed', 'eds', and 'edn', respectively.

  A stop is placed at the end of the chapter titles.

  The publisher's name, shortened if necessary, is placed before the place of publication. For publishers operating in several places, it is sufficient to given the name of the first place listed on the title page of the cited book as the publisher's address

Page numbers or volume and page numbers referred to, are placed after the place of publication.

No full stops used at the end of the entries.

No elements are underlined.

References : Abbott K M 1974 References-a new system used by CSIR. Scientiae 15:27-28.ANSI Z39.5 1969 Abbreviation of tides for periodicals, American National Standards Institute, New York

BIOSIS list of serials. BIOSIS/Biological Abstracts, Philadelphia

BS 4148 1970 The abbreviation of titles of periodicals.

Part 1. Principles. British standards Institution, London

BS 4148 1975 the abbreviation of titles of periodicals.

Part 2. Word abbreviation list. British Standards Institution, London

ELSE Working Group 1977 Recommendations on references. Earth Life Sci Ed 5:7-8

Index Medicus. US Dept of Health, Education and Welfare, Public Health

Service, National Institutes of Health, US Government Printing Office, Washington, DC

ISO DIS 690 Bibliographic references to monographs and serials

ISO 833 Documentation-International list of periodicals title word abbreviations

IUB-CEBJ 1973 The citation of bibliographic references in biochemical journals. Recommendations (1971). Biochem J 135:1-3 [and elsewhere]

This document evolved from discussions before, during and after an ELSE-Ciba Foundation Workshop on the consolidation and Adoption of a Rational System for References, held at the Ciba Foundation, London, on 25 November 1977. The Workshop, funded largely by the Ciba Foundation, was held in order that the ELSE Working Group's recommendations on references (1977) and the ensuing discussions and attempts at formulating generally acceptable guidelines could be discussed by a wider group. The participants in the Workshop represented the earth sciences, life sciences, chemistry and biochemistry, physics and engineering.

Rule for Publicity : This code is reproduced by kind permission of the editor of the British Medical Journal.

For disciplines other than medicine this code could be modified as necessary.

- The publication of advertisements has become a recognized function of medical journals, but any advertisement may be refused without explanation.
- The advertisements in a journal, like the text, are a source of information for readers. This information is provided by the advertiser, who is responsible for its accuracy; but care should be taken that no advertisement contravenes the principles set out below.
- Advertisements should not imply or promise benefit which, after due consideration and, if necessary, consultation with experts, appears highly improbably. Claim should be supported by trustworthy evidence.
- No therapeutic product should be advertised unless its essential constituents and their quantity in each dose, are disclosed to the editor of the journal. Methods of manufacture need not be disclosed.
- Advertisements should not impugn the dignity of the medical profession or offend against good taste or recognized standards of medical practice.
- Advertisements of drugs or appliances should not contain testimonials, anonymous or otherwise. This

does not exclude dated references to reputable medical journals, but such advertisements must not include misleading quotations from articles.

- Advertisements of books may contain quoted matter from reviews so long as 4 dated reference to the review is given, but not the name of the reviewer.
- Opinions expressed by contributors to medical journals must not be quoted in away that makes them look like editorial opinions.
- The distinction between the advertisement columns and the text should be kept so clear that no ordinary reader can mistake one for the other.
- Publication of an advertisement means that in the Editor's judgement it does not contain misleading statements: but such publication does not necessarily mean that the journal endorses the claims made, and such endorsement must not be implied in advertisements of the same product in the lay press.
- medical journals should not accept advertisements of products that are improperly advertised in the pay press or elsewhere.
- Advertisements should be considered on their own merits. An advertisement that is otherwise acceptable is not necessarily made unacceptable by the fact that the advertiser is putting forward improper claims for other products.
- disparaging references: no advertisement should be published which appears to bring discredit on the products of other manufacturers.

Reviews of Books : Length and form of review: 700-1000 words, typed double-spaced starting on the attached page.

Date by which review should be sent in: [date within two/four weeks of book being posted to reviewer]. If for any reason you cannot review the book by this date, please telephone the book review editor as soon as possible.

Fee: the editor regrets that no fee is payable for book reviews; the review copy, however, remains your property.

Anonymity: reviews in the journal are normally signed If you have a particular reason of remaining anonymous, please discuss this with the book review editor; if he agrees to anonymity, please mark your review accordingly.

Please note that the journal requires fair and balanced reviews. Even if your review is a negative one, please use temperate language in your evaluation of the arguments in the book and avoid attacking the authors/editors personally. There is no need to comment on the price of the book unless it is outstandingly expensive (or cheap): readers can judge for themselves, with the help of your evaluation, whether a book is worth what the publisher is charging for it. Paper-backs are not in themselves cheaper than hardbacks; when they cost less than a hardback book of the same length it is only because the publisher expects to sell a very large number of copies and can price the paper-back accordingly.

In your review, please:

- Describe the contents briefly.
- Indicate the intended readership.
- Evaluate the book first on its own terms, saying how well you think the authors/editors have achieved their stated aims. You may then want to criticise those aims and the way the subject has been handled, taking into account the following questions (where relevant), amongst others that may occur to you:

  Is the material well selected and well organized?

  Are the arguments clear and logically correct?

  Are the statements of fact accurate?

  Are the conclusions convincing, original and important for the discipline as a whole, or for the special topic of the book?

Where experimental work is discussed, is the experimental design satisfactory?

Is the style clear, concise and readable?

- Comment briefly on any or all of the following:

  the general appearance of the book,

  the legibility of the typeface,

  the incidence of typographical errors,

  the clarity of the illustrations,

  the accuracy, up-to-dateness and coverage of the reference and the usefulness of the index (if there is one).

- Please return the review (which should include your name and address).

Upliftment Stages

Very good reporters almost always get offers to become editors, sometimes early in-their careers. Some turn them down because they would rather stay in the front lines with their typewriters. This is for the reporter who didn't turn down the offer, or won't turn it down, when it comes. It reviews the editor's problems of designing and managing investigative reporting. It also should help the beginning investigative reporter understand the problems of the man he's working for.

Probing News : To develop an investigative program, the newspaper editor should consider adopting the following plan. It consists of nine steps:

1. Decide that you want an investigative tone in the local news report and that you are willing to accept the pressures this decision implies.
2. Carefully marshal the reasons for your decision and discuss them with the publisher, telling him you won't raise the budget or hire new people just yet.
3. Convey your investigative attitude to sub-editors and reporters. Reinforce it by asking challenging questions

and assigning reporters to make aggressive follow-ups on stories that have been treated superficially. Make it concrete by asking reporters and editors for lists of investigative ideas. Study, screen, and merge these ideas into a few attractive, feasible story ideas, then settle on one.

4. Pick the staff member who shows the best combination of investigative attributes, give him at least a week to study the feasibility of the story before reporting back directly to you.
5. If the reporter's study confirms the feasibility of the project, clear him of other duties so he can begin basic research. Set up a schedule of meetings, at least one a week, to review progress and discuss problems.
6. When the reporter believes he is ready for the key interview, evaluate his research and discuss the key interview plan with him.
7. After the interview, block out the time to do a "feet up" editing job, the kind Neale, Copple describes in Depth Reporting. This editing entails a single, clear-cut sentence of your purpose and thesis, a background to help the reader understand the circumstances surrounding the story, and interpretation. Interpretation is used here as a super definition of the why of the investigation. And the details of the investigation, the facts beneath the surface, and fitting the story into the reader's world. Make you hypothesis work or knock it down.
8. After you are sure the story is solid, let the publisher know it is coming. Be prepared to argue for it but don't try to slip by him if he is not used to high-risk, hard-nosed reporting. If he is not prepared for strong public reaction, it could cost you and the reporter your jobs.
9. A week after the story has run, get the staff together and discuss the story's impact. The way in which individuals respond will help identify other

investigative reporting prospects on the staff. The meeting will also help reinforce in staff members; minds your own commitment to quality journalism. Such commitment is a sine qua non for further development.

Of course, the whole project may blow up in your face at appoint from Step 2 to Step 9. If it does, you will have to decide what to do about it. You have to make things happen. You can't be half-hearted. If, for example you run a story about shady retailing practices but delete the names of offending stores, the word will spread quickly. "If there's obvious lack of feeling for a subject by an editor," says Al Delugach, "it's going to be communicated by an attitude, even unspoken, to a reporter. The guidance is negative."

Conversely, your direct expressive of interest motivation, support and counsel for good and feasible projects will stimulate at first a nervous trickle, then a steady stream of ideas-too many, in fact. Readers will be phoning in tips or walking in with inconclusive documents and fascinating but unprovable their and ideas. Reporters will be baying for scalps Than's when your editing judgement will be put to its severest test. You have to keep on top.

Picking the Players : The first rule to honour in keeping on top is to pick good people. My first piece of advice is simple: don't hire an investigative reporter from out to own. Why?

* Established, responsible investigative reporters are very expensive, Until your paper has a track record-at least a couple of years of persistent performance against tough opposition-you will have a hard time hiring the sectioned investigator. The experienced ones are wise, indeed cynical, about pioneering their craft for a paper whose editor and publisher have not proved their commitment.
* Some self-styled investigative reporters float from city to city, looking for chances to collect scalps mid prizes without accepting responsibility. One of these may

blow your way and knock over the police chief in six weeks. But he ray also skimp on research, hang it all on "confidential sources" and leave your holding a court summons.

* Even if you find a diamond in the rough, he'll take several months to get the feel of your town, its local power structure and political scene, Unless you and the publisher are prepared to wait. You may be disappointed. My second piece of advice, therefore, is equally simple: pick people on your own staff. Either that or size up new recruits who seem to have investigative potential. Here are the qualitative to look for in a reported who has investigative possibilities:

Self-discipline : Whether he works on a team or alone, the best reporter, keeps himself under control. He does not act hastily. He things constantly aid analytically.

Mental Toughness : He has the ability to stand up under fire, to outstare, outtalk, and outthink people who try to foil him. It is the quality of being decisive. It is the kind of determination that produces results. It is difficult to assess this quality in an interview: performance is the best measure.

Persistence : Similar to mental toughness, persistence implies a sort of Oriental patience. When direct tactics cannot be applied, persistence will pay off. When the front door is closed, the investigator walks around the block and finds the landlord, the delivery man, or a telephone mechanic to help him get to the people inside.

Deferred Gratification : The investigative reporter does not live for tomorrow's by-line. He enjoys the business of dogged pursuit, of careful deduction, of patient construction of a framework of facts. He doesn't expect a by-line until he has a story that he can stand behind, word for word. Then, of course, he wants it very much.

Single-mindedness : As Ben Bradlee says, "It was not accident that both Bob Woodward and Carl Bernstein were young and divorced... nobody clutching them at home, nobody saying, 'Let's slip away for a long weekend,' "Bradlee was talking about the willingness" "to put in the time, to invest a sheer god awful number of hours' once an investigation gets under way.

Personal Integrity : This quality connotes a devotion to truth. It also implies an integration of self, a wholeness of personality that enables the reporter to withstand personal abuse, uncertainty, frustration, jealousy, backbiting, loneliness.

A Board and Open-mind : Two traits are paramount in the investigative reporter: he abides rigidity of ideology or investigative theory, and he looks far and wide for patterns. He sees both the forest and the trees, and he then picks out which trees have been planted in rows and which have sprung up from windblown seeds. The true professional also talks openly about his work. He is willing to defend it against criticism is not afraid to take a problem to his editor, is not crushed when the editor makes a considered and well-articulated no-go decision.

Independence of Thought : This quality comes as standard equipment with any model of investigative reporter, new or used, It is his most valuable tool. He is not awed by the folklore of journalism. He does not believe "you can't touch that story." He does not believe the best way to do some thing is "the way we've always done it." He examine subjects an institutions with fresh vigour.

A Sense of Outrage : This term is Les Whitten's and it means about the same thing as Bill Lambert's "low threshold of indentation." It is an essentially humanist orientation, most often manifested as a desire to defend the little guy against the big guy. Only a shade or a degree away from obsession or cant. 'Ibis attribute can easily turn into a pursuit of devil theories, blinding its advocate to plausible explanations. But to some degree, it is present in virtually every investigator. It is the vision that enables him to see that the king is naked.

Competency in Writing : The nature of investigative writing sometimes makes it less exciting than a dramatic rescue story. But you must look foot a clear writer, one who puts together a well-structured story. Read sample of his writing and check with his last editor to see if the work was his own or needed extensive rewriting. Find out whether he writes easily and automatically, or slowly and laboriously. Is he able to accept criticism? Does an experienced editor on the staff have time to work over his writing.

Evaluate all these factors. Then pick a person who averages four on a five point scale on all traits.

Coaching the Individual : Training your own investigative people entails headaches, false starts, and frustrations. A reporter needs lots of testing before he can be turned loose. He needs to develop judgement and poise. If he can spell and write declarative sentences-and shows a lot of ambition—hire him and send him to the police station. Dave Nimmer, ex-investigator turned managing editor of the Minneapolis tar, put it this way: "If a guy hadn't covered cops, then I don't believe he had his as kicked around enough to develop the tough mindedness for investigative reporting."

The police station and the editor can't carry the burden of training alone. Fledgling investigators can benefit as well from seminars and academic training, though these should not substitute for practical experience. The American Press Institute in Restom Va., schedules two week seminars for investigative reporters. These are intensive experiences with lecturers recruited not only from the top ranks of the Washington and New York press corps, but also from among editors and reporters on newspapers of all sizes.

Most major schools of journalism offer courses that immerse advanced students in investigative concepts and techniques. Some of the best programs are at American University, Ohio State, Northwestern, and Stanford.

Coaching the Team : The outstanding journalist seems to get himself trained-and to get stories by flashes of genius. He often substitutes intuition about a source's reliability for some of the drudgery of by building a massive documentary case. But for most mortals—reporters and editors alike tackling a large institutional or system story in pairs or teams is more practical and efficient. Teaming helps encourage the flow of ideas; teammates check each other and increase the effectiveness of key interviews. A team following a good plan can be far more productive than two journeymen working separately on day-to-day assignments from a city editor.

Jim Steele and his partner Donald Barlett are Exhibit A in support of the team idea. In six years they won fourteen national reporting awards. Such a success rate is reason enough to consider the advantages of team reporting.

The Permanent Team : Permanent teams have been highly successful not only for the Philadelphia Inquirer, but also for Newsday (the modern pioneer in teaming), the Chicago Tribune, and the Boston Globe. Their teams range from two to six persons, occasionally supplemented by others for specific projects. The goal of each team is to conceive and develop original investigative stories. Team members took for stories no one else has done, ideally for the story none else has even thought of. Although some teams-notably those of Newsday and the Tribune—aim for slow, planned turnover, all lean toward synergistic personal relationships with a high degree of permanence. The advantages of the permanent team are worth analysing:

Volume : Team members become familiar with a wide variety of reference works, basic and special sources of documents, and bureaucracies. They can move on several lines of inquiry simultaneously rather than sequentially, a fact that can be crucial in probing a changing, developing situation. The lone reporter may be simply outpaced by events. Changes in policy, elections, personnel turnover, death or transfer of key persons, loss of sources-these may cloud or negate the meaning of facts gathered nine of ten months (or two years) earlier. Most teams plan their projects to last no more than two or three months from conception to publication.

Attainment of Goal

Success Rates : Largely because they are more thorough, team projects generally produce greater public impact-changes in laws or policies, rises or falls of businesses or government agencies.

Breadth of Contacts : Members of permanent teams usually have had experience on two half a dozen beats, and they are assiduous about keeping up those contacts. On a given project, a team may split tasks on the basis of members' back rounds. Or, as Bill Lambert points out, a team can merge information from individual members sources and effectively conceal the origin of key leads. Thus a team merely has to generate and develop as many new sources on a project as does an individual reporter.

Synergism : The effect of three or four minds analyzing a problem is more than the sum of the parts. At times, the effect seems most exponential. It can produce unconventional ways of viewing a set of facts, of putting together observations.

Interviewing : When a key interview comes up, the solo reporter must choose between going it alone or briefing another reporter to accompany him. But the team member already has one or more fully briefed veterans working with him. They can concentrate on scripting the interview. On planning roles and tactics, rather than each worrying about whether the other understands the problem. And in the critical phase after key interviews, the team can produce a complete series or story- and side bars, promptly. This speed of production minimizes the risk of a leak to the opposition or a counter-attack by the target.

Continuity and Momentum : Perhaps the major advantage of the permanent team is that it permits one project to follow another quickly without cumbersome phases of slowdown and start-up. Sometimes base-building for a long-term project may begin while a current project is being wrapped up. The Tribune's great vote-fraud effort of 1972, for instance, called for nearly a year of inside work by task-force member William Mullen in the election commissioner's office. While Mullen was occupied there, task force leader George Bliss and others were carrying out a highly successful nursing-home investigation.

Self-checking : The best reporter, trying to write a five-part series from 200 pages of notes, a 50-page chronology, 165 index cards and two congressional committee reports, must worry about errors of memory and understanding. If team members check each other's daily notes and story drafts, the risk of error is sharply reduced.

Self-regulation : At the end of a long, hard job, even good reporters can fall into devil theories or impute evil motives to characters who may only be incompetent or stupid. The presence of one to three colleagues, each presumably a strong and independent thinker, reduces this risk of lost perspective.

Simpler Management : An experienced team can be easier to supervisor than a number of individuals. The wise editor holds the team leaders accountable. He spends a good deal of time with the leader but finds this much easier than having to resolve the individual problems and conflicting needs of three or four persons.

Training : About once a year, a new member is taken abroad the Chicago Tribune Task Force, while one veteran returns to general assignments or a beat. This rotation reduces jealousy among other staff members. It also helps to test and train.

Team Problems : But team operation, like any other, is not without costs and problems. Because the team works with more direction and fewer burdens than most reporters, as Barlett notes, its salaries may be more efficiently spent, but all investigative work costs money. Further, security is harder to achieve when five people (including the line editor) know something than when a single reporter knows it.

To be able to carry on several lines of inquiry at once is an advantage-but not if gaps are being left or if the same trail is being crossed several times. These errors and omissions sometimes occur in a team effort. The team leader must ensure that every member of the team knows, day by day, what others have found out. Each team member must not only write his own daily memo, but also read the notes of his colleagues. Bob Greene is wont to bring in a pot of coffee laced with Scotch and pass it around at the end of a day. Says Greene: 'We talk about what we have found out. One says, 'I think the next person I should go to is this.. We work it out that night, approximately what we're going to do the next day." Then, as described in Greene reads all the memos and "breaks" them for duplicating and distribution the next day.

The ego and the navel are also matters to reckon with in team efforts. The stereotypical investigative reporter has a strong ego. He may refuse to let others share his prized sources. He may complain that "nobody else does any work." If a person with an excessive ego turns up on a team, he will upset his colleagues and will himself operate at less than maximum capacity. The risk of passing into a contemplation of the level is greatest in a two-person team hidden away in a private office. If two successive projects fall short of expectations, the publisher starts asking what return is coming from that $50,000 line in the budget, and the team may indulge in excessive caution, restudy of procedures, reorganization of files, self-criticism-anything other than tackling a new project aggressively. David Nimmer remarks: "They had better report to somebody [an editor] every day, just for their own benefit. If they re out chasing butterflies, it's very easy to get down on themselves. They've got to feel part of a newsroom."

If, on the other hand, the team starts winning prizes-especially if it achieves results against great odds-an aura of mysticism may arise around its members. The very good ones can handle it. But some are never the same. Some become sticklers. Because methodology paid off they become infatuated with it. They spend time drawing plans and writing daily memos to themselves and as a result fall behind in the real work. Others get snooty. The victims of snootiness spend much time lecturing about journalism; they may even write books. They don't want to move on a story unless the work plan has been screened by the Pulitzer Prize advisory committee. Such case are sometimes cured by enchanting the classic definition of a courageous managing editor: he's the one who fired a Pulitzer winner.

And reporters not on the team can, of course, become jealous. They can refuse to pass alone tips and ignore tips given them by team members. They complain about their own work loads and resent the time investigator spend reading books, encyclopaedias, and magazines.

The good editor-the coach-has to manage things to minimize the problems and maintain the advantages of the team.

Ad hoc Team : The temporary team put together for a specific story is even more work for the editor than a permanent team. It can, nonetheless, produce spectacular results. After the project is finished, team members return to their beats. The ad hoc team might include one expert and a few specialists picked to supplement his skills and knowledge. Or it might include several experts who don't need the help of specialists. One reason it worked so well is that we had used ad hoc teams on at least five major stories in the three previous years (two won national awards).

With a couple of notable exceptions, the strengths of an ad hoc team are the same as those of a permanent one. They can handle about the same research volume, bring in a breadth of contacts, react synergistically. Train the new member, and check each other. If anything, ad hoc teams are more conservative than permanent ones-more inclined to discuss difficult questions at length and less inclined to take chances. Elitism is also less of a problem because team members know they are going back to other tasks when the project is done.

The cost per project is about the same as for a permanent team; however rather than four or five major projects a year, the ad hoc concept envisages only one or two, so the annual cost for this type of teaming is usually lower.

But three strengths of the permanent learn-simpler management because of a strong team leader, standard writing procedures for keeping daily reports and producing final drafts, and especially continuity and momentum are lost with an ad hoc team. The permanent team practically runs on its own. The editor has to intervene more with the ad hoc team. With little operating continuity, he must take special pains to see that the team is protected from other assignments, that the schedule is followed, that the daily reports are written, that the project files are maintained. The editor has to assign writing-duties to the team, explain the general approach, then mediate disagreements between reporters, such as an argument about turning a sideboard into a major story. Instead of having reporters continually defining new ideas and exploring feasibility, the editor finds the burden now falls on him. When he assigns feasibility studies, he finds they must be sandwiched into other routines. When a report comes back, the editor may have to make an undesirably quick judgement on a half-developed idea. And when he does decide to form a new team, he must shuffle beats, brief team members, set up a schedule of progress conferences, and arrange new file facilities.

There is also the greater danger of leaks. Especially if the effort drags on for months and several people pop into and out of it, word of the project will get on the grapevine. Less experienced reporters tend to be less scrupulous about keeping their files-and their Mouths locked. So security is also a problem with the ad hoc team.

What is less of a danger, however are ego trips. They are less of a problem than on a permanent team. The editor, though, must make sure the work is properly apportioned and that people who do the routine records work and peripheral interviews get appropriate credit.

The ad hoc team, then, represents the editor's conscious trade off of continuity and momentum for a more tightly controlled budget. It is an effective check, certainly, on "head hunting" or make-work by irresponsible persons, but it can also become a damper on reporters' motivation.

Single Ace : When you have a Seymour Hersh, a Nick Gage, a Gene Cunningham—or a staff of Stanley Penns and Jonathan Kwitnys—you are a better off to leave them alone, asking only that they talk once or twice a week with a senior editor. Such persons develop their own working styles, their own solid sources. Though they may appear to operate instinctively, they work efficiently. They keep their own files. They know most of the standard hustles and games people play, so they know where to look for the chinks in the system. They combine indignation, logical judgement personal strength, and physical stamina. They have the peculiar self-motivation that management can rarely improve on and can indeed stifle with too many restrictions. Their most common problem is a occasional fit of cynicism or gloom.

Although his salary and expenses may seem high, the solo performer can be very cost-efficient. The editor must develop, with his business manager, a pay policy that permits him to work the hours he feels necessary. Putting the reporter on fixed salary-adjusted for expected extra effort-is one practical approach. If he produces as many as three of four major stories or series a year-stories that build the paper's credibility and cause other good things to happen he is a bargain. He will also spin of scores of tips and ideas for other staff members and will usually motivate them to do better day-to-day reporting. He may arouse jealousy among the time-services, but the editor has an easy response to those people: "You get the same results, friend, and you can have the same deal."

The strongest reason for finding your own ace is to avoid the danger of playing safe. An editor has plenty of controls tilting him toward the status quo: his publisher, his elite friends, his conservative staff members. The law, the traditions and codes of professional associations. If he wants his newspaper to do its public duty, he should always find room for one or two iconoclasts on the staff.

Editing the Players : If there ever was a time for feet-up editing, it is when the investigative reporter's first draft arrives. Investigative editing calls for the same kind of sleuthing as investigative reporting. The editor should take the draft into his office, shut off his phone calls and read it through several times. He not only has thousands of his budget dollars in the piece, he had the newspaper's reputation for accuracy, honesty, and fairness on the line. Although the reporter is willing to stand behind every word, the editor is the one who will be called to account for whatever recriminations ensue. Therefore, the editor should read that story through not once or twice, but six times. Six times? Yes. And each of those times, he examines the story from a different point of view, as we shall see.

First reading. Is the thesis proved? Is it clearly stated and is there enough documented, attributable evidence so that a reasonable reader may understand the conclusions? If not, make notes about what is missing and go on to the next reading.

Second reading. Is the thesis important? Will a significant number of readers see it as important? In short, who will give a damn?

Third reading. Does the story flow? Does it move in a continuous logical line? Or does it pause frequently to branch off into details explanation of some legal point or translation of bureaucratic or technical jargon?

Fourth reading. How can it be trimmed? A story in which the reporter has invested weeks or months will probably be laden with detail, excessive restatement, tedious qualification, and unnecessary attribution. It may help to pencil an Outline of the story as written, identifying the essential points so you can decide how much support each point needs. If one sharp quote captures a key thought, are three reinforcing quotes needed? If three sets of records support a contention, is it necessary to detail all three, or will a single sentence ("City purchase records confirmed the- transaction") be enough? Draw a line or put a light X beside each possible cut or computation. Try to arrive at a balance between enlightenment and boredom. You want to get the story told quickly with strong, clear words. This is the time, for example, to strip out quotes that simply make an interviewee look silly without contributing information about his motives.

Fifth reading. After the cuts and adjustments, will the story read? Will making a side bar out of the fifth and sixth paragraphs make mysterious gibberish out of everything after the sixteenth paragraph? This is simply standard editing "to conform," calls for special care in a long, complex piece.

Sixth reading. Now it is time, to test the reporter. If he is a pro, he can stand it. If he cannot, you would rather know now than after the story is printed. Put yourself in the position of the subject of the key interview-or his attorney. Write down in blunt words every question you can think of that challenges the accuracy of the reporter's arithmetic, the credibility of his quoted sources, the logic of his assertions.

By now you have spent at least a couple of hours with the story and have made marks all over the copy, plus a list of pertinent and impermanent questions. It is time to call the reporter in and to through the list.

Resolution of Problem : Your jobs is to keep things moving briskly towards reasonable solution of the problem: how to get the piece in print. A good reporter appreciates it. "I'd hate to sell a story to a person who didn't think of asking the right questions," says Dick Lyneis "I want them to be real tough. I want them to set incredibly high standards. I want him to pin me up against the wall. I want them to make me defend everything I've got."

If your questions from the first and last readings are substantive, it is wise to tackle them first. You may have at least a temporary no go situation, and you need to determine if it is worthwhile to send the reporter back for more work.

If you can establish that the story has a sound thesis, proved by evidence, the next step is to deal with the hard questions that came up in the last reading. These are questions you, the editor, may have to answer in a phone call or visit from the aggrieved person or his attorney. The reporter should have answers to every one of them. If he does not if he appears confused or claims "confidential source" too often you must articulate your reservations now. This can be a delicate problem in human relations as well as one of the most crucial aspects of editing. Presumably, the reporter has been pouring heart and soul into the project, day and night for weeks on end. Whenever possible, suggest that further checking is in order that perhaps some other source or record can be found to fill whatever gap has shown up. But if the reporter has simply failed to talk to an obvious person because "he wouldn't tell us anything anyway," then draw a hard-line. Such a reporter is making unwarranted assumptions.

If you have a competent reporter at work, there is no serious confrontation on 99 stories out of 100. But you are making a terrible mistake if you avoid the challenging questions. This kind of self-evasion leads to decisions such as, "We've put so much work into it, I suppose we have to run something." That attitude is a disservice to your readers.

Once the critical questions from the sixth reading are answered, the rest of the conference should be a breeze.

The important tasks now ire to strip the main piece to greyhound shape, to pull out and rework the side bars, and to set up the accompanying graphics with the layout specialist while the reporter rewrites. If the main story involves penetrating some corporate labyringth, you may decide on a simple chart—boxes and connecting lines-to clarify the relationships. If the story is heavy with statistics, simple line or bar graphs can help clear up major points.

Call the company lawyer and tell him there will be a piece for him to go over tomorrow. Stop in the publisher's office and, as bravely, as possible, assure him that the "big piece" is in hand and, so far, all books well.

Final Huddle : During the time between your acceptance of the reporter's story and its publication, you as an editor have hard and critical work to do. You must allow ample time to do it well.

The first step is to seek out a trusted colleague—city editor, editorial writer, veteran reporter-who has not been involved in the story and show him the rewrite. Don't ask for a detailed editing but a fresh viewpoint and a candid evaluation of the thesis, approach, and structure.

Next visit the lawyer, Lawyers think in terms of evidence and proof. That's not a bad viewpoint to have just before you publish. Have the lawyer read everything-side bars, charts and graphs, headlines, cutline. Unwitting level in heads or cutlines is common. Occasionally, the lawyer will also react like a typical reader and tell you he doesn't understand some compressed thought that the copy editor tried to squeeze into a fourteen count headline. The lawyer's lay judgement, as well as his profession can be helpful.

After the page is made up. Read it again. 'Ibis may disrupt normal shop procedure, but it should be done in the interest of accuracy. Have the reporter read the page, too.

If time allows, have yet one more new person look at the page. The sports editor, the life-style editor, the wire editor, or some other trusted but uninvolved staffer may spot an error everyone else has missed. Even a simple complain—"I don't quite follow what this paragraph means'!—may suggest a changed that adds the final polish to the story.

The final huddle complete, stop and congratulate the reporter for persistence and professional performance. And make sure that he or the city editor is greeted for follow-up-not just the next day but two weeks from now or a month from now.

Skill of Knitting

Editing is both an art and a craft. The art of any kind of editing lies in knowing which manuscripts to accept outright, which to reject and which to accept in spite of their imperfections. The craft of scientific editing lies in revising and preparing material for publication as promptly as possible and in a form acceptable to readers. But what exactly do scientific editors do? How do they learn to find the best authors or select the best articles for multi-author books or journals? How do they operate a refereeing system? How do they develop a method for revising, or teaching others to revise, the presentation of scientific work?

What are their responsibilities to authors, to readers and to science itself? The people most in need of answers to these questions are those who have been enticed into editing by assurances that there is really nothing much to it and that it will not take much of their (unpaid) time. Neither statement is true. Editing is complex, time-consuming, and often exhausting. It can also be absorbing and highly satisfying, as this book will show.

Editors need good judgement, tempered with imagination and intuition, and a wide and sound knowledge of the disciplines covered in their publications. They should be endowed with a firm command of language—perhaps extending to more than one language and a well-controlled passion for accuracy. They must exercise tact in dealing with authors and common sense in revising the language or structure of papers. And they must be able to cope with, or arrange for others to cope with, the numerous practical problems of getting typescripts into print and then into the hands of readers.

In general, the aims of scientific editors are to choose the best and most original work available at the time on a particular topic or in a particular branch of science, and to bring that work to they attention of interested readers as promptly as possible, in a form that is both readable and retrievable. Scientific editors, alone or with the help of advisers and assistants, save readers' time and tempers (and some authors reputations) by rejecting or revising any mediocre, badly presented or misleading work.

These aims are the same as those of editors in other branches of scholarship, Scientific editors differ from others perhaps only in requiring a particularly crisp and exact style of writing and in preferring certain conventions and methods of presentation that have come to be regarded as indispensable in science.

The exact functions of scientific editors vary with the fields in which they work. Some of their work is creative, some of it consists of substantive and technical editing, and the rest is administrative.

Editors in other Subjects : In the less mathematical, more literary fields such as psychology, sociology, archaeology and some parts of theoretical biology, editors are concerned more with assessing the quality of ideas than with improving the way those ideas are expressed. Authors in these fields may even refuse to have their manuscripts edited.

When the subject is one in which experimental data or reproducible observations are impossible to obtain, authors are perhaps justified in being less than precise. In the more material sciences, however, certain ways of presenting results and arguments are widely accepted, and systems of nomenclature are continually being proposed, debated and (occasionally) agreed; clarity and conciseness are vital, and logic essential. Editors must therefore be familiar with the standards and usages of their disciplines and be prepared to tighten author's presentations accordingly.

Whether editors obtain material for publication by seeking out the best authors to contribute to a book or by selecting the best manuscripts from the many submitted to a journal, the problems are the same: good authors are rare and prescriptions for success in compiling good scientific books or journals are rarer still.

What, in fact, are the criteria for judging quality? Chase found that, a ranked by 191 successful scientists, those criteria are: logical rigour, reputability of research techniques, clarity and conciseness of writing style, originality, mathematical precision, coverage of significant published work, compatibility with generally accepted disciplinary ethics, theoretical significance, pertinence to current research in the discipline, and applicability to practical or applied problems in the field. In Chase's sample this ranking order varied with the discipline: natural scientists placed more emphasis on replicability of research techniques, originality, mathematical precision and coverage of the published work, while social scientists gave higher ranking to logical rigour, theoretical significance and applied significance.

Even with these criteria as guides, the ability to choose the best work to publish remains an indefinable and elusive talent owing as much to intuition as to a deep knowledge of the subject. Since a talent of this kind cannot be taught, though it develops with experience, the rest of this chapter concentrates on outlining the other aspects of editing multi-author books, conference proceedings and journals.

The first section goes into some detail over the editing and publishing of multi-author books, since these do not receive a separate chapter to themselves later, unlike the other two categories and since some of this first section also applies to conference proceedings-which are of course another form of multi-author book. The three sets of outlines are intended to place the various editorial procedures in context for editors or potential editors of any type of scientific publication.

The Contribution : The term 'multi-author books' refers here to books with chapters by different authors on different aspects of a single topic and to collections of review papers such as those in year-books and similar series. The principles described apply to textbooks as well, but their planning is not covered in detail. The compilation of a multi-author book can be justified only if the subject is such that one person could not handle it adequately. The subject should therefore be one with facets in many disciplines, or be especially complex, or so new that it is essential for previously unpublished developments in different institutions to be described by the original workers, Monographs, review series and textbooks may all meet these criteria.

Editors of multi-author books have to make sure that the subject is covered adequately and in a balanced way. They select authors so that this goal can be reached, arrange to fill gaps if anyone fails to submit a chapter in time, and edit the text so that the book has unity and a coherent style. They need two almost contradictory qualifications.

They must know their subject very well indeed so that they know what kind of book is needed in that area of science and can choose the appropriate authors to collaborate in producing it. At the same time they must be able to put themselves in the place of readers who are not as knowledgeable as the contributors to the book; they must then edit the chapters so skilfully that readers will not only understand the different contributions but also appreciate the connections between the chapters and the structure of the subject as a whole.

Multi-author books may be initiated by a scientist with an idea for a book, or by a scientific society or institution, or by a publisher's ,acquisitions editor' who asks a scientist to do the editing. Before approaching a potential scientific editor, an acquisitions editor makes sure that market exists for the proposed book.

Scientists or a scientific organisation with an idea for a book or series of books should themselves examine what competition there is from recently published work, as they will have to convince a publisher that the book or series meets a need and has an assured market in established disciplines or professions. No one should compile a book first and hope to find a publisher afterwards: if publishers disagree with a scientist's assessment of the market the work will all be wasted.

After the initial idea for a book has been mulled over and knocked into shape, therefore, the editor writes an outline of what it will contain and draws up a list of potential contributors. An editor who wants to stay sane keeps the list short: the fewer authors there are, the easier it is to keep in touch with them and the less likely it is that manuscripts will be delivered late, or not at all. For a yearbook or annual review, however, some editors find it advisable to invite more authors than will eventually be needed: then if authors fail to submit their chapters in time the book can still be produced on schedule, and the chapters received after the deadline can be updated and printed in the next year's volume.

The outline helps to show the editor which kinds of expertise are needed for the various chapters, and the writers may then almost select themselves. But even if the possible authors are an editor's friends (or perhaps especially if they are), their latest work has to be examined critically before they are invited to contribute. Is their knowledge of research developments still comprehensive and sound, or have they turned into overworked administrators? Do they have good reputations for keeping to deadlines? Have their recent papers had to be heavily edited before they could be published?

When contributors are being chosen, editors may be subjected to certain pressures. Formal or informal advisers occasionally make suggestions that are not strictly disinterested. This kind of pressure can usually be recognized easily enough and the editor can be ready to deal with it firmly but tactfully.

Pressure from a sponsoring society may be more difficult to cope with. If the book is one of series covering a wider field, a sponsoring organization sometimes ask for topics to be included which do not fit into the editor's plans for that particular publication, or the sponsor may ask for certain topics to be excluded because they are to be covered in other books in the series. Or the society may want some of its officers to be invited to contribute even though they are not particularly qualified to do so. Again, editors have to be ready with prompt and tactful solutions to this kind of problem.

Another type of pressure may be felt if a book has two or more editors. Joint editors must discuss the aims and scope of their book in some detail before they approach possible contributors or a publisher.

They should be quite sure that they agree completely on what the book is about and to whom it is addressed, what work each of them will do during its preparation, which disciplinary conventions they will use, and what general procedures they will follow. Usually, each editor is responsible for a different section of the book. But to ensure consistency and prevent overlapping of chapters, at least one editor should read all the manuscripts before the material goes to the printer. If co-editors edit each other's chapters in the book, they are probably wise if they agree to exchange comments in writing rather than face to face.

Although the editor of a multi-author book usually asks potential contributors informally at an early stage whether they are interested in collaborating on the book, it is better not to send out formal invitations to write chapters until after certain practical details have been agreed with a publisher. Scientific editors who have to find a publisher will want one who can provide, or at least promise, good production arrangements, attractive presentation, rapid printing, and rapid and efficient worldwide distribution and promotion. Book reviews, publishers' catalogues, publishers' advertisements in journals, and the advice of librarians and of colleagues who are authors of editors can all help when a short list of suitable publishers is being drawn up. Directories of publishers show how well established different publishers are, what agencies they have in other countries, how many books they publish each year and what kind of books they publish (it is no good sending a book on nuclear physics to a publisher specializing in poetry). Publishers who handle perhaps 50 books a year can give a book individual attention, but getting it into print is only the first step: wide distribution is essential too, and small or new publishers may not have the necessary machinery for this.

If a book in English is to be published by a British publishing house which has no branch in the USA, or by an American publisher without a UK subsidiary, the potential editor should ask what arrangements will be made for handling sales in North America or the UK market, respectively. Worldwide publication is not automatic unless the publisher has world rights in a book or arranges to assign certain rights to another publisher who operates in areas not covered by the first publisher.

Another point the potential editor should investigate is who in the publishing house will be assigned to watch over the book during the publication cycle. A publishing house editor normally acts as the scientific editor's contact on all matters to do with the book's production and promotion. A contact of this kind is essential if the scientific editor is not to waste time looking for the right person every time a query arises. And if copy-editing is being done in the publishing house the scientific editor should also find out how much the copy editor will do and arrange to see the manuscripts again after they have been copy-edited but before they are typeset or retyped as camera ready copy.

For their part, publishers want authoritative and reliable texts, neither too short nor too long, that are likely to reach them in readily publishable form, preferably with some well-known names amongst the authors. European publishers who want to sell books on the American market are happy to see American authors among the contributors and *vice-versa*. Editors looking for publishers should therefore send all those on their short list the outline of the book, the list of potential authors (including a few words about the qualifications of each), and some indication of the book's length, the level of readership and the range of disciplines to be covered. Detailed questions about production schedules, marketing arrangements and so on can be left until a publisher shows definite interest, but it is worth asking at this stage about the total production time and possible price for the book.

Once a scientific editor and a publisher reach an understanding in principle, a formal agreement is negotiated, dealing with some or all of the following: the approximate length of the typescript; the date by which the typescript should be handed to the publishers; the target publication date; royalties or fees; copyright and other rights; responsibility for costs incurred during editing; responsibility for copy-editing; indexing and proof-reading; responsibility for libel; arrangements for reprints and free copies; and other matters affecting production, design, promotion and distribution, including sanctions to be invoked if the agreement is broken.

Before any agreement is signed it is probably wise for new editors to consult a lawyer who knows something about authors, rights, or take advice from colleagues who are experienced editors or authors. Editors who insist on tight production schedules must remember at this stage that they will have to keep their side of the bargain by producing manuscripts promptly at the agreed time. The publisher is unlikely to try to influence the content of a book once the agreement has been signed, but if the book later turns out to be very different in length or scope from what was agreed originally, the publisher has a legitimate complaint and a new agreement may then have to be negotiated.

Most publishers offer editors either a fee or a standard royalty based on either the list price of the book or the net receipts from sales, the arrangement to base royalties on net receipts being more common in the USA than in the UK, In the UK, 10% of list price is a common royalty on a hardback book, though 121/2 % or 15% may be offered. To produce the same amount as a 10%, 12 1/2% or 15% royalty based on list price, the royalty based on the publisher's actual income from sales would have to be higher-about 15%, 19% and 23%, respectively, assuming an average discount of 35%. A sliding scale may be agreed by which the royalty increases (or starts) when, say, 1000 or 2000 copies have been sold. On a paper-back edition the royalty may be 7 1/2% of list price, or perhaps only 5% or 6%.

Publishers price books, usually, at about five times the production cost per copy (the unit cost), or at a price per page which works out at roughly the same as five times the unit cost. A breakdown of list price might look like this.

Production cost	20%
Average discount (to book-sellers. etc.)	35%
Royalty	10%
Marketing and Overheads	25%
Publisher's profit	10%

The publisher makes 10% profit only when every copy has been sold, and makes no profit at all until a certain sales figure, the break even point, has been reached.

Editors who have their readers' interests at heart rather than their own often want to know why books are highly priced. The answer is that if the book is in English the publisher has to pay to produce, advertise and distribute the book of a worldwide market, yet the total expected sales may be very small. A highly specialized monograph of interest only to graduate research workers in a limited field of study might sell, say, 500-1500 copies in three years before it goes out of date; a collection of review papers in a series that every library feels obliged to buy may sell 2000-3000 copies; and a textbook for undergraduates may sell anything from 10,000 copies upwards, depending on how wide its appeal is and how long it remains up to date.

The comparative cheapness of paper-backs is entirely due to the publisher's expectation of high sales, not to the lower cost of a paper cover: the unit production cost for a paper-back is usually very little less than that of the hardback version. Similarly, text-books or other books with large markets are cheaper than specialized monographs of the same length because the production cost for a large number of copies is not much more than for a small number and the unit cost therefore falls.

Even though the main appeal of a scientific book lies in the quality of its contents, its appearance has a certain importance. Long before manuscripts are ready for the printer, the editor should discuss the design of the book with the publisher or the publisher's designer and ask to see specimen pages showing the style of headings, references, the typeface, type size and so on.

The Adjustment : When general arrangements with the publisher have been completed, the editor can draw up a timetable for receipt of manuscripts. For a book likely to run to, say 2504M pages, about 12 months might be a reasonable time between formal invitations going to the authors and manuscripts being sent to be printed. Longer may be needed if authors have to write long chapters or several chapters each, or if the authors have particularly heavy professional commitments which leave little time for writing (but it is better to avoid choosing these as contributors in the first place). Within 12-month schedule authors may be allowed, say, four months for writing their contributions, with reminders about the approaching deadline being sent to them after 10 weeks and again after 15 weeks.

If a manuscript fails to arrive the editor decides whether to drop the chapter or find a substitute author who can Ate it in time. The rest of the 12 months is needed for consultation, editing, revising and writing any introductory or linking material. Depending on the production method, the printer's capacity and capability, the contributors' cooperation and the editor's sense of urgency publication of the book itself will then take 5-12 months from the time the printer receives the last typescript from the editor: first profits will be ready in six to eight weeks, or longer; authors may be given-or take-up to four weeks to return corrected proofs; correction of first proofs and production and proof-reading of second proofs may take another four to six weeks; and final printing, binding and so on may take six to eight weeks, or longer.

As soon as the timetable for receipt of manuscripts has been drawn up the editor can send formal invitations to contributors. The letters should outline the book and indicate the level of readership the editor has in mind. The editor suggests what each person should write about and how long the chapter should be, gives the date by which a working title and synopsis should be supplied and the date the manuscript has to be ready, and may want to say what action will be taken if the typescript does not arrive in time.

The publisher should be named, as should the other contributors, with those who have not yet agreed to contribute being distinguished from any who have already informally agreed to do so. Authors should be told whether secretarial or other expenses will be met, whether a fee or a share of the royalty will also be paid, when proofs (if any) can be expected, and whether a free copy of the book, or reprints of chapters, or both, will be provided by the publisher.

If an editor has decided that unsatisfactory chapters will be rejected even though people have been invited to write them, authors have to be warned that the editor reserves the right to do this. If chapters are to be seen by an editorial board or other referees, authors ought to be informed of this too. A form of assignment of copyright may be enclosed with the invitation.

The editor also prepares a style guide and, before sending

it to the authors who accept the invitation, may test its practical value by writing a chapter for the book to the guide's specifications. Alternatively, the editor might ask authors to follow the guidelines of an appropriate journal in the field and simply add a few instructions about specific requirements for the book. Later, when the contributing authors have supplied working titles and synopses for their chapters, the editor distributes these, or a detailed summary based on them, to all contributors.

The editor's main problem in the easier stages of the preparations the book will be to get all the authors to deliver a publishable manuscript on time, so that dilatory contributors do not undo the good work of the punctual ones. A draconian solution is to commission a new author if a chapter has not arrived in spite of frequent reminders. If a small amount of money is available for editorial and writing costs, one way of using it is to pay extra secretarial and other fees to help authors who are asked to write a chapter at short notice.

When manuscripts begin to arrive, the editor logs them in and checks whether authors have covered the subjects arranged at the agreed length, and whether they have presented their material appropriately for the intended audience, written passages that overlap too much with other chapters, left gaps they were expected to fill or introduced contradictions with other chapters. The editor then revises the content or style as necessary, and writes linking pieces if the subject changes too abruptly between chapters'.

When most of the material is ready for the printer, the editor either writes or asks someone else to write a preface of foreword outlining the book and its aims. Instead of a preface, or sometimes in addition to it, the editor or one of the contributors may write an introductory chapter setting the scene for the rest of the book in more detail than a short preface allows. Introductions or prefaces, together with any passages written to link different sections, do much to give multi-author books the unit they often lack.

After all the manuscripts have been referred for outside opinion necessary edited and revised copy-edited and assembled in what seems a local order, the editor considers the book as a whole once more, to see that it has the required unity and consistency of style.

At this stage, as well as when ending each chapter, the editor must keep the readers clearly in mind. The book has to be made intelligible to the least experienced readers and to workers in other disciplines, but these readers should not be patronized, nor should more knowledgeable readers be given the feeling that the text is over-explanatory. The editor's role is to see that the chapters are on the same level of intelligibility and shown authors where over-familiarity with their subject has led them to condense too much, fogging the readers' understanding. In the interests of clarity the editor must be ready to insert sub-headings, define symbols and neologisms, and substitute plain language for laboratory shortened or for the impenetrable prose that is unfortunately far too common in science.

When work on the text is finished, the 'front matter' or 'prelims'-the title page, preface, contents and so forth—are prepared and the typescripts are sent to the printer, usually via the publisher. The publisher will then probably ask the editor to write descriptive blurbs for the jacket and provide other promotion material. The publisher will want advice on individuals, societies and institutions who might be included in a mailing list of possible buyers and a list of journals or people who might review the book. The editor may also be asked to choose designs and colours for, the binding and dust jacket.

Depending on the production policy agreed with the publisher there may be two proof stages, or one, or none. Proofs are and a master set is returned to the publisher by the date agreed. If there are two proof stages, authors normally receive only the first but the editor receives the second as well.

As soon as paged proofs are available, the editor either compiles an index or has it prepared by a professional indexer Once the index proof has been checked, the editor need only wait expectantly for publication day and the comments of contributors, other colleagues and—eventually-book reviewers.

The Difference : Conference proceedings differ in several ways from other multi-author books, and their editors often face an additional set of problems. The editors may have had no opportunity of influencing the choice of papers presented at the conference, and they may even have their editorial functions thrust on them after a meeting has ended.

They then have to try to construct a satisfying book out of several unrelated building-blocks separated by yawning gaps. When this goal is reached it is usually only because the editor has cajoled speakers to produce good manuscripts, rewritten some passages, interpolated linking paragraphs, or written whole chapters to replace missing manuscripts. But many people who have been seduced into editing conference proceedings at a late stage find themselves forced to allow a motley collection of papers to be published, in a book that is later deservedly attacked by reviewers for the unevenness of its contents.

The responsibilities of editors of conference proceedings range from rewriting most of the papers and re-drawing the illustrations to doing nothing more strenuous than giving permission for their names to grace the title page-an unethical practice that should be anathema to any scientist with a reputation to consider. In general, the work of the conference editor depends partly on the size of the conference and partly on how much help and advice the publisher-if there is an outside publisher—can provide.

If the sponsoring organization publishes its own conferences but has no regular system for doing so, the editor will probably not only undertake the scientific editing but will also be expected to deal with printers and arrange for marketing and distribution.

Another route to publication for conferences is in journals or journal supplements, a solution which does away with some of the criticisms made about the publication of conference proceedings.

The aim of most conferences is to generate interaction amongst those who attend them. The aim of the published proceedings is to preserve all worth-while material presented during the meeting and make it available to readers who did not attend the conference. Both sets of purposes should be clearly defined by the organizing committee at the outset and adhered to afterwards, otherwise both meeting and book will be less than adequate. The editor has to recognize the different goals of meeting and book, and work with the conference organizers and with any co-editors in achieving both sets of aims.

For some conferences intended for publication, all speakers are invited by the organizing committee; for others, especially large congresses, anyone who wishes may submit a paper or abstract for consideration by the committee; in a third type, the programme may consist of a mixture of invited an submitted papers. The organizing committee then has to make a number of decisions about publication. Should all papers on the programme be published, or only some? Are papers to be selected for publication? Will they be refereed? By what date must they be submitted? Are full papers, or only synopses, to be circulated before the meeting? In the published book, will discussion sections be included? Who will publish or print the proceedings?

Ideally, the editor is a member of the organizing committee when these questions are discussed. Even if other people choose the speakers, the course of publication runs more smoothly when the editor can see to it that invitations and circularise contain clear and firm general information for authors on the requirements for synopses and manuscripts. Fully detailed instructions are more conveniently given in a separate set of guidelines for contributors. The sample guidelines for multi-author books can be adapted for conference proceedings.

Publishers who specialize in conference proceedings can help the editor by providing advice about the style guide and by assisting with copy-editing and proof-reading. As well as covering the items already listed for multi-author books, the agreement drawn up between the publisher and the sponsoring organization may define what assistance will be provided and make it clear how discussions will be handled, if these are to be published. If the sponsoring organization itself is the publisher, the editor and organizing committee may negotiate an agreement specifying the exact role of the editor in the publication of the proceedings. If, as often happens, points like these are not covered in the formal agreement, they should nevertheless be agreed in writing by those concerned.

Royalties for, and sales of, conference proceedings are similar to the figures given for multi-author books, though conference editors are perhaps more likely to be paid a fee for their work than royalties, and volumes of proceedings rarely, if ever, have such high sales as text-books.

Once the date for a conference has been arranged, other dates can be fixed around it. These dates depend on what the organizers decide to circulate before the meeting. A good compromise is to send out a programme containing synopsis-preferably rather extended, factually informative ones-about three to four weeks before the conference. Speakers should be asked to send these summaries to the editor or organizers some 10 to 12 weeks before the meeting. With repeated reminders, it should be possible to obtain over 90% of the summaries in time to be printed with the programme. Some organisers make receipt of the synopsis by a certain date a condition of the author being allowed to speak.

In some ways handling a large conference is easier than handling other multi-author books; a would be contributor who fails to deliver a paper at the meeting, for example, can hardly insist on it being included in the published proceedings. The main problems for the editor therefore lie in obtaining synopses in good time, and perhaps in arranging for the recording and transcription of impromptu papers and discussions.

A particularly important part of the editor's work on proceedings is the conversion of a good oral presentation into a publishable paper if authors have not succeeded in doing this. Where discussions are included, the editor's most valuable contribution lies in preparing them for publication in a way that satisfied both readers and participants.

Work on manuscripts for conference proceedings is similar to that on manuscripts for other multi-author books. The main principle of editing conference proceedings is also the same as for other multi-author books: a single intelligence-the editor's must hold the various parts together in spite of disparities in the scientific level of contributions and in the communicative skills of the authors. For conferences another important principle to follow is that the proceedings must be published quickly if they are to be of any use to readers. This means establishing firm timetables and keeping to deadlines. Delays in the early stages can easily lead to a volume being out of date before it leaves the binders.

The Organs : A journal is, in effect, a third kind of multi-author book, but one that appears weekly, monthly, quarterly, or perhaps irregularly, with most of its contents submitted by authors for their own reasons rather than solicited by editors for theirs. Editors of journals are responsible to the scientific community as well as to their sponsors (often learned societies). At the same time they usually have great freedom in controlling the content and form of what is published. It is this freedom that allows editors to put an individual stamp on their journals, even though many different authors contribute to each issue.

Scientific journals, whether sponsored by learned societies

or by commercial publishers, vary from the ultra specialized to the general, from the rich giant to the impoverished dwarf, and from the academically detached to the politically engage. The scale of the editor's work varies accordingly, but the basic responsibilities remain the same for every kind of journal. Editors must define or re-define the aims and scope of their journals and choose ankles and other features congruent with those aims.

They have to decide whether to select articles after consulting referees or mainly on their own unassisted judgement. They must determine whether poorly presented but scientifically valuable papers should be published as they stand or be improved before publication and, if papers are to be improved, whether the work should be done by the editorial staff or by the authors. Editors must also organize an efficient handling system for typescripts and proofs, ensure prompt publication by the most suitable printing method, and cooperate with secondary services (abstracting and title-listing) and data banks in making primary articles readily retrievable. Some editors are also responsible for the efficient distribution, promotion and economic viability of their journals.

Most journals, whoever sponsors them, have an editorial board or committee whose ostensible purpose is to advise the editor on anything and everything to do with running the journal. In practice, boards range from the purely decorative to the strictly functional. Most commonly, board members act as referees or as section editors, or they may recommend other people who would be suitable as referees. When a journal is new, board members well known in their disciplines may be persuaded to write several of its first articles, as an encouragement to other contributors. The only material regard for board members is likely to be a free subscription to the journal: apart from this, publication of their names is the best compensation most journals can offer.

The editorial boards or committees of journals sponsored by learned societies are elected or co-opted in the same way as other committees of these societies. If the society is a local or national one, the members of the committee may meet form ally once a year or more often, and their duties usually include establishing the policy of the journal. Members of editorial boards of commercially sponsored journals, on the other hand, are invited to join the board by the editor and publishers, and they may never have any formal meetings at all, still less any discussions of policy. Committee or board members may be asked to serve for a set number of years or for an unlimited term, but a set time is preferable: good advisers can always be asked to serve another term on the board but replacing bad or inert advisers can be difficult if membership is for an unspecified time.

For most journals, but not all, reference help editors to select papers for publication. The criteria for selection of papers are those listed at the beginning of this chapter.

Journal editors also have to decide whether to publish a wide variety of articles and features or whether to restrict the journal to one or two types of section, and they must choose the specifications which apply to each section. The possible sections include:

Original Articles: will there be a maximum permitted length or specified form?

Solicited Aesearch Articles : Short notes, e.g. on methodology: same handling as for full length articles, or with special arrangements for speedy publication?

Review Articles: solicited, unsolicited, or both?

Hypotheses not stemming from the author's own results comments on other published papers, without new data Correspondence.

Corrections: how to bring them to the reader's attention? Editorials: never, occasionally or in every issue? Linked to articles in the same issue or independent? Political or apolitical? Singed?

Synopses of papers to be presented at meetings of the sponsoring society Other society business (including presidential addresses and the like) Guidelines for authors: in every issue?

Book reviews

Advertisements

University and other appointments vacant and wanted

This list seems formidable, but many of the decisions may be simple to make, or may be made by the editorial board, the sponsoring society, or the publishers. The simplest list of what to publish would probably be:

Original, unsolicited articles (or letters, for a 'Letters' journal) Corrections (otherwise known as Errata)

Guidelines for authors

Even this short list can produce problems, as can be seen from Lis DeBakey's book The scientific journal in which experienced journal editors provide guidelines for others, revealing as they do so a wide range of opinion, and even disagreement on certain points. The main questions are:

(a) are referees to be used, and if so how are conflicts of opinion between them and the authors to be resolved and

(b) is the presentation of articles to be improved and, if so, how much and by whom? On the second point, it is generally recognized that the journal editor's role is to uphold standards, both by rejecting poor articles and improving good ones. Solicited articles, including editorials, review articles and book reviews should, however, be edited with a light hand, especially it they are signed—another policy decision that has to be made.

Although journal editors may commission review articles and other items, they spend much of their time dealing with unsolicited manuscripts submitted for publication by hopeful authors. The general principles of selection have already been mentioned and the mechanics of handling manuscripts. The editor, or the editorial office personnel of the larger journals or organizations, examines each manuscript when it arrives and, if referees are used, decides who is best qualified to assess it. Occasionally it will immediately be obvious that a paper can be accepted or rejected without being sent to anyone else. If the journal does not use a refereeing system the editor is the only arbiter anyway. Selection there has to be: apart from questions of quality, few journals could afford to publish all the papers submitted.

The work of journal editors and referees is made easier if each journal provides clear instructions or guidelines for authors. Guidelines can never, of course, improve the quality of the research described in submitted papers, but they can influence authors to think more carefully about the style and form of their typescripts. If an author submits a paper that has clearly been prepared without reference to the guidelines, the editor may decide to return it, after first considering the principles.

Most new editors want to change the format, layout and covers of their journals, but surprisingly, perhaps this involves much more than individual taste. Restraints on six, for example, have been imposed by postal authorities and laid down by standard organizations. Changes should not be initiated lightly. Designers, publishers, printers and librarians have to be consulted and various production methods and the relevant cost factors have to be taken into account. Another temptation that must be resisted is changing a journal's tide, as this causes endless confusion for the secondary services as well as producing problems for readers, authors and other editors.

The Readership : Journal editors have to decide who their clients are. If they aim to serve authors they will develop a system that allows either for rapid publication of submitted articles or for equally rapid rejection. If their chief clients are the readers, careful and critical review will be the main aim together with much editorial work on the accepted articles to make these as comprehensible, interesting and retrievable as possible. To attract readers, these editors will probably encourage correspondence, comments on published work, hypotheses and so forth. If they see themselves as committed neither to authors nor to readers as separate groups, but to the advancement of science as such they may take one of two directions. Either they will demand extensive and rigorous proof of every statement made-and here they will rely heavily on the approval of the referees; or they will decide to publish only the most original work, even when it yields conclusion contrary to the prevailing consensus (or dogma).

In practice, most editors try to serve authors, readers and science: it is a question of deciding with what priorities and by what mechanisms. Of course, the image of the reader as someone who subscribes personally to the journal, opens it eagerly as it arrives and reads it through from cover to cover is old-fashioned, if not mythical. Readers are those who are alerted to individual articles either by a secondary (title-listing or abstracting) service or by their own browsing through the contents pages of current periodicals in a library.

Editors who keep this concept of 'reader' firmly in mind ask authors to add key phrases to their titles, for inclusion on the contents pages of the journal. They place the contents in consistent form on one of the outside covers. They arrange for the name of the journal and its volume number and date, as well as the page number, to appear on each page of the journal, so that a full reference is included on photo-copied articles or parts of articles. Conscientious editors also draw special attention to correction the unthinking or insecure editor hides them away. The first course of action promotes scientific progress; the second impedes it. Attention to details of these kinds distinguishes the considerate editor active in the service of science from the arrogant or merely conservative arbiter of which articles deserve publication.

Unlike most editors of books, editors of some scientific journals may have to contend with the financial problems of keeping their journals going. Here we need only point out that economic pressures force editors to make their journals as attractive as possible, whether by selecting the best articles and publishing them much faster than any competitors, or by offering a superb and rapid editorial service to those who are not masters of language or by commissioning informed comment on work being published in the same issue of the journal. If, in these and other ways, an editor can create a superlative product, people are likely to pay what is asked for it- a proposition that may remain true even in times of shrinking library and research budgets.

These outlines already show that editing is not a simple task. The expansion or exposition of the scientific information system that has been in progress since the 1950s has exposed editors of primary publications to increasingly heavy pressures from would be authors. At the same time editors have had to learn to cope with the requirements of the secondary services and with the problems posed by new techniques of information transmission. To keep the information system running smoothly editors must be stringent in selecting only first rate original work for publication. Thy must be punctilious in ensuring that readers can obtain or identify published material as quickly as possible. And, as discussed in the next chapter, they should arrange for authors to receive whatever editorial guidance they need and it is practicable to give them.

7

Reporter's Duty

The contents of a newspaper can be broadly divided into four parts-news; articles and features; opinion pieces such as editorials, comments, letters to the editor, reviews, columns; and advertisements.

News constitutes about 60% of the space in a newspaper. It pertains to some recent event which is a matter of interest to readers or listeners. News implies new thing or latest information.

The Concept

A few definitions of 'news' are:

> "News may be defined as any accurate fact or idea that will interest a large number of readers."
>
> "News is anything timely that is interesting and significant to readers in respect of their personal affairs or their relation to society, and the best news is that which possesses the greatest degree of this interest and significance for the greatest number."

> "News may be defined as an accurate, unbiased account of the significant facts of a timely happening that is of interest to the readers of the newspapers that print the account."
>
> "News is the first report of significant events which have interest for the public."
>
> "News is an account of a current idea, event or problem that interests people."
>
> "News is the record of the most interesting, important and accurate information obtainable about the things man thinks and says, sees, describes, plans and does."

According to Mr. B.G. Verghese, former Editor-in-Chief *The Hindustan Times,* "the standard definition that only 'man bites dog' is news is obsolete and inaccurate. In view of the 'communication gap' in a democratic society that which is reported becomes news and that which is not reported remains non-news. Sensationalization, disaster, fraud and the like is news but it is not 'sole news or the highest news'." Mr. Verghese advocates reporting of more constructive developments and trends in great social, economic and political changes, technological advances, modernization processes rather than concentrating only on political news.

Various Items of News

News stories are particularly of two types-straight news and interpretative *or* explanatory or opinionated writing. A straight news story gives factual account of what has happened in a simple, clear and accurate manner. This type of story never distorts, misrepresents or gives wrong facts. It draws no conclusions, makes no accusations, offers no opinions and does not indulge in any speculation. Interpretative news story, on the other hand, reports happenings in depth, gives all sides of the picture, provides background and puts some meaning into the news so that the reader can better understand and appreciate the event.

Most of the definitions of news agree on the point that news is which is of interest to the public. The interest, however, differs from person to person and place to place. Some other characteristics of news are immediacy, proximity, oddity, conflict, suspense, curiosity, and consequences.

The following are the important elements of news:

1. Immediacy or timeliness is of great importance. The new thing: or latest information makes all the difference. As news ages, it lose its potency. The nearness of an event in time is vital to daily newspapers.
2. Truth and objectivity is another quality of news. The balanced picture of an event or a happening or accuracy in reporting events enhances the value of news.
3. Nearness or propinquity, i.e., closeness in space, is yet another element of news. The newsworthiness of an event is in direct ratio to its physical nearness to the public served by the newspaper appraising it. An accident or a crime near at home has much greater news value than a bigger accident or crime abroad.
4. News should be of interest or concern or significance to readers. The interest, however, differs. It may be of interest to a section of the community or of local, regional, national or international interest.
5. Names of individuals also make news. The person may be widely known because of his position, wealth or status. Even an unknown person can make news because of some oddity, eccentricity or unusual occupation or some other factor.
6. Timing and place of occurrence of an event are also important elements of news. The hour of an event may decide its news importance, so also where the thing happens is important. Suicide in a city may not be big news, but in a small place such news may hit the headlines.
7. Numbers and size make news. An accident in which

a large number of people have died or injured makes news. If very few people are involved in the accident and nobody died, the news value becomes less important.

8. Suspense and mystery adds to the value of news. It holds readers' interest in the news. The more the suspense, the greater is the curiosity of readers in the news.

The other elements which are dominant in news stories are action, movement and mobility; combat, struggle, contrast, rivalry; sex and scandal; beauty and romance; adventure and pathos including exploration, discovery, excavation, invention; novelty and humour; and stories about children and animals.

In brief, news is associated with something new or something novel; or relates to a famous person; or of importance to a large number of people; or pertains to conflict, mystery, crime; or reveals something confidential; or forecasts the future; or deals with a funny situation; or romance; or sex, suicide, murder, etc.

Duty of a Reporter

To be a successful reporter, one must have news sense or flair or nose for news. He should have the ability to recognize the news value in ordinary things. The qualities necessary in a reporter are: patience and perseverance to get a story; eye for details; capacity for hard work; gift of imagination; skill for clear and concise presentation of news and views; and spirit of enterprise and adventure.

The reporter has to work with great speed under stress and strain. He will succeed only if he has an understanding of time value and necessary flexibility and adaptability to change himself to the changing situation.

The reporter must report the news accurately and fairly without prejudice and personal opinion. The following remarks of the late Mr. Frank Moraes, Editor-in-Chief of the *Indian*

Express, about the qualities necessary in a news reporter are very pertinent: "What do I regard as the most important quality in a news reporter? I would unhesitatingly say-accuracy. This, and the ability to express himself clearly and concisely. The average newspaper reader is a man in a hurry. He should never be required to read a sentence twice to get its meaning."

To sum up, the essentials of good reporting are-accuracy, balance, brevity and speed. Loose writing and unverified details create a number of difficulties and should be avoided. Reporters cover a variety of assignments-accidents, court cases, crime, proceedings of legislatures, communal incidents, demonstrations, deaths, etc. besides political, social, economic and cultural events and sports.

In covering accidents, a competent authority, an identifiable official spokesman should be quoted. The time, place and cause of the accident and if possible an eye witness account is to be given. The reporter should give the names of casualties only if he can verify their accuracy. He should show respect to the dead and avoid horrid details. Legal complications would arise if a person is reported to have 'died', but who is actually alive. The nature of accident should be described accurately. He must attribute his report to some authority. The source should be identified at the very start. The context in which the announcement of the accident is made, for instance, 'Press Conference' or 'Interview' as the case may be, should be mentioned.

In reporting court cases, care is to be exercised in not giving cause to libel or contempt. Anything that reflects directly or indirectly on the personal character or conduct of identifiable persons or institution or criticises or hinders the process of law should be scrupulously avoided. The report should be 'a fair summary' of evidence tendered, the statements made by the counsel and the ruling given by the court. If charges made by the prosecution are reported, the reply of the defendant must also be incorporated in the story. The onus of proving that the report was in public interest will be on the agency or newspaper.

In reporting crime, murder, suicide, fire, sabotage, etc. the statement pertaining to the name of the person involved, motive, cause, etc. should be attributed to police or an appropriate source. The term 'arrest' is different from 'taken into custody' or 'detained' for interrogation and as such, correct nomenclature should be used. A person is presumed to be innocent until he is found guilty by a court. So it is advisable to use expressions like 'alleged assailant and ,allegedly stabbed'. All information provided by police should be attributed to them. A reporter should refrain from making comments or speculating the circumstances under which the crime was committed, nor should he draw any conclusion or support or discount a particular theory.

The communities are generally not identified as 'Hindus' or 'Muslims' while reporting communal clashes. Generalized allegation and accusation of being anti-national should not be made against a whole community. Fullest verification is necessary before giving any facts and figures. Nothing should be included in the report which will whip up communal passions. The source from which casualty figures, etc. are taken should be indicated. If the figures are not confirmed, the report must indicate that the figures are 'unconfirmed'. News of efforts aiming at resolving peace and harmony should be highlighted.

The death story should include the cause of death, its time and place. Age of the dead and by whom survived, as well as the name of the disease are to be mentioned. If the name of the disease is not intelligible to readers, it should be explained in layman's language.

In, demonstrations and meetings, avoid adjectives and superlatives. Give as far as possible a factual account.

In covering presentation of budgets in Parliament and Assemblies, the new tax proposals, deficit, surplus, comparison between the past and present budget tax proposals, new schemes, reactions, etc. are to be reported. In reporting debates, the name of the speakers are followed by their party affiliations. In reporting- question-hour, identification is not necessary. The report of the proceedings show be fair and objective and remarks, if any made, should be in public interest. The expunged portions should not be included in the report.

The reporter has to interview people for news. He should study the subject and should have at least a broad background of it before conducting interview, particularly on specialized subjects. Knowledge of shorthand and typing will help him a great deal. While interviewing people, he should be a good listener and keep up a pleasant and cheerful disposition. The reporter should have mastery over the techniques of interviewing people.

The reporter should also clearly understand the difference between the classifications of news. 'Flash' is a one-line news item about an event of major significance. It has an element of suddenness and tells about something unexpected. 'Snap' is used for important sports or commercial news. 'Top priority' story consists of one or two paragraphs, while 'priority' story may run upto three or more paragraphs.

Press correspondents and reporters, possessing press authority from newspapers or news agencies, can send press telegrams including flash press telegrams to the concerned paper or agency. The rates charged for ordinary and express inland telegrams for minimum first. 50 words are Re. 1 and Rs. 2 respectively, and for every 5 additional words Paise 10 and Paise 20 respectively. The flash telegrams are limited to a maximum of 100 words, and are charged at the same rate as that of inland express private telegram. The press telegrams may be accepted without payment, if the newspaper or news agency had obtained previous sanction from the postal authorities.

The news story must be written effectively. The introductory sentence or paragraph, the lead or the beginning, is crucial to the story. The function of the lead is not only to summarize the story but also to attract readers to the story. It sets the tone and the temper of the story. The news story should have the most important points in the first paragraph, but the temptation to 'tell' too many things in the introduction should be avoided.

Brevity is the quality of presentation of news. In the news story there is not much scope for subsidiary and background material. The news is written in terse, concise and matter-of-fact manner. There is not much room for colour, ornamentation, or dramatization. It is a hurriedly written piece to meet the deadline. Since it is limited to time and place, no attempt should be made to make it a self-contained story.

Items of Special News

Every news agency or newspaper follows its own 'style'. But a few general guidelines, in regard to the style of writing, are given below:

1. Use short words, short sentences, short paragraphs-and produce a clean copy.
2. Avoid needless adjectives so that the risk of exaggeration or under-estimation is eliminated. Distinguish between factual and propagatory material which is available from your sources whether official or non-official.
3. Guard against word-wasting abstractions.
4. Where there is no risk of ambiguity or awkwardness, drop the point from groups of initials such as CIP, SP, IAF, PIB and AIR. But where confusion may occur, use points as in U.N. (United Nations), U.S. (United States), W.H.O. (World Health Organization).
5. Do not abbreviate names, use Mohammed (not Mohd.), Choudhary (not Ch.).
6. The standard abbreviations are:

   kg, km, kw, kv (for both singular and plural); Mr., Mrs., Dr. (preceding a name); Jr., Sr. (following a name); Academic degree: B.A., M.A., M.S., Ph.D., M.D.; M.P.

(Member of Parliament); GMT (Greenwich Mean Time), (Indian Standard Time), Hrs. (hours); For ships: M.V. JAL JAWAHAR (Motor Vessel) or S.S. AKBAR (Steamship); I.P.C. (Indian Penal Code), Cr. P.C. (Criminal Procedure Code).

7. Do not abbreviate the days of the week, and the months of the year in the body of the copy. Similarly, use Rupees, not Rs. except in tables.
8. Use the following abbreviations for Service ranks: Lieutenant—Lt; Lieutenant Commander—Lt Cdr; Commander—Cdr; Captain—Capt; Major—Maj; Lieutenant—Colonel—Lt Col; Colonel—Col; Brigadier—Brig; Major General—Maj Gen; Lieutenant General—Lt Gen; General—Gen; Flight Sergeant—Flt Sgt; Flight Lieutenant—Flt Lt; Squadron Leader—Sqn Ldr; Wing Commander—Wg Cdr; Group Captain—Group Capt; Commodore—Cmdr; Warrant Officer—WO.

   In the first instance, the rank should be given in full.
9. Except May, June and July, the months are to be abbreviated in dateline: JAN, FEB, MAR, APR, AUG, SEP, OCT, NOV, DEC.

   The months of the year and the days of the week are, however not abbreviated in the body of the copy.
10. Use October 30 and not 30th October as a way of style.
11. Calendar years to be mentioned in full: 1966 (not 66) and financial year: 1976-77.
12. Except in quotes, the time should be rendered on the basis of 24 hour cycle. Use 1115 hrs and 2130 hrs.
13. GMT time should be converted into IST and both should be mentioned-occurred at 1100 hrs IST (0530 hrs GMT).
14. All editing should be done in capital letters only. Heavily edited copy should be retyped.
15. Type 'no' and 'now' twice. Also type twice uncommon names of persons and places, Example: "He said now

now..." This is to ensure "now" does not appear as 'no' in transmission, which happens quite often.

16. Numbers up to eleven should be spelt out and beyond that in figures. For money use lakhs and crores, not millions. However, for expressing the number of men and other things use millions. For example: A grant of rupees five lakhs.. ., but 5,00,000 people (in figure)... six million shoes... 96.50 million tonnes of foodgrains.
17. Except when confusion is likely to result, the following are not put in quotes: names of newspapers or magazines; trade names; makes or models of cars and aircraft; sports events or trophies; fictional or stage character; ships or pets; names of royal, official or historical houses and castles.
18. The following are normally put in quotes: nicknames or pen names; titles of books, poems, songs, plays and films; private houses or properties in general.
19. Avoid abbreviations like i.e., e.g., n.b., viz., etc. and use their equivalents: that is; for example; note carefully; namely; and so forth.
20. Do not use in the copy trade names for the products of the same type manufactured by others. Use words like detergent powder (not surf); transparent wrapping (not cellophane); vacuum flask (not thermos); synthetic fabric (not terylene); petroleum jelly (not vaseline); aspirin (not aspro) and edible oil (not vanaspati).

Upgraded Items

The term press release is generally used for releases covering news. The press release should contain worthwhile material which has some news value. It will not only mean unnecessary expenditure but will also damage the reputation of the concerned Publicity/ Information Department if the release is based on a very trivial matter.

A press release should be written in journalistic style. It should provide facts or information of interest to the readers and should attempt to cover all aspects of a specific subject. There should not be any loose end. The press release should be on a current subject or which is in news. The release should not be generally lengthy. It should be concise and to the point. It has not much scope for subsidiary or background material. The release should be a piece of clear writing without any ambiguity, without any effort towards colour or ornamentation. The drafting should be done in a manner that if the last paragraphs are deleted by the newspaper, no damage is done to the news story in the press release.

The introduction or lead should be in a summary format as we have in a news story. The relative value of the various ingredients of the subject in the press release are weighed and evaluated and the most pertinent portion of them are included in the lead.

The releases should have a consistent format. Generally, the name of the organization from where the release emanates, is given on the top. The date and place are indicated on the top right side. The release should have a title and a sub-title also, if necessary. It should have a suitable introductory paragraph. In the case of releases from non-official organizations, it is also desirable to mention the designation of the person issuing the release and his telephone number.

The press releases covering news in the case of government are mainly of four types-Press Communiques, Press Notes, Handouts, and Unofficial Handouts.

The press communiques are issued when some important government decisions or announcements are made, such as cabinet appointments, conclusion of the foreign dignitaries' visit, international agreements, etc. The press communique is formal in character. It carries the name of the Ministry or Department and place and date at the bottom left hand corner of the press release. Generally, the press is expected to reproduce the press communique without any substantial change. No heading or sub-heading is given.

The second category of press release is press notes. The press notes are less formal in character. These are also issued on important official matters, e.g., raising or lowering of tariff rates, etc. The press note also carries the name of the Ministry or Department and place and date at the bottom left-hand corner. Headings or sub-headings are given in press notes. Unlike the press communique, the newspapers can edit or condense the press note.

Both the press communique and the press note are the responsibility of the government department and not that of the Press Information Bureau (PIB), the Central government agency which deals with the press on behalf of all ministries and departments of the Government of India, nor that of they State Directorates of Public Relations/ Information, which deal with the State government departments.

The third category of press release is handouts. The handouts are issued on a variety of subjects like the day-to-day activities of the ministry or departments, VIP speeches, questions and answers in Parliament, etc. The hand-out is a less formal type of release and not issued under the government's formal authority.

It covers the name of the PIB or other releasing agency on the top without any mention of the ministry or department to which the release pertains. One of the important common categories of handouts relates to speeches of ministers or other high officials. Handout is issued only when the speech is related to the governmental activity. No official handout is issued, if the minister has spoken in his personal capacity as a member of a political organization. The place and date are indicated on top at right-hand side.

The speech, when released to the press in the form of a handout, is summarized and properly edited. Formal introductory and concluding remarks, are omitted and redundant and repetitive material taken out. Proper title and sub-title are given. The important aspect or aspects, which are to be stressed, are included in the introductory paragraph or in the lead. The full text of the speech is not released unless the subject is of very great importance.

While covering inaugural and other functions, where VIPs make speeches, the press release should stress on the significance of the function, and try to spell out in concrete terms the benefits it gives to the community rather than reproducing the speech. For instance, the opening of a new branch of a bank or of a power house at a particular place should be an opportunity to the communicator to bring out in the press release the specific gains which would accrue to the people of that area rather than spotlighting on the dignitary and his speech.

The speech of the Prime Minister or of a very important dignitary, on formal occasions or at important gatherings, is generally released in full to ensure correct reporting. The full text is also helpful to the editors and column writers. It is also utilized for reference purposes in the future. If the speech of the Prime Minister or the dignitary is extempore, advance arrangements will have to be made for reporters and tape-recorders.

Unofficial handouts are issued on a subject where the government would not like to assume official responsibility in the matter, but feels that there may be a positive advantage in making the information public unofficially. These handouts are supplements to oral briefings. These are given across the table to press correspondents and no general release is made. The unofficial handouts would not have the imprint of the PIB or other releasing agency. The date and place are indicated at the bottom left-hand corner.

The Press Information Bureau and the State Information Departments handle press relations work on behalf of the Central and State governments respectively. The PIB provides information to the press on government activities; it feeds Indian and foreign correspondents with news and background material, and keeps the government informed of press and public reaction to governmental activities. It endeavours to give special assistance to small newspapers in regional languages.

There is a positive advantage in having centralized releases on behalf of the different departments at one point. It is convenient to press representatives. It also guards against release of material pertaining to one ministry or department, which is critical or contradictory or not in good taste of other departments. The Press Information Bureau and the State Public Relations Departments are in a position to take an overall view of the functioning of the government, and as such can provide effective coordination.

Releases for Press

There are many other forms of releases, which do not cover news but give information in an indirect way and help in building the image of the government or an organization. More widely-known releases of this type are backgrounders, biographical sketches, contradictions, articles and features, newsletters, releases on reports, broadcast talks, etc.

Contradiction or denial of news story is to be issued only when - there is a serious mistake or the facts in the story are patently incorrect. Since denials give more publicity, it should be avoided as far as possible, particularly when the story is substantially correct. The best way for the publicist is to publish a positive story after a lapse of some time. The opportunity should be utilized to present a correct statement of facts without referring to what has been incorrectly published in the past. Negative statement or refutation of a news story, except in very exceptional circumstances, is not a good strategy.

Background material providing additional information and useful details is essential for journalists, newspapers and periodicals. Events should be anticipated and necessary background material is prepared well in advance. It may also be supplied on ad hoc requests. The backgrounder should be a self-contained release as far as possible. It would be useful for leader and column writers. The backgrounder should give a detailed run-down for better appreciation of decisions or activities.

Whenever the government or other reports are to be given to the press, it is necessary that a summary should also be released, which should be brief. The constructive side of the report is to be highlighted in the summary. Out of these reports, self-contained items can be taken out and released separately. If a report that is to be presented to Parliament, it should be ensured that it is not given to the press before it has been distributed to members of Parliament, or laid on the Table of either House of Parliament.

The press release from business houses also follows more or less the same format. It should also include the name of the organization, address, name of the concerned officer, telephone number, etc. to facilitate the work of the newspaper representative to get speedy clarification and additional information, if required.

No payment is required to be paid to newspapers if the releases, discussed above, are published in newspapers.

In these releases, the name of releasing agency is given at the top. The place and date are indicated on top right-hand side. The type of release is mentioned in a box on top left-hand side. Title and sub-title are also given.

One important point to remember is about the timing of the releases. If the publicist wants to reach both 'dak' ('dak' editions are meant for outstations and up-country centres and, therefore, printed earlier in the evening) and city editions of the newspapers, the release must be in the hands of the news editor by noon, latest.

Even when the objective is to get into city edition only, it is a good policy to send the release before 1500 hrs. In certain cases, the copy can be sent a day in advance with an embargo put both at the top and at the bottom of the release. Embargo is to be indicated in either of the two ways: (i) For publication/ broadcast on or after__________ hours on __________20; or (ii) Not to be published/ broadcast before__________hours on__________20

Newspapers have a lot of prepared material for the magazine section of their Sunday editions. As such, it will not be in the publicist's interest to send unimportant items on Saturday, Sunday and other holidays. It is preferable to send such items on other than these days for publication. Through the technique of embargo, the publicist can release his story simultaneously from different centres in the country. While putting the embargo, the requirements of radio should also be taken into consideration. For instance, when it is desired that the embargo story is to appear in papers, say, on Saturday morning, the embargo should only be for the Friday evening, so that the news can be used in radio news bulletins on Friday evening.

Bibliography

Ahuja, B.N. : *Theory and Practice of Journalism,* Surjeet Publications, Delhi, 1979.

Alfred, John : *Mass Communication in the New Millennium,* Prime Publication, New Jersey, 2003.

Apter, Michel : *The New Technology of Education,* MacMillan, London, 1968.

Aronson, James : *The Press and the Cold War,* Beacon Press, Boston, 1970.

Awasthy, G.C. : *Broadcasting in India,* Allied Publishers Private Ltd., Bombay, 1965.

Bard, F. Eraser : *An Introduction to Journalism,* The MacMillan Co., New York, 1958.

Bernard, H. W. : *Principles of Journalism: A Basic Text,* Allied Publishers Private Ltd., New Delhi, 1998.

Bhatia, A. : *Journalism in Modern India,* Asia Publishing House, Bombay, 1964.

Brank, S.M. : *Journalism Characteristics and School Learning,* Harper, New York, 1976.

Carrol, L. : *Occupational Information,* Prentice Hall, New York, 1961.

Cattell, B.B. : *Media Structure, Growth and Action,* Houghton Mifflin Co., Boston, 1999.

Chatterjee, R.K. : *Mass Communication,* National Book Trust, New Delhi, 2002.

Chauhan, S.S. : *A Textbook of Mass Communication*, Sterling Publishers, New Delhi, 2001.

Cottle, W.C. : *Interest and Personality Inventories*, Houghton Miffling Co., New York, 1968.

Cream, David : *Explaining Teaching Machines and Programmes*, Featon, San Fracisco, 1961.

Critchfield, Richard : *The Indian Reporter's Guide*, Allied Pacific Pvt. Ltd., Bombay, 1962.

Curfis, D. : *Interpretotive Reporting*, MacMillan Co., New York, 1957.

Dale, Edgare : *Audio-Visual Method in Teaching*, Dryden Rinehart and Winston, New York, 1969.

Das, R.C. : *Educational Technology*, Sterling Publishers, New Delhi, 2000.

Donald, H. : *Developmental Counselling*, The Ronald Press, New York, 1966.

Donald, Mc. : *The Art of Radio*, Faber & Faber, London, 1961.

Emery, Edwin : *The Press and America*, Prentice Hall, New Jersey, 1999.

Eve, A. A. : *Micro-teaching Theory into Practice*, Oxford, New York, 1969.

Frank, H. Krouse : *Media Technique with Youth*, Charles and Mervil, Ohio, 1990.

Gagne, R.M. : *The Conditions of Learning*, Holt Binsort and Winston, New York, 1965.

Gaur, J.S. and Saraswat, R.K. : *Mass Media*, NCERT, New Delhi, 1998.

Ghiselli, Edwin E. : *Personnel and Industrial Media*, McGraw Hill Book Co., New York, 1955.

Gunning, Robert : *The Technique of Clear Writing*, McGraw Hill Book Co., New York.

Haban, F. : *Movies that Teach*, Dryden Press, New York, 1945.

Hancock, Alan : *Planning for Educational Mass Media*, Longmans, London, 1977.

Hercleread, A.V. : *Instruction: Materials and Methods,* Mc Graw Hill Book Co., New York, 1964.

Hoppock, Rebert : *Occupational Information,* McGraw Hill Book Co., New York, 1997.

Hudson, Kenneth : *The Dictionary of Diseased English,* The MacMillan Co., Bombay, 1977.

James, S. : *Audio-Visual Materials and Techniques,* American Book Company, New York, 1959.

John, A. : *The Asian Newspaper's Reluctant Revolution,* The Iowa State University Press, Iowa, 1977.

John, Hohenberg : *The Professional Journalist,* Rinehort and Winston, New York, 1969.

Johnson, Stanley and Julian Harriss : *The Complete Reporter,* The MacMillan Co., New York, 1942.

Joseph and Jospeth : *Idyels Past and Present: An Editor's Wet Copy,* Orient Longman, Bombay, 1979.

Kaul, B.N. : *Studies in Mass Media,* Har Anand, New Delhi, 1998.

Knight, R. : *Intelligence and Intelligence Tests,* Methuen and Co. Ltd. London, 1943.

Kothari, O.S. : *Report of the Indian Education Commission, 1964-66,* Publication Divison, New Delhi, 1966.

Krug, R.E. : *Ability Testing in Developing Countries: A Handbook of Principles and Techniques,* Praeger, New York, 1972.

Laxman, N.J. : *Introduction to Media Technology,* Oxford Publishing Company, New Delhi, 2003.

Lowman, J. : *Mastering Techniques of Media,* Prentice Hall, New York, 1999.

Luhan, Mc : *Understanding Media,* Routludge, London, 1964.

Mahler, C.A. : *Media Counselling in the Schools,* Houghton Mifflin, Boston, 1969.

Matheson, Alastair : *The Communication Materials and Methods,* McGraw Hill Book Company, New Delhi, 1964.

McCully, C.H. : *The Media—Instrument of Change*, National College Record, Bombay, 2001.

Mehta, D.S. : *Mass Communication and Journalism in India*, Allied Publishers Pvt. Ltd., Bombay, 1979.

Menon, Narayan : *The Communication Revolution*, National Book Trust, New Delhi, 1976.

Miller, Care G. : *Modern Journalism*, Rinehart and Winston, New York, 1962.

Miller, Carroll, H. : *Foundations of Guidance*, Harper and Brothers, New York, 1961.

Mitchell, V. : *Reporting*, Rinehart and Winston, New York, 1960.

Mohanty, J. : *Educational Broadcasting: Radio & Television in Education*, Sterling Publishers, New Delhi, 1984.

Mojar, N.F. : *Current Trends in Mass Communication*, Deep & Deep Publications, New Delhi, 2001.

Mokam, K.B. : *Dynamics of Mass Media in India*, Deep & Deep Publications, New Delhi, 2000.

Mosan, N.N. : *Indian Education in the Emerging Society*, Sterling Publishers, New Delhi, 1982.

Moven, Kiran : *Studies in Educational Broadcasting*, Deep & Deep Publications, New Delhi, 1996.

Mujuni, J.P. : *Studies in Media Education*, Deep & Deep Publications, New Delhi, 1995.

Muni, K.W. : *Media Technology*, Deep & Deep Publications, New Delhi, 2003.

Murthy, Nadig Krishna : *Indian Journalism*, University of Mysore, Prasaranga, 1966.

Natrajan, J. : *History of Indian Journalism*, Publications Division, New Delhi, 1999.

Natrajan, S. : *A History of the Press in India*, Asia Publishing House, Bombay, 1962.

Oscar, Krisen : *Encyclopaedia of Mass Media and Journalism*, Oxford, New York, 1998.

Ottaway, A.K.C. : *Press and Society*, Routldge and Kegan Paul, London, 1962.

Oxtoby, J.S. : *Media and Cultural Environment*, Methuen, London, 1969

Page, C.M. : *Society and Media*, MacMillan, London, 1950.

Panda, K.C. : *Role of Mass Media in School Learning*, RCE, Bhubaneswar, 1978.

Parikh, R.D. : *The Press and Society*, Popular Prakashan, Bombay, 1965.

Quirk, A. : *Editor and Editorial Writer*, Rinehart & Co., New York, 1955.

Reston, James : *The Artillery of the Press: Its Influence on American Foreign Policy*, Harper & Row, New York, 1967.

Rewntreu, Desk : *Media Technology in Curriculum Development*, Harper and Row Publishers, London, 2001.

Richder L. : *Handbook of Broadcasting*, McGraw- Hill Book Co., New York, 1957.

Roland, E. : *Exploring Journalism*, Prentice Hall, New Jersey, 1958.

Sadanand, K.R. : *New Media: Memo to Educational Planners*, John, Wiley, London, 2002.

Sahni, J.N. : *Truth About the Indian Press*, Allied Publishers, Bombay, 1974.

Schramm, Wilbur : *Big Media, Little Media*, Edward Arnold, London, 2000.

Sethi, Patanjali : *Professional Journalism*, Orient Longman, Bombay, 1974.

Shaw, David : *Journalism Today*, Harper's College Press, London, 1977.

Shelly, C. : *Fundamentals of Mass Media*, Houghton Miffin Co., Boston, 1976.

Thedore, M. : *Headlines and Deadlines*, Columbia University Press, New York, 1961.

Thorndike, R.L. : *Media Psychology and Education*, Wiley Eastern Pvt. Ltd., New Delhi, 2001.

Ullan, J. : *Technical Reporting*, Rinehart and Winston, New York, 1963.

Vedanayagam, G. : *Media Teaching Technology for College Teachers*, Sterling Publishers, New Delhi, 1989.

Viner, B. : *The Practice of Journalism*, Heinemann, London, 1963.

Warich, D. : *Modular Circula: International Encyclopaedia*, Pergamone Publications, London, 1994.

Whinnie, Donald : *The Art of Broadcasting*, Faber & Faber, London, 1961.

Willian, Charvat : *Handbook for Writers*, Prentice Hall, New Jersey, 1962.

Wolseley, E. : *How to Report and Write the News?*, Prentice Hall, New Jersey, 1961.

Zanda, B. : *Journalism as Guidance*, MacMillan Co., New York, 1998.

Zohar, B. : *Principles and Techniques of Journalism*, Vikas Publishing House, New Delhi, 1982.

Index

N

O

P

J

K

L

M

R

S

T

U

V

W